MW01603226

This book is dedicated to our loyal subscribers and readers who believe in our mission to introduce ancient wisdom to modern minds.

THE
ESSENTIAL
GREEKS

AN ANTHOLOGY OF CLASSICAL GREEK LITERATURE

EDITED BY ANYA ELIZABETH LEONARD AND VAN BRYAN
PREFACE BY ANYA ELIZABETH LEONARD
INTRODUCTION BY BEN POTTER
CHAPTER INTRODUCTIONS BY VAN BRYAN
SPECIAL THANKS TO NATALIE KO

CLASSICAL WISDOM WEEKLY

Front and back cover by Santiago Alvira

First Edition: 2015

ISBN 978-0-9861084-0-2

Printed in the United States of America

TABLE OF CONTENTS

PREFACE

Why Read the Classics?

Before I read the classics, they were read to me. My mother weaned us all, my brothers and I, on Homer's twin epics, *The Odyssey* and *The Iliad*. I remember her reading them to us at night, before bed. The crashing waves...the beckoning sirens...the ferocious monsters...it was all so very real. The tales, at once compelling and enlightening, transported us from the land of the waking to the realm of the dreamtime. The line between fiction and reality always blurred.

It was an experience for which I am eternally grateful. Moreover, it was also the beginning of a lifelong relationship with the books that have shaped my life.

For my mother, it was the mythology that captured her imagination. My brothers – perhaps not altogether surprisingly for a couple of young, would-be ruffians – it was the battles, the dragons, the Cyclops and gaping Charybdian that teased at their inquisitive natures.

As for me, I was intrigued by the travel...both geographically and, in a sense, through time itself. Here were stories from far off places that had traversed not only oceans and land, but also thousands of *years* to reach my ears. I identified with the characters – their struggles and victories, fears, pains and exaltations–in ways I just couldn't experience in contemporary pop culture.

'How could people living so long ago, in such a different world, have so many of the same feelings we have nowadays' I wondered? Our reactions to varied circumstances and the timeless lessons we draw from experience was something that always fascinated me. It does to this day.

The beauty of the classics also reached me through art. When I was still very young- maybe ten or twelve years of age–my mother took me to a pre-Raphaelite exhibition with works by John Everett Millais, Dante Gabriel Rossetti and, my favorite then and still, John William Waterhouse. The works are captivating; ethereal women with long locks in soft, languid settings; a kind of wispy dreamscape for the imagination. I was entranced...and not only because of the skill of the artists. The paintings captured those same mythological fables and tall tales my mother loved to recall. Waterhouse's beckoning sirens still stand out in my mind...

The canvases brought our favorite stories to life in the most magical way, a melding of mythology and art, folklore and canvas, legend and brushstroke.

In my teenage years I made it a mission to see the world's best art. I was fortunate enough to have Europe as my backyard and used every opportunity to view, in person, the masterpieces I loved to study. I would stare at the piece of work and imagine the artist's hand actually putting on the final touches. A physical representation of spanning time, it was as if I was personally connected to the artist by just seeing their actual, physical work.

I remember traveling to the Vatican museum and falling in love with Hellenistic art. Time was limited on this particular visit (we arrived a bit later, if memory serves), and so the encounter was equally brief and intoxicating. A friend and I dashed throughout the corridors, trying to ensure we took in all our favorite works. Careening around one corner or another (to the distaste of more mature visitors, it now occurs to me) I came upon the *pièce de résistance*: Laocoön and his two sons, in all their magnificence. The Trojan priest who knew the Greeks' equine gift was treacherous was struck down, along with his progeny, by a God-sent snake. The twists and turns, the sheer agony on his face make the Hellenistic exemplar a powerful piece, a tangible moment from *The Iliad*.

Finally in college, I delved into the books with the seriousness and dedication they deserve. I studied Ancient Greek and Latin, discussed the various translations, and pontificated on the philosophies, histories and literatures found within.

But maybe this last point deserves less attention. The classics aren't about degrees, but rather a love of learning. You see, in my mind, the classics are a journey, a lifelong experience that takes us around the world in pursuit of art, that plunges us into debate with others, that recalls to our mind the stories and philosophies that have fascinated us for so long.

And, in no small way, the classics also inspire us to pursue our own humble contribution to the preservation of the texts themselves and the experiences they can help unlock for others.

It was with this in mind we set out to build *Classical Wisdom Weekly*, our newsletter dedicated to all things classics-related, and also to the creation of the book you have now in your own hands, *The Essential Greeks*. It was a desire to continue a journey that I myself love, as well as a way to help others discover the stories and art from the past. To this end, I've had the great fortune of working with Bill Bonner to make this all a reality, someone who shares this interest and sees the value of the classics.

It would appear to us, the classics lovers, that this value is obvious and self-evident, though, sadly, this is not always the case. It appears that from time to time we must come forth and champion our cause. We must remind others of the importance of our ancient past, and how her works can reveal the value of being a good person, demonstrate how to be happy, or illustrate lessons from the past that we wish not to make again.

But, amazingly, the ancient Greek classics do even more than that.

The men and women before us initiated the process of investigation and inquiry into previously unknown fields and began a journey that following generations of artists, philosophers, historians and scientists continue to this day. As the foundation of almost all western knowledge, studying these great texts allows us to know the shoulders on which we stand.

Consequently, the inquisitive reader will discover no shortage of classical references throughout the history of art, philosophy, literature and science. In fact, until as late as the 19th century, a classical education was considered a prerequisite for any European intellectual. Just about every discipline refers to the classics as inspiration, justification or as a platform from which to disagree. Knowing their original sources illuminates the latter works, providing context and insights.

Just as viewing Laocoön and his sons brought the *Iliad* to life, I find reading the original texts breaths new vigor into ancient history. There are plenty of people who content themselves with the facts found on Wikipedia, but other, more curious folks will want to live the moments and thoughts as described by Herodotus, Thucydides, Plato or Aristotle.

For instance, a reader may know how Socrates died in 399 BC, but without reading the *Apologia*, or any of the other texts describing the great philosopher's wit and wisdom, are they moved by his death and demonstrations?

Of course the main reason to study and preserve the classics is that they inspire and enlighten on every level. Some will shine new light on old problems or illuminate past solutions to current issues. Others will provoke questions that maybe you've never asked yourself before. Then there are the texts that elicit creativity, passion, empathy or further curiosity.

Indeed, the ancient Greek texts can shine as brightly today as they did so long ago, filled with battles, journeys, discoveries and great beauty. They have inspired and educated individuals for thousands of years and, hopefully, will continue to do so for thousands more. Our mission here at *Classical Wisdom Weekly* is to help that come true... and we sincerely hope this book will be a worthy enough start.

Sincerely,

Anya Leonard
Co-Founder and Project Director
Classical Wisdom Weekly
Classicalwisdom.com

INTRODUCTION

When I was first approached by a fledgling, but fascinating online publication to contribute to a course of lectures and publications under the tentative title of 'The Essential Greeks' I was, in almost equal parts, flattered and excited. But more than anything else, I was deeply apprehensive!

I was, of course, flattered to have been chosen above many other worthy candidates, and excited to be given the opportunity to share a passion of mine with a wider audience.

My concern, however, was not restricted to an anxiety about 'producing the goods', though any writer worth his salt would do well to contemplate such a factor. No, what daunted me was the task of compiling a list of Greeks which could, in any way, be considered 'essential'.

Making any catalogue of this nature will invariably lead to the exclusion of many, perhaps most, of people's personal favourites. What is more, with such a cull taking place in that most public (and least urbane) of surroundings, the internet, any ire experienced by the modern representatives of the snubbed ancients would be swiftly and 'firmly' expressed.

A small disclaimer: the feat we wished to achieve was not the last word on the good and the great of ancient Greece. On the contrary, our aim was to provide a solid grounding in, or convenient review of, the men (and, possibly in Homer's case, woman) who shaped Western civilisation.

To prevent the project from escalating out of all proportion whilst simultaneously providing our readership with a firm foundation, it was decided that ten 'slots' would be enough to supply a sufficient, but not overly daunting induction into all things Greco.

So, when whittling down our (rather long) short-list, it was decided that the criterion 'importance' was not, in itself, enough. We also wanted to present the readers with characters about whom our introductions could be just that... tasters or teasers, hors-d'oeuvre to whet the appetite for a feast to be devoured privately.

It is no coincidence therefore that all of our selections, with the troublesome exception of that gadfly, Socrates, are men of literature.

It is partly for this reason that perhaps the most famous Greek of them all, Alexander the Great, did not make our cut.

Additionally, Mr. A.T.Great would require a great deal more time and attention than the scope of our project would allow – not to mention the fact that some purists do not even consider him to be legitimately 'Greek'.

Other notable politicians and statesmen such as Draco, Solon, Peisistratus, Leonidas I, Pericles, Alcibiades, Nicias, Cleon, Philip II et al are, of course, worthy of time and attention, but most of these, and many others, are dealt with within the pages of the historians Herodotus and Thucydides.

This was one of many reasons that helped the two fathers of historiography make our team.

The historian Xenophon may have some justification in feeling unfairly snubbed in this instance. However, as he was a contemporary of Thucydides in both time and space, it seemed excessive to include both.

And if his spleen was venting before, Xenophon could be forgiven for belching bloody bile at being twice overlooked, this time as an authority on Socrates.

As stated above, Socrates is the only one of our 'essentials' who didn't write. However, many of his words and deeds are recorded in the pages of Plato and the hapless Xenophon.

We, like the majority of classical scholars, chose Plato as the biographer-in-chief for the movements of Socrates. Though we also included Plato as a character in his own right, because if one begins a discussion with Socrates then it must inevitably continue with Plato. From there the natural place for it to conclude is, of course, with Aristotle; it is he who completes our philosophical triumvirate.

Though numerous other contenders were jostling for position with these three heavyweights, the fact that they lived in the same city, followed each other in time and left a good deal of biographical information (as well as intellectual content) meant that they would have been impossible to leave off the list.

Almost identical reasons can be applied to the chosen playwrights. While cries of 'what about Thales? Pythagoras? Heraclitus? Diogenes?' understandably follow our philosophical trio, there is little controversy in our choice of dramatists.

Clearly a hullabaloo would have ensued had we left Aeschylus, Sophocles or Euripides off our list. For these great scribes it had to be all or none and, as they also succeeded each other in technique and theatrical innovation, as well as wrote some of the most approachable, relevant and entertaining work extant from the ancient world, their inclusion was not merely an essential, but also a greatly pleasurable one.

It was with great pain that my own personal favourite (see, even I'm not satisfied with the final draft!), the comedic playwright Aristophanes, was excluded. As brilliant, hilarious and culturally significant as he is, his work is perhaps slightly too esoteric. Also, nothing takes the sheen off a joke like an academic explaining it in minute detail!

Not that Aristophanes stands alone in being cast aside with a heavy heart.

The practical necessities of our format meant that the inclusion of great sculptors such as Praxiteles, Polycleitus, Myron and, especially, Phidias was a non-starter.

For similar reasons the world of science and mathematics is unfairly underrepresented with Aristarchus, Archimedes and Euclid barely getting an 'honourable mention'.

The Lesbian lyrics of Sappho and the fables of Aesop were harder to reject. However, if there is one Greek whose absence from our menu of mastery sticks out like a sore thumb, it's that poet who considered the supernatural and the soil of equal interest and importance; the enigmatic Hesiod.

The reason for his non appearance is simple, though will cause further chagrin amongst his champions, it was deemed necessary to give (at least) two of our ten slots to Homer.

While Hesiod's works are admittedly more approachable and digestible than Homer's, the latter's contribution to Greek literature, art, culture and society as a whole is almost impossible to overstate.

Indeed, one could make the claim that none of our other 'essentials' could have achieved what they had without the hand of Homer laying heavy on their shoulders.

So there we have it, our very own apologia of our decision. Though, as you know (or will very soon) an apologia and an apology are very different things indeed.

As stated before, to attempt to compile a definitive anthology of influential Greeks would be a work of futility and impossibility. In our case, it would be a great compliment to be accused to have merely 'scratched the surface' of the classical Greek world.

A culture of such depth, breadth, delight and brilliance is one that a lifetime of devout study would not do justice to, to make the slightest scuff in its shell is a worthy achievement for any student interested in art, beauty, history and the human condition.

More than anything else we hope that our chosen poets, historians, philosophers and playwrights will expand your horizons, inflame your passions, offer reflection or contemplation… and provide a little entertainment. For that is, by and large, what they lived to do and, had they not succeeded in that goal, would not have survived the countless miles and thousands of years that bring them into our homes today.

Enjoy.

—Ben Potter (January, 2015)

MAP OF THE MEDITERRANEAN

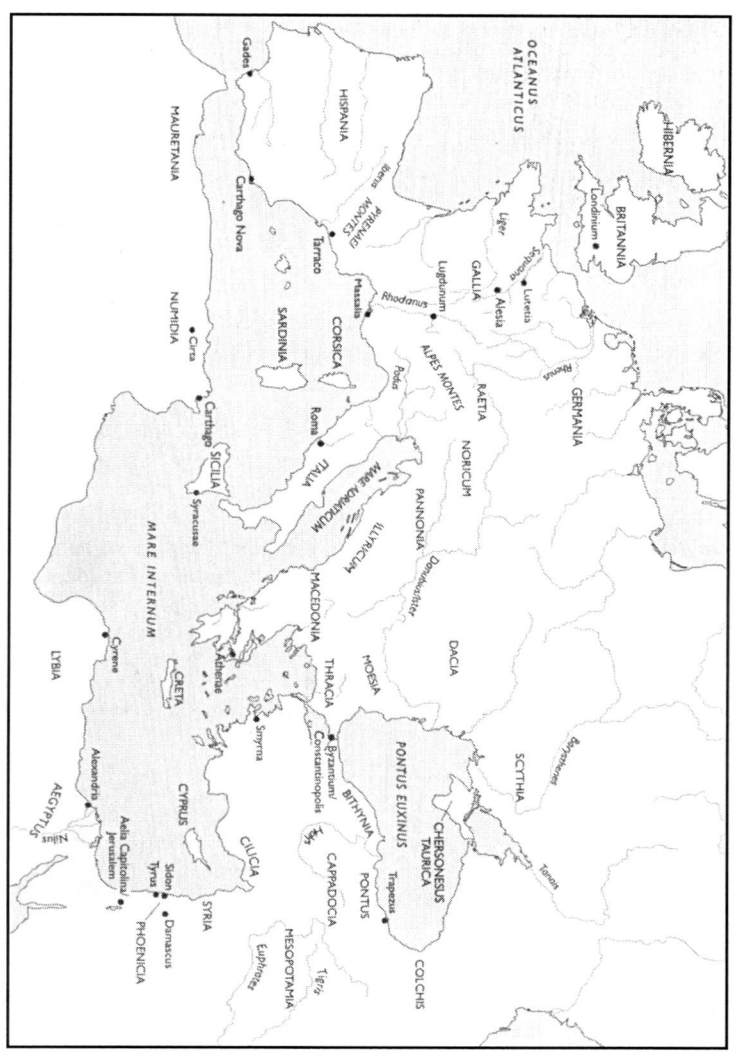

MAP OF GREECE AND THE AEGEAN

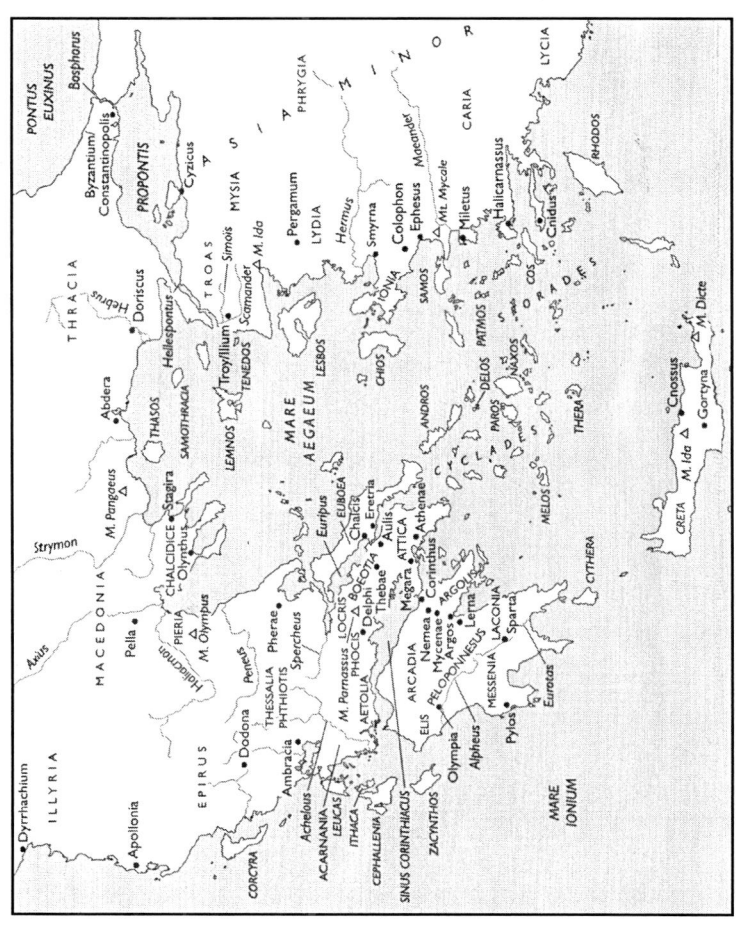

MAP OF ITALY

The Book Of The Dead
Homer
The Odyssey, Book XI
Translated by Samuel Butler

In book XI of The Odyssey, which has received the nickname "The Book of the Dead", Odysseus follows the instructions of the witch, Circe, and travels to the river Oceanus in the land of the Cimmerians.

Here, Odysseus must concoct an exotic brew of honey, milk, wine, and the blood of two sacrificial sheep. In doing so, he will attract the ghosts of long-dead heroes and be allowed to visit with some favorites like Ajax, Achilles, and even Agamemnon.

The official reason for Odysseus' assembly with these departed souls is so that he might confer with the blind prophet, Tiresias, and learn of the best way to continue his voyage home to Ithaca.

This task, however, is taken care of rather quickly. With his official purpose fulfilled, Odysseus spends the rest of his time reacquainting with old friends and comrades. What follows is a who's who of characters from classical literature and ancient mythology alike.

The purpose of these meetings seems to be purely for the benefit of the reader who may have been pondering the fate of the souls of particular characters who died, often violently, before the events of The Odyssey.

Is Achilles satisfied with his legacy as a warrior? Does Ajax regret taking his own life? How is it that Agamemnon, King of the Greeks, came to dwell in the halls of Hades? All this and more will be answered.

Then, when we had got down to the sea shore we drew our ship into the water and got her mast and sails into her; we also put the sheep on board and took our places, weeping and in great distress of mind. Circe, that great and cunning goddess, sent us a fair wind that blew dead aft and stayed steadily with us keeping our sails all the time well filled; so we did whatever wanted doing to the ship's gear and let her go as the wind and helmsman headed her. All day long her sails were full as she held her course over the sea, but when the sun went down and darkness was over all the earth, we got into the deep waters of the river Oceanus, where lie the land and city of the Cimmerians who live

1

enshrouded in mist and darkness which the rays of the sun never pierce neither at his rising nor as he goes down again out of the heavens, but the poor wretches live in one long melancholy night. When we got there we beached the ship, took the sheep out of her, and went along by the waters of Oceanus till we came to the place of which Circe had told us.

Here Perimedes and Eurylochus held the victims, while I drew my sword and dug the trench a cubit each way. I made a drink-offering to all the dead, first with honey and milk, then with wine, and thirdly with water, and I sprinkled white barley meal over the whole, praying earnestly to the poor feckless ghosts, and promising them that when I got back to Ithaca I would sacrifice a barren heifer for them, the best I had, and would load the pyre with good things. I also particularly promised that Teiresias should have a black sheep to himself, the best in all my flocks. When I had prayed sufficiently to the dead, I cut the throats of the two sheep and let the blood run into the trench, whereon the ghosts came trooping up from Erebus- brides, young bachelors, old men worn out with toil, maids who had been crossed in love, and brave men who had been killed in battle, with their armour still smirched with blood; they came from every quarter and flitted round the trench with a strange kind of screaming sound that made me turn pale with fear. When I saw them coming I told the men to be quick and flay the carcasses of the two dead sheep and make burnt offerings of them, and at the same time to repeat prayers to Hades and to Proserpine; but I sat where I was with my sword drawn and would not let the poor feckless ghosts come near the blood till Teiresias should have answered my questions.

The first ghost 'that came was that of my comrade Elpenor, for he had not yet been laid beneath the earth. We had left his body unwaked and unburied in Circe's house, for we had had too much else to do. I was very sorry for him, and cried when I saw him:'Elpenor,' said I, 'how did you come down here into this gloom and darkness? You have here on foot quicker than I have with my ship.'

"'Sir,' he answered with a groan, 'it was all bad luck, and my own unspeakable drunkenness. I was lying asleep on the top of Circe's house, and never thought of coming down again by the great staircase but fell right off the roof and broke my neck, so my soul down to the house of Hades. And now I beseech you by all those whom you have left behind you, though they are not here, by your wife, by the father who brought you up when you were a child, and by Telemachus who is the one hope of your house, do what I shall now ask you. I know that when you leave this limbo you will again hold your ship for the Aeaean island. Do not go thence leaving me unwaked and unburied behind you, or I may bring heaven's anger upon you; but burn me with whatever armour I have, build a barrow for me on the sea shore, that may tell people in days to come what a poor unlucky fellow I was, and plant over my grave the oar I used to row with when I was yet alive and with my messmates.' And I said, 'My poor fellow, I will do all that you have asked of me.'

Thus, then, did we sit and hold sad talk with one another, I on the one side of the trench with my sword held over the blood, and the ghost of my comrade saying all this to me from the other side. Then came the ghost of my dead mother Anticlea, daughter to Autolycus. I had left her alive when I set out for Troy and was moved to tears when I saw her, but even so, for all my sorrow I would not let her come near the blood till I had asked my questions of Teiresias.

Then came also the ghost of Theban Teiresias, with his golden sceptre in his hand. He knew me and said, 'Ulysses, noble son of Laertes, why, poor man, have you left the light of day and come down to visit the dead in this sad place? Stand back from the trench and withdraw your sword that I may drink of the blood and answer your questions truly.'

So I drew back, and sheathed my sword, whereon when he had drank of the blood he began with his prophecy.

"You want to know,' said he, 'about your return home, but heaven will make this hard for you. I do not think that you will escape the eye of Neptune, who still nurses his bitter grudge against you for having blinded his son. Still, after much suffering you may get home if you can restrain yourself and your companions when your ship reaches the Thrinacian island, where you will find the sheep and cattle belonging to the sun, who sees and gives ear to everything. If you leave these flocks unharmed and think of nothing but of getting home, you may yet after much hardship reach Ithaca; but if you harm them, then I forewarn you of the destruction both of your ship and of your men. Even though you may yourself escape, you will return in bad plight after losing all your men, [in another man's ship, and you will find trouble in your house, which will be overrun by high-handed people, who are devouring your substance under the pretext of paying court and making presents to your wife.

"When you get home you will take your revenge on these suitors; and after you have killed them by force or fraud in your own house, you must take a well-made oar and carry it on and on, till you come to a country where the people have never heard of the sea and do not even mix salt with their food, nor do they know anything about ships, and oars that are as the wings of a ship. I will give you this certain token which cannot escape your notice. A wayfarer will meet you and will say it must be a winnowing shovel that you have got upon your shoulder; on this you must fix the oar in the ground and sacrifice a ram, a bull, and a boar to Neptune. Then go home and offer hecatombs to an the gods in heaven one after the other. As for yourself, death shall come to you from the sea, and your life shall ebb away very gently when you are full of years and peace of mind, and your people shall bless you. All that I have said will come true].'

"This,' I answered, 'must be as it may please heaven, but tell me and tell me and tell me true, I see my poor mother's ghost close by us; she is sitting by the blood without saying a word, and though I am her own son she does not remember me and speak to me; tell me, Sir, how I can make her know me.'

"That,' said he, 'I can soon do Any ghost that you let taste of the blood will talk with you like a reasonable being, but if you do not let them have any blood they will go away again.'

On this the ghost of Teiresias went back to the house of Hades, for his prophecyings had now been spoken, but I sat still where I was until my mother came up and tasted the blood. Then she knew me at once and spoke fondly to me, saying, 'My son, how did you come down to this abode of darkness while you are still alive? It is a hard thing for the living to see these places, for between us and them there are great and terrible waters, and there is Oceanus, which no man can cross on foot, but he must have a good ship to take him. Are you all this time trying to find your way home from Troy, and have you never yet got back to Ithaca nor seen your wife in your own house?'

"'Mother,' said I, "I was forced to come here to consult the ghost of the Theban prophet Teiresias. I have never yet been near the Achaean land nor set foot on my native country, and I have had nothing but one long series of misfortunes from the very first day that I set out with Agamemnon for Ilius, the land of noble steeds, to fight the Trojans. But tell me, and tell me true, in what way did you die? Did you have a long illness, or did heaven vouchsafe you a gentle easy passage to eternity? Tell me also about my father, and the son whom I left behind me; is my property still in their hands, or has some one else got hold of it, who thinks that I shall not return to claim it? Tell me again what my wife intends doing, and in what mind she is; does she live with my son and guard my estate securely, or has she made the best match she could and married again?' My mother answered, "Your wife still remains in your house, but she is in great distress of mind and spends her whole time in tears both night and day. No one as yet has got possession of your fine property, and Telemachus still holds your lands undisturbed. He has to entertain largely, as of course he must, considering his position as a magistrate, and how every one invites him; your father remains at his old place in the country and never goes near the town. He has no comfortable bed nor bedding; in the winter he sleeps on the floor in front of the fire with the men and goes about all in rags, but in summer, when the warm weather comes on again, he lies out in the vineyard on a bed of vine leaves thrown anyhow upon the ground. He grieves continually about your never having come home, and suffers more and more as he grows older. As for my own end it was in this wise: heaven did not take me swiftly and painlessly in my own house, nor was I attacked by any illness such as those that generally wear people out and kill them, but my longing to know what you were doing and the force of my affection for you- this it was that was the death of me.'

Then I tried to find some way of embracing my mother's ghost. Thrice I sprang towards her and tried to clasp her in my arms, but each time she flitted from my embrace as it were a dream or phantom, and being touched to the quick I said to her, 'Mother, why do you not stay still when I would embrace you? If we could throw our arms around one another we might find sad comfort in the sharing of our sorrows even in the house of Hades; does Proserpine want to lay a still further load of grief upon me by mocking me with a phantom only?'

"My son," she answered, "most ill-fated of all mankind, it is not Proserpine that is beguiling you, but all people are like this when they are dead. The sinews no longer hold the flesh and bones together; these perish in the fierceness of consuming fire as soon as life has left the body, and the soul flits away as though it were a dream. Now, however, go back to the light of day as soon as you can, and note all these things that you may tell them to your wife hereafter."

Thus did we converse, and anon Proserpine sent up the ghosts of the wives and daughters of all the most famous men. They gathered in crowds about the blood, and I considered how I might question them severally.

In the end I deemed that it would be best to draw the keen blade that hung by my sturdy thigh, and keep them from all drinking the blood at once. So they came up one after the other, and each one as I questioned her told me her race and lineage.

The first I saw was Tyro. She was daughter of Salmoneus and wife of Cretheus the son of Aeolus. She fell in love with the river Enipeus who is much the most beautiful river in the whole world. Once when she was taking a walk by his side as usual, Neptune, disguised as her lover, lay with her at the mouth of the river, and a huge blue wave arched itself like a mountain over them to hide both woman and god, whereon he loosed her virgin girdle and laid her in a deep slumber. When the god had accomplished the deed of love, he took her hand in his own and said, 'Tyro, rejoice in all good will; the embraces of the gods are not fruitless, and you will have fine twins about this time twelve months. Take great care of them. I am Neptune, so now go home, but hold your tongue and do not tell any one.'

Then he dived under the sea, and she in due course bore Pelias and Neleus, who both of them served Jove with all their might. Pelias was a great breeder of sheep and lived in Iolcus, but the other lived in Pylos. The rest of her children were by Cretheus, namely, Aeson, Pheres, and Amythaon, who was a mighty warrior and charioteer.

Next to her I saw Antiope, daughter to Asopus, who could boast of having slept in the arms of even Jove himself, and who bore him two sons Amphion and Zethus. These founded Thebes with its seven gates, and built a wall all round it; for strong though they were they could not hold Thebes till they had walled it.

Then I saw Alcmena, the wife of Amphitryon, who also bore to Jove indomitable Hercules; and Megara who was daughter to great King Creon, and married the redoubtable son of Amphitryon.

I also saw fair Epicaste mother of king Oedipodes whose awful lot it was to marry her own son without suspecting it. He married her after having killed his father, but the gods proclaimed the whole story to the world; whereon he remained king of Thebes, in great grief for the spite the gods had borne him; but Epicaste went to the house of the mighty jailor Hades, having hanged herself for grief, and the avenging spirits haunted him as for an outraged mother- to his ruing bitterly thereafter.

Then I saw Chloris, whom Neleus married for her beauty, having given priceless presents for her. She was youngest daughter to Amphion son of Iasus and king of Minyan Orchomenus, and was Queen in Pylos. She bore Nestor, Chromius, and Periclymenus, and she also bore that marvelously lovely woman Pero, who was wooed by all the country round; but Neleus would only give her to him who should raid the cattle of Iphicles from the grazing grounds of Phylace, and this was a hard task. The only man who would undertake to raid them was a certain excellent seer, but the will of heaven was against him, for the rangers of the cattle caught him and put him in prison; nevertheless when a full year had passed and the same season came round again, Iphicles set him at liberty, after he had expounded all the oracles of heaven. Thus, then, was the will of Jove accomplished.

And I saw Leda the wife of Tyndarus, who bore him two famous sons, Castor breaker of horses, and Pollux the mighty boxer. Both these heroes are lying under the earth, though they are still alive, for by a special dispensation of Jove, they die and come to life again, each one of them every other day throughout all time, and they have the rank of gods.

After her I saw Iphimedeia wife of Aloeus who boasted the embrace of Neptune. She bore two sons Otus and Ephialtes, but both were short lived. They were the finest children that were ever born in this world, and the best looking, Orion only excepted; for at nine years old they were nine fathoms high, and measured nine cubits round the chest. They threatened to make war with the gods in Olympus, and tried to set Mount Ossa on the top of Mount Olympus, and Mount Pelion on the top of Ossa, that they might scale heaven itself, and they would have done it too if they had been grown up, but Apollo, son of Leto, killed both of them, before they had got so much as a sign of hair upon their cheeks or chin.

Then I saw Phaedra, and Procris, and fair Ariadne daughter of the magician Minos, whom Theseus was carrying off from Crete to Athens, but he did not enjoy her, for before he could do so Diana killed her in the island of Dia on account of what Bacchus had said against her.

I also saw Maera and Clymene and hateful Eriphyle, who sold her own husband for gold. But it would take me all night if I were to name every single one of the wives and daughters of heroes whom I saw, and it is time for me to go to bed, either on board ship with my crew, or here. As for my escort, heaven and yourselves will see to it."

Here he ended, and the guests sat all of them enthralled and speechless throughout the covered cloister. Then Arete said to them:

"What do you think of this man, O Phaecians? Is he not tall and good looking, and is he not Clever? True, he is my own guest, but all of you share in the distinction. Do not he a hurry to send him away, nor niggardly in the presents you make to one who is in such great need, for heaven has blessed all of you with great abundance."

Then spoke the aged hero Echeneus who was one of the oldest men among them, "My friends," said he, "what our august queen has just said to us is both reasonable and to the purpose, therefore be persuaded by it; but the decision whether in word or deed rests ultimately with King Alcinous."

"The thing shall be done," exclaimed Alcinous, "as surely as I still live and reign over the Phaeacians. Our guest is indeed very anxious to get home, still we must persuade him to remain with us until to-morrow, by which time I shall be able to get together the whole sum that I mean to give him. As regards- his escort it will be a matter for you all, and mine above all others as the chief person among you."

And Ulysses answered, "King Alcinous, if you were to bid me to stay here for a whole twelve months, and then speed me on my way, loaded with your noble gifts, I should obey you gladly and it would redound greatly to my advantage, for I should return fuller-handed to my own people, and should thus be more respected and beloved by all who see me when I get back to Ithaca."

"Ulysses," replied Alcinous, "not one of us who sees you has any idea that you are a charlatan or a swindler. I know there are many people going about who tell such plausible stories that it is very hard to see through them, but there is a style about your language which assures me of your good disposition. Moreover you have told the story of your own misfortunes, and those of the Argives, as though you were a practiced bard; but tell me, and tell me true, whether you saw any of the mighty heroes who went to Troy at the same time with yourself, and perished there. The evenings are still at their longest, and it is not yet bed time- go on, therefore, with your divine story, for I could stay here listening till to-morrow morning, so long as you will continue to tell us of your adventures."

"Alcinous," answered Ulysses, "there is a time for making speeches, and a time for going to bed; nevertheless, since you so desire, I will not refrain from telling you the still sadder tale of those of my comrades who did not fall fighting with the Trojans, but perished on their return, through the treachery of a wicked woman.

"When Proserpine had dismissed the female ghosts in all directions, the ghost of Agamemnon son of Atreus came sadly up to me, surrounded by those who had perished with him in the house of Aegisthus. As soon as he had tasted the blood he knew me, and weeping bitterly stretched out his arms towards me to embrace me; but he had no strength nor substance any more, and I too wept and pitied him as I beheld him. 'How did you come by your death,' said I, 'King Agamemnon? Did Neptune raise his winds and waves against you when you were at sea, or did your enemies make an end of you on the mainland when you were cattle-lifting or sheep-stealing, or while they were fighting in defence of their wives and city?'

"'Ulysses,' he answered, 'noble son of Laertes, was not lost at sea in any storm of Neptune's raising, nor did my foes despatch me upon the mainland, but Aegisthus and my wicked wife were the death of me between them. He asked me to his house, feasted me, and then butchered me most miserably as though I were a fat beast in a slaughter house, while all around me my comrades were slain like sheep or pigs for the wedding breakfast, or picnic, or gorgeous banquet of some great nobleman. You must have seen numbers of men killed either in a general engagement, or in single combat, but you never saw anything so truly pitiable as the way in which we fell in that cloister, with the mixing-bowl and the loaded tables lying all about, and the ground reeking with our-blood. I heard Priam's daughter Cassandra scream as Clytemnestra killed her close beside me. I lay dying upon the earth with the sword in my body, and raised my hands to kill the slut of a murderess, but she slipped away from me; she would not even close my lips nor my eyes when I was dying, for there is nothing in this world so cruel and so shameless as a woman when she has fallen into such guilt as hers was. Fancy murdering her own husband! I thought I was going to be welcomed home by my children and my servants, but her abominable crime has brought disgrace on herself and all women who shall come after- even on the good ones.'

"And I said, 'In truth Jove has hated the house of Atreus from first to last in the matter of their women's counsels. See how many of us fell for Helen's sake, and now it seems that Clytemnestra hatched mischief against too during your absence.'

"'Be sure, therefore,' continued Agamemnon, 'and not be too friendly even with your own wife. Do not tell her all that you know perfectly well yourself. Tell her a part only, and keep your own counsel about the rest. Not that your wife, Ulysses, is likely to murder you, for Penelope is a very admirable woman, and has an excellent nature. We left her a young bride with an infant at her breast when we set out for Troy. This child no doubt is now grown up happily to man's estate, and he and his father will have a joyful meeting and embrace one another as it is right they should do, whereas my wicked wife did not even allow me the happiness of looking upon my son, but killed me ere I could do so. Furthermore I say- and lay my saying to your heart- do not tell people when you are bringing your ship to Ithaca, but steal a march upon them, for after all this there is no trusting women. But now tell me, and tell me true, can you give me any news of my son Orestes? Is he in Orchomenus, or at Pylos, or is he at Sparta with Menelaus- for I presume that he is still living.'

"And I said, 'Agamemnon, why do you ask me? I do not know whether your son is alive or dead, and it is not right to talk when one does not know.'

"As we two sat weeping and talking thus sadly with one another the ghost of Achilles came up to us with Patroclus, Antilochus, and Ajax who was the finest and goodliest man of all the Danaans after the son of Peleus. The fleet descendant of Aeacus knew me and spoke piteously, saying, 'Ulysses, noble son of Laertes, what deed of daring will you undertake next, that you venture down to the house of Hades among us silly dead, who are but the ghosts of them that can labour no more?'

"And I said, 'Achilles, son of Peleus, foremost champion of the Achaeans, I came to consult Teiresias, and see if he could advise me about my return home to Ithaca, for I have never yet been able to get near the Achaean land, nor to set foot in my own country, but have been in trouble all the time. As for you, Achilles, no one was ever yet so fortunate as you have been, nor ever will be, for you were adored by all us Argives as long as you were alive, and now that you are here you are a great prince among the dead. Do not, therefore, take it so much to heart even if you are dead.'

"'Say not a word,' he answered, 'in death's favour; I would rather be a paid servant in a poor man's house and be above ground than king of kings among the dead. But give me news about son; is he gone to the wars and will he be a great soldier, or is this not so? Tell me also if you have heard anything about my father Peleus- does he still rule among the Myrmidons, or do they show him no respect throughout Hellas and Phthia now that he is old and his limbs fail him? Could I but stand by his side, in the light of day, with the same strength that I had when I killed the bravest of our foes upon the plain of Troy- could I but be as I then was and go even for a short time to my father's house, any one who tried to do him violence or supersede him would soon me it.'

"'I have heard nothing,' I answered, 'of Peleus, but I can tell you all about your son Neoptolemus, for I took him in my own ship from Scyros with the Achaeans. In our councils of war before Troy he was always first to speak, and his judgement was unerring. Nestor and I were the only two who could surpass him; and when it came to fighting on the plain of Troy, he would never remain with the body of his men, but would dash on far in front, foremost of them all in valour. Many a man did he kill in battle- I cannot name every single one of those whom he slew while fighting on the side of the Argives, but will only say how he killed that valiant hero Eurypylus son of Telephus, who was the handsomest man I ever saw except Memnon; many others also of the Ceteians fell around him by reason of a woman's bribes. Moreover, when all the bravest of the Argives went inside the horse that Epeus had made, and it was left to me to settle when we should either open the door of our ambuscade, or close it, though all the other leaders and chief men among the Danaans were drying their eyes and quaking in every limb, I never once saw him turn pale nor wipe a tear from his cheek; he was all the time urging me to break out from the horse- grasping the handle of his sword and his bronze-shod spear, and breathing fury against the foe. Yet when we had sacked the city of Priam he got his handsome share of the prize money and went on board (such is the fortune of war) without a wound upon him, neither from a thrown spear nor in close combat, for the rage of Mars is a matter of great chance.'

"When I had told him this, the ghost of Achilles strode off across a meadow full of asphodel, exulting over what I had said concerning the prowess of his son.

"The ghosts of other dead men stood near me and told me each his own melancholy tale; but that of Ajax son of Telamon alone held aloof- still

11

angry with me for having won the cause in our dispute about the armour of Achilles. Thetis had offered it as a prize, but the Trojan prisoners and Minerva were the judges. Would that I had never gained the day in such a contest, for it cost the life of Ajax, who was foremost of all the Danaans after the son of Peleus, alike in stature and prowess.

"When I saw him I tried to pacify him and said, 'Ajax, will you not forget and forgive even in death, but must the judgement about that hateful armour still rankle with you? It cost us Argives dear enough to lose such a tower of strength as you were to us. We mourned you as much as we mourned Achilles son of Peleus himself, nor can the blame be laid on anything but on the spite which Jove bore against the Danaans, for it was this that made him counsel your destruction- come hither, therefore, bring your proud spirit into subjection, and hear what I can tell you.'

"He would not answer, but turned away to Erebus and to the other ghosts; nevertheless, I should have made him talk to me in spite of his being so angry, or I should have gone talking to him, only that there were still others among the dead whom I desired to see.

"Then I saw Minos son of Jove with his golden sceptre in his hand sitting in judgement on the dead, and the ghosts were gathered sitting and standing round him in the spacious house of Hades, to learn his sentences upon them.

"After him I saw huge Orion in a meadow full of asphodel driving the ghosts of the wild beasts that he had killed upon the mountains, and he had a great bronze club in his hand, unbreakable for ever and ever.

"And I saw Tityus son of Gaia stretched upon the plain and covering some nine acres of ground. Two vultures on either side of him were digging their beaks into his liver, and he kept on trying to beat them off with his hands, but could not; for he had violated Jove's mistress Leto as she was going through Panopeus on her way to Pytho.

"I saw also the dreadful fate of Tantalus, who stood in a lake that reached his chin; he was dying to quench his thirst, but could never reach the water, for whenever the poor creature stooped to drink, it dried up and vanished, so that there was nothing but dry ground- parched by the spite of heaven. There were tall trees, moreover, that shed their fruit over his head- pears, pomegranates, apples, sweet figs and juicy olives, but whenever the poor creature stretched out his hand to take some, the wind tossed the branches back again to the clouds.

"And I saw Sisyphus at his endless task raising his prodigious stone with both his hands. With hands and feet he' tried to roll it up to the top of the hill, but always, just before he could roll it over on to the other side, its weight would be too much for him, and the pitiless stone would come thundering down again on to the plain. Then he would begin trying to push it up hill again, and the sweat ran off him and the steam rose after him.

"After him I saw mighty Hercules, but it was his phantom only, for he is feasting ever with the immortal gods, and has lovely Hebe to wife, who is daughter of Jove and Juno. The ghosts were screaming round him like scared birds flying all whithers. He looked black as night with his bare bow in his hands and his arrow on the string, glaring around as though ever on the point of taking aim. About his breast there was a wondrous golden belt adorned in the most marvellous fashion with bears, wild boars, and lions with gleaming eyes; there was also war, battle, and death. The man who made that belt, do what he might, would never be able to make another like it. Hercules knew me at once when he saw me, and spoke piteously, saying, my poor Ulysses, noble son of Laertes, are you too leading the same sorry kind of life that I did when I was above ground? I was son of Jove, but I went through an infinity of suffering, for I became bondsman to one who was far beneath me- a low fellow who set me all manner of labours. He once sent me here to fetch the hell-hound- for he did not think he could find anything harder for me than this, but I got the hound out of Hades and brought him to him, for Mercury and Minerva helped me.'

"On this Hercules went down again into the house of Hades, but I stayed where I was in case some other of the mighty dead should come to me. And I should have seen still other of them that are gone before, whom I would fain have seen- Theseus and Pirithous glorious children of the gods, but so many thousands of ghosts came round me and uttered such appalling cries, that I was panic stricken lest Proserpine should send up from the house of Hades the head of that awful monster Gorgon. On this I hastened back to my ship and ordered my men to go on board at once and loose the hawsers; so they embarked and took their places, whereon the ship went down the stream of the river Oceanus. We had to row at first, but presently a fair wind sprang up.

—Translated by Samuel Butler

13

The Rage of Achilles, The Death of Hector
Homer
The Iliad, Book XXII
Translated by Samuel Butler

A driving theme of The Iliad *is the rage of Achilles. The opening lines of the epic invoke the muses to sing of the rage of Achilles and how it brought about such terrible destruction for the Greeks and Trojans alike.*

For most of the epic, however, Achilles refuses to participate in the war. He is quarreling with King Agamemnon, who has stolen the captured woman Briseis from him, and the warrior refuses to fight until proper retribution has been paid.

Achilles remains on strike and is only prompted to rejoin the fray once his comrade and lover, Patroclus, is slain by the Trojan prince, Hector. Equipped with new armor forged by the god Hephaestus, Achilles dives into battle once more, intent on seeking his vengeance.

Achilles' need for revenge is inevitably self-destructive. It has been foretold by his mother, Thetis, that if Achilles seeks the death of Hector, he will be fated to perish soon after.

Achilles' rage, however, cannot be contained. He would rather die young and victorious than live out his days in obscurity. The action comes to a head in Book XXII when Achilles finally faces Hector outside the walls of Troy.

The old man tore his grey hair as he spoke, but he moved not the heart of Hector. His mother hard by wept and moaned aloud as she bared her bosom and pointed to the breast which had suckled him. "Hector," she cried, weeping bitterly the while, "Hector, my son, spurn not this breast, but have pity upon me too: if I have ever given you comfort from my own bosom, think on it now, dear son, and come within the wall to protect us from this man; stand not without to meet him. Should the wretch kill you, neither I nor your richly dowered wife shall ever weep, dear offshoot of myself, over the bed on which you lie, for dogs will devour you at the ships of the Achaeans."

Thus did the two with many tears implore their son, but they moved not the heart of Hector, and he stood his ground awaiting huge Achilles as he drew nearer towards him. As serpent in its den upon the mountains, full fed with deadly poisons, waits for the approach of man- he is filled with fury and his eyes glare terribly as he goes writhing round his den- even so Hector leaned his shield against a tower that jutted out from the wall and stood where he was, undaunted.

"Alas," said he to himself in the heaviness of his heart, "if I go within the gates, Polydamas will be the first to heap reproach upon me, for it was he that urged me to lead the Trojans back to the city on that awful night when Achilles again came forth against us. I would not listen, but it would have been indeed better if I had done so. Now that my folly has destroyed the host, I dare not look Trojan men and Trojan women in the face, lest a worse man should say, 'Hector has ruined us by his self-confidence.' Surely it would be better for me to return after having fought Achilles and slain him, or to die gloriously here before the city. What, again, if were to lay down my shield and helmet, lean my spear against the wall and go straight up to noble Achilles? What if I were to promise to give up Helen, who was the fountainhead of all this war, and all the treasure that Alexandrus brought with him in his ships to Troy, aye, and to let the Achaeans divide the half of everything that the city contains among themselves? I might make the Trojans, by the mouths of their princes, take a solemn oath that they would hide nothing, but would divide into two shares all that is within the city- but why argue with myself in this way? Were I to go up to him he would show me no kind of mercy; he would kill me then and there as easily as though I were a woman, when I had off my armour. There is no parleying with him from some rock or oak tree as young men and maidens prattle with one another. Better fight him at once, and learn to which of us Jove will vouchsafe victory."

Thus did he stand and ponder, but Achilles came up to him as it were Mars himself, plumed lord of battle. From his right shoulder he brandished his terrible spear of Pelian ash, and the bronze gleamed around him like flashing fire or the rays of the rising sun. Fear fell upon Hector as he beheld him, and he dared not stay longer where he was but fled in dismay from before the gates, while Achilles darted after him at his utmost speed. As a mountain falcon, swiftest of all birds, swoops down upon some cowering dove- the dove flies before him but the falcon with a shrill scream follows close after, resolved to have her- even so did Achilles make straight for Hector with all his might, while Hector fled under the Trojan wall as fast as his limbs could take him.

15

On they flew along the waggon-road that ran hard by under the wall, past the lookout station, and past the weather-beaten wild fig-tree, till they came to two fair springs which feed the river Scamander. One of these two springs is warm, and steam rises from it as smoke from a burning fire, but the other even in summer is as cold as hail or snow, or the ice that forms on water. Here, hard by the springs, are the goodly washing-troughs of stone, where in the time of peace before the coming of the Achaeans the wives and fair daughters of the Trojans used to wash their clothes. Past these did they fly, the one in front and the other giving ha. behind him: good was the man that fled, but better far was he that followed after, and swiftly indeed did they run, for the prize was no mere beast for sacrifice or bullock's hide, as it might be for a common foot-race, but they ran for the life of Hector. As horses in a chariot race speed round the turning-posts when they are running for some great prize- a tripod or woman- at the games in honour of some dead hero, so did these two run full speed three times round the city of Priam. All the gods watched them, and the sire of gods and men was the first to speak.

"Alas," said he, "my eyes behold a man who is dear to me being pursued round the walls of Troy; my heart is full of pity for Hector, who has burned the thigh-bones of many a heifer in my honour, at one while on the of many-valleyed Ida, and again on the citadel of Troy; and now I see noble Achilles in full pursuit of him round the city of Priam. What say you? Consider among yourselves and decide whether we shall now save him or let him fall, valiant though he be, before Achilles, son of Peleus."

Then Minerva said, "Father, wielder of the lightning, lord of cloud and storm, what mean you? Would you pluck this mortal whose doom has long been decreed out of the jaws of death? Do as you will, but we others shall not be of a mind with you."

And Jove answered, "My child, Trito-born, take heart. I did not speak in full earnest, and I will let you have your way. Do without let or hindrance as you are minded."

Thus did he urge Minerva who was already eager, and down she darted from the topmost summits of Olympus.

Achilles was still in full pursuit of Hector, as a hound chasing a fawn which he has started from its covert on the mountains, and hunts through glade and thicket. The fawn may try to elude him by crouching under cover of a bush, but he will scent her out and follow her up until he gets her- even so there was no escape for Hector from the fleet son of Peleus. Whenever he made a set to get near the Dardanian gates and under the walls, that his people might help him by showering down weapons from above, Achilles would gain on him and head him back towards the plain, keeping himself always on the city side. As a man in a dream who fails to lay hands upon another whom he is pursuing- the one cannot escape nor the other overtake- even so neither could Achilles come up with Hector, nor Hector break away from Achilles; nevertheless he might even yet have escaped death had not the time come when Apollo, who thus far had sustained his strength and nerved his running, was now no longer to stay by him. Achilles made signs to the Achaean host, and shook his head to show that no man was to aim a dart at Hector, lest another might win the glory of having hit him and he might himself come in second. Then, at last, as they were nearing the fountains for the fourth time, the father of all balanced his golden scales and placed a doom in each of them, one for Achilles and the other for Hector. As he held the scales by the middle, the doom of Hector fell down deep into the house of Hades- and then Phoebus Apollo left him. Thereon Minerva went close up to the son of Peleus and said, "Noble Achilles, favoured of heaven, we two shall surely take back to the ships a triumph for the Achaeans by slaying Hector, for all his lust of battle. Do what Apollo may as he lies grovelling before his father, aegis-bearing Jove, Hector cannot escape us longer. Stay here and take breath, while I go up to him and persuade him to make a stand and fight you."

Thus spoke Minerva. Achilles obeyed her gladly, and stood still, leaning on his bronze-pointed ashen spear, while Minerva left him and went after Hector in the form and with the voice of Deiphobus. She came close up to him and said, "Dear brother, I see you are hard pressed by Achilles who is chasing you at full speed round the city of Priam, let us await his onset and stand on our defence."

And Hector answered, "Deiphobus, you have always been dearest to me of all my brothers, children of Hecuba and Priam, but henceforth I shall rate you yet more highly, inasmuch as you have ventured outside the wall for my sake when all the others remain inside."

Then Minerva said, "Dear brother, my father and mother went down on their knees and implored me, as did all my comrades, to remain inside, so great a fear has fallen upon them all; but I was in an agony of grief when I beheld you; now, therefore, let us two make a stand and fight, and let there be no keeping our spears in reserve, that we may learn

17

whether Achilles shall kill us and bear off our spoils to the ships, or whether he shall fall before you."

Thus did Minerva inveigle him by her cunning, and when the two were now close to one another great Hector was first to speak. "I will-no longer fly you, son of Peleus," said he, "as I have been doing hitherto. Three times have I fled round the mighty city of Priam, without daring to withstand you, but now, let me either slay or be slain, for I am in the mind to face you. Let us, then, give pledges to one another by our gods, who are the fittest witnesses and guardians of all covenants; let it be agreed between us that if Jove vouchsafes me the longer stay and I take your life, I am not to treat your dead body in any unseemly fashion, but when I have stripped you of your armour, I am to give up your body to the Achaeans. And do you likewise."

Achilles glared at him and answered, "Fool, prate not to me about covenants. There can be no covenants between men and lions, wolves and lambs can never be of one mind, but hate each other out and out an through. Therefore there can be no understanding between you and me, nor may there be any covenants between us, till one or other shall fall and glut grim Mars with his life's blood. Put forth all your strength; you have need now to prove yourself indeed a bold soldier and man of war. You have no more chance, and Pallas Minerva will forthwith vanquish you by my spear: you shall now pay me in full for the grief you have caused me on account of my comrades whom you have killed in battle."

He poised his spear as he spoke and hurled it. Hector saw it coming and avoided it; he watched it and crouched down so that it flew over his head and stuck in the ground beyond; Minerva then snatched it up and gave it back to Achilles without Hector's seeing her; Hector thereon said to the son of Peleus, "You have missed your aim, Achilles, peer of the gods, and Jove has not yet revealed to you the hour of my doom, though you made sure that he had done so. You were a false-tongued liar when you deemed that I should forget my valour and quail before you. You shall not drive spear into the back of a runaway- drive it, should heaven so grant you power, drive it into me as I make straight towards you; and now for your own part avoid my spear if you can- would that you might receive the whole of it into your body; if you were once dead the Trojans would find the war an easier matter, for it is you who have harmed them most."

He poised his spear as he spoke and hurled it. His aim was true for he hit the middle of Achilles' shield, but the spear rebounded from it, and did not pierce it. Hector was angry when he saw that the weapon had sped from his hand in vain, and stood there in dismay for he had no second spear. With a loud cry he called Diphobus and asked him for one, but there was no man; then he saw the truth and said to himself, "Alas! the gods have lured me on to my destruction. I deemed that the hero Deiphobus was by my side, but he is within the wall, and Minerva has inveigled me; death is now indeed exceedingly near at hand and there is no way out of it- for so Jove and his son Apollo the far-darter have willed it, though heretofore they have been ever ready to protect me. My doom has come upon me; let me not then die ingloriously and without a struggle, but let me first do some great thing that shall be told among men hereafter."

As he spoke he drew the keen blade that hung so great and strong by his side, and gathering himself together be sprang on Achilles like a soaring eagle which swoops down from the clouds on to some lamb or timid hare- even so did Hector brandish his sword and spring upon Achilles. Achilles mad with rage darted towards him, with his wondrous shield before his breast, and his gleaming helmet, made with four layers of metal, nodding fiercely forward. The thick tresses of gold wi which Vulcan had crested the helmet floated round it, and as the evening star that shines brighter than all others through the stillness of night, even such was the gleam of the spear which Achilles poised in his right hand, fraught with the death of noble Hector. He eyed his fair flesh over and over to see where he could best wound it, but all was protected by the goodly armour of which Hector had spoiled Patroclus after he had slain him, save only the throat where the collar-bones divide the neck from the shoulders, and this is a most deadly place: here then did Achilles strike him as he was coming on towards him, and the point of his spear went right through the fleshy part of the neck, but it did not sever his windpipe so that he could still speak. Hector fell headlong, and Achilles vaunted over him saying, "Hector, you deemed that you should come off scatheless when you were spoiling Patroclus, and recked not of myself who was not with him. Fool that you were: for I, his comrade, mightier far than he, was still left behind him at the ships, and now I have laid you low. The Achaeans shall give him all due funeral rites, while dogs and vultures shall work their will upon yourself."

Then Hector said, as the life ebbed out of him, "I pray you by your life and knees, and by your parents, let not dogs devour me at the ships of the Achaeans, but accept the rich treasure of gold and bronze which my father and mother will offer you, and send my body home, that the Trojans and their wives may give me my dues of fire when I am dead."

Achilles glared at him and answered, "Dog, talk not to me neither of knees nor parents; would that I could be as sure of being able to cut your flesh into pieces and eat it raw, for the ill have done me, as I am that nothing shall save you from the dogs- it shall not be, though they bring ten or twenty-fold ransom and weigh it out for me on the spot, with promise of yet more hereafter. Though Priam son of Dardanus should bid them offer me your weight in gold, even so your mother shall never lay you out and make lament over the son she bore, but dogs and vultures shall eat you utterly up."

Hector with his dying breath then said, "I know you what you are, and was sure that I should not move you, for your heart is hard as iron; look to it that I bring not heaven's anger upon you on the day when Paris and Phoebus Apollo, valiant though you be, shall slay you at the Scaean gates."

When he had thus said the shrouds of death enfolded him, whereon his soul went out of him and flew down to the house of Hades, lamenting its sad fate that it should en' youth and strength no longer. But Achilles said, speaking to the dead body, "Die; for my part I will accept my fate whensoever Jove and the other gods see fit to send it."

As he spoke he drew his spear from the body and set it on one side; then he stripped the blood-stained armour from Hector's shoulders while the other Achaeans came running up to view his wondrous strength and beauty; and no one came near him without giving him a fresh wound. Then would one turn to his neighbour and say, "It is easier to handle Hector now than when he was flinging fire on to our ships" and as he spoke he would thrust his spear into him anew.

When Achilles had done spoiling Hector of his armour, he stood among the Argives and said, "My friends, princes and counsellors of the Argives, now that heaven has vouchsafed us to overcome this man, who has done us more hurt than all the others together, consider whether we should not attack the city in force, and discover in what mind the Trojans may be. We should thus learn whether they will desert their city now that Hector has fallen, or will still hold out even though he is no longer living. But why argue with myself in this way, while Patroclus is still lying at the ships unburied, and unmourned- he Whom I can never forget so long as I am alive and my strength fails not? Though men forget their dead when once they are within the house of Hades, yet not even there will I forget the comrade whom I have lost. Now, therefore, Achaean youths, let us raise the song of victory and go back to the ships taking this man along with us; for we have achieved a mighty triumph and have slain noble Hector to whom the Trojans prayed throughout their city as though he were a god."

On this he treated the body of Hector with contumely: he pierced the sinews at the back of both his feet from heel to ancle and passed thongs of ox-hide through the slits he had made: thus he made the body fast to his chariot, letting the head trail upon the ground. Then when he had put the goodly armour on the chariot and had himself mounted, he lashed his horses on and they flew forward nothing loth. The dust rose from Hector as he was being dragged along, his dark hair flew all abroad, and his head once so comely was laid low on earth, for Jove had now delivered him into the hands of his foes to do him outrage in his own land.

—Translated by Samuel Butler

Xenia And The Swineherd
Homer
The Odyssey, Book XIV
Translated by Samuel Butler

By book XIV, Odysseus has made his way back to Ithaca. He is, however, not yet successful in reclaiming his oikos, or household, from the 108 suitors who have taken up residence during his absence.

Before he can undertake such a task, Odysseus first encounters his old friend and swineherd, Eumaeus. Eumaeus does not recognize Odysseus, who is disguised as a beggar, but still welcomes the man into his home and offers him food and drink.

Eumaeus tells the beggar, Odysseus, the state of affairs on Ithaca. The king has been gone for decades now, fighting in the Trojan War. The suitors, believing Odysseus dead, do not feel compelled to leave his home. Nonetheless, Penelope, Odysseus' wife, has obstinately refused the advances of the suitors, opting to remain loyal to her husband.

Eumaeus is often pointed to as a good example of a character adhering to the customs of xenia, *the ancient Greek traditions regarding hospitality between a guest and a host.*

By inviting the disguised Odysseus into his home and offering him food and conversation, Eumaeus is obeying the laws of xenia. *His loyalty to these customs is even more significant given his lowly status as a swineherd.*

The good behavior of Eumaeus is starkly juxtaposed to that of the suitors, who continue to feast in the home of Odysseus without him being present and who have most certainly worn out their welcome.

Xenia, *although perhaps unfamiliar to us, was of great importance to the ancient Greeks. Within* The Odyssey, *we can often tell which characters are heroic or wicked based upon their adherence to* xenia. *Moreover, those who deny the customs of xenia will certainly be punished for their transgressions.*

Ulysses now left the haven, and took the rough track up through the wooded country and over the crest of the mountain till he reached the place where Minerva had said that he would find the swineherd, who was the most thrifty servant he had. He found him sitting in front of his hut, which was by the yards that he had built on a site which could be seen from far. He had made them spacious and fair to see, with a free ran for the pigs all round them; he had built them during his master's absence, of stones which he had gathered out of the ground, without saying anything to Penelope or Laertes, and he had fenced them on top with thorn bushes. Outside the yard he had run a strong fence of oaken posts, split, and set pretty close together, while inside lie had built twelve sties near one another for the sows to lie in. There were fifty pigs wallowing in each sty, all of them breeding sows; but the boars slept outside and were much fewer in number, for the suitors kept on eating them, and die swineherd had to send them the best he had continually. There were three hundred and sixty boar pigs, and the herdsman's four hounds, which were as fierce as wolves, slept always with them. The swineherd was at that moment cutting out a pair of sandals from a good stout ox hide. Three of his men were out herding the pigs in one place or another, and he had sent the fourth to town with a boar that he had been forced to send the suitors that they might sacrifice it and have their fill of meat.

When the hounds saw Ulysses they set up a furious barking and flew at him, but Ulysses was cunning enough to sit down and loose his hold of the stick that he had in his hand: still, he would have been torn by them in his own homestead had not the swineherd dropped his ox hide, rushed full speed through the gate of the yard and driven the dogs off by shouting and throwing stones at them. Then he said to Ulysses, "Old man, the dogs were likely to have made short work of you, and then you would have got me into trouble. The gods have given me quite enough worries without that, for I have lost the best of masters, and am in continual grief on his account. I have to attend swine for other people to eat, while he, if he yet lives to see the light of day, is starving in some distant land. But come inside, and when you have had your fill of bread and wine, tell me where you come from, and all about your misfortunes."

On this the swineherd led the way into the hut and bade him sit down. He strewed a good thick bed of rushes upon the floor, and on the top of this he threw the shaggy chamois skin- a great thick one- on which he used to sleep by night. Ulysses was pleased at being made thus welcome, and said "May Jove, sir, and the rest of the gods grant you your heart's desire in return for the kind way in which you have received me."

To this you answered, O swineherd Eumaeus, "Stranger, though a still poorer man should come here, it would not be right for me to insult him, for all strangers and beggars are from Jove. You must take what you can get and be thankful, for servants live in fear when they have young lords for their masters; and this is my misfortune now, for heaven has hindered the return of him who would have been always good to me and given me something of my own- a house, a piece of land, a good looking wife, and all else that a liberal master allows a servant who has worked hard for him, and whose labour the gods have prospered as they have mine in the situation which I hold. If my master had grown old here he would have done great things by me, but he is gone, and I wish that Helen's whole race were utterly destroyed, for she has been the death of many a good man. It was this matter that took my master to Ilius, the land of noble steeds, to fight the Trojans in the cause of king Agamemnon."

As he spoke he bound his girdle round him and went to the sties where the young sucking pigs were penned. He picked out two which he brought back with him and sacrificed. He singed them, cut them up, and spitted on them; when the meat was cooked he brought it all in and set it before Ulysses, hot and still on the spit, whereon Ulysses sprinkled it over with white barley meal. The swineherd then mixed wine in a bowl of ivy-wood, and taking a seat opposite Ulysses told him to begin.

"Fall to, stranger," said he, "on a dish of servant's pork. The fat pigs have to go to the suitors, who eat them up without shame or scruple; but the blessed gods love not such shameful doings, and respect those who do what is lawful and right. Even the fierce free-booters who go raiding on other people's land, and Jove gives them their spoil- even they, when they have filled their ships and got home again live conscience-stricken, and look fearfully for judgement; but some god seems to have told these people that Ulysses is dead and gone; they will not, therefore, go back to their own homes and make their offers of marriage in the usual way, but waste his estate by force, without fear or stint. Not a day or night comes out of heaven, but they sacrifice not one victim nor two only, and they take the run of his wine, for he was exceedingly rich. No other great man either in Ithaca or on the mainland is as rich as he was; he had as much as twenty men put together. I will tell you what he had. There are twelve herds of cattle upon the mainland, and as many flocks of sheep, there are also twelve droves of pigs, while his own men and hired strangers feed him twelve widely spreading herds of goats. Here in Ithaca he runs even large flocks of goats on the far end of the island,

and they are in the charge of excellent goatherds. Each one of these sends the suitors the best goat in the flock every day. As for myself, I am in charge of the pigs that you see here, and I have to keep picking out the best I have and sending it to them."

This was his story, but Ulysses went on eating and drinking ravenously without a word, brooding his revenge. When he had eaten enough and was satisfied, the swineherd took the bowl from which he usually drank, filled it with wine, and gave it to Ulysses, who was pleased, and said as he took it in his hands, "My friend, who was this master of yours that bought you and paid for you, so rich and so powerful as you tell me? You say he perished in the cause of King Agamemnon; tell me who he was, in case I may have met with such a person. Jove and the other gods know, but I may be able to give you news of him, for I have travelled much."

Eumaeus answered, "Old man, no traveller who comes here with news will get Ulysses' wife and son to believe his story. Nevertheless, tramps in want of a lodging keep coming with their mouths full of lies, and not a word of truth; every one who finds his way to Ithaca goes to my mistress and tells her falsehoods, whereon she takes them in, makes much of them, and asks them all manner of questions, crying all the time as women will when they have lost their husbands. And you too, old man, for a shirt and a cloak would doubtless make up a very pretty story. But the wolves and birds of prey have long since torn Ulysses to pieces, or the fishes of the sea have eaten him, and his bones are lying buried deep in sand upon some foreign shore; he is dead and gone, and a bad business it is for all his friends- for me especially; go where I may I shall never find so good a master, not even if I were to go home to my mother and father where I was bred and born. I do not so much care, however, about my parents now, though I should dearly like to see them again in my own country; it is the loss of Ulysses that grieves me most; I cannot speak of him without reverence though he is here no longer, for he was very fond of me, and took such care of me that whereever he may be I shall always honour his memory."

"My friend," replied Ulysses, "you are very positive, and very hard of belief about your master's coming home again, nevertheless I will not merely say, but will swear, that he is coming. Do not give me anything for my news till he has actually come, you may then give me a shirt and cloak of good wear if you will. I am in great want, but I will not take anything at all till then, for I hate a man, even as I hate hell fire, who lets his poverty tempt him into lying. I swear by king Jove, by the rites

25

of hospitality, and by that hearth of Ulysses to which I have now come, that all will surely happen as I have said it will. Ulysses will return in this self same year; with the end of this moon and the beginning of the next he will be here to do vengeance on all those who are ill treating his wife and son."

To this you answered, O swineherd Eumaeus, "Old man, you will neither get paid for bringing good news, nor will Ulysses ever come home; drink you wine in peace, and let us talk about something else. Do not keep on reminding me of all this; it always pains me when any one speaks about my honoured master. As for your oath we will let it alone, but I only wish he may come, as do Penelope, his old father Laertes, and his son Telemachus. I am terribly unhappy too about this same boy of his; he was running up fast into manhood, and bade fare to be no worse man, face and figure, than his father, but some one, either god or man, has been unsettling his mind, so he has gone off to Pylos to try and get news of his father, and the suitors are lying in wait for him as he is coming home, in the hope of leaving the house of Arceisius without a name in Ithaca. But let us say no more about him, and leave him to be taken, or else to escape if the son of Saturn holds his hand over him to protect him. And now, old man, tell me your own story; tell me also, for I want to know, who you are and where you come from. Tell me of your town and parents, what manner of ship you came in, how crew brought you to Ithaca, and from what country they professed to come- for you cannot have come by land."

And Ulysses answered, "I will tell you all about it. If there were meat and wine enough, and we could stay here in the hut with nothing to do but to eat and drink while the others go to their work, I could easily talk on for a whole twelve months without ever finishing the story of the sorrows with which it has pleased heaven to visit me.

"I am by birth a Cretan; my father was a well-to-do man, who had many sons born in marriage, whereas I was the son of a slave whom he had purchased for a concubine; nevertheless, my father Castor son of Hylax (whose lineage I claim, and who was held in the highest honour among the Cretans for his wealth, prosperity, and the valour of his sons) put me on the same level with my brothers who had been born in wedlock.

When, however, death took him to the house of Hades, his sons divided his estate and cast lots for their shares, but to me they gave a holding and little else; nevertheless, my valour enabled me to marry into a rich family, for I was not given to bragging, or shirking on the field of battle. It is all over now; still, if you look at the straw you can see what the ear was, for I have had trouble enough and to spare. Mars and Minerva made me doughty in war; when I had picked my men to surprise the enemy with an ambuscade I never gave death so much as a thought, but was the first to leap forward and spear all whom I could overtake. Such was I in battle, but I did not care about farm work, nor the frugal home life of those who would bring up children. My delight was in ships, fighting, javelins, and arrows- things that most men shudder to think of; but one man likes one thing and another another, and this was what I was most naturally inclined to. Before the Achaeans went to Troy, nine times was I in command of men and ships on foreign service, and I amassed much wealth. I had my pick of the spoil in the first instance, and much more was allotted to me later on.

"My house grew apace and I became a great man among the Cretans, but when Jove counselled that terrible expedition, in which so many perished, the people required me and Idomeneus to lead their ships to Troy, and there was no way out of it, for they insisted on our doing so. There we fought for nine whole years, but in the tenth we sacked the city of Priam and sailed home again as heaven dispersed us. Then it was that Jove devised evil against me. I spent but one month happily with my children, wife, and property, and then I conceived the idea of making a descent on Egypt, so I fitted out a fine fleet and manned it. I had nine ships, and the people flocked to fill them. For six days I and my men made feast, and I found them many victims both for sacrifice to the gods and for themselves, but on the seventh day we went on board and set sail from Crete with a fair North wind behind us though we were going down a river. Nothing went ill with any of our ships, and we had no sickness on board, but sat where we were and let the ships go as the wind and steersmen took them. On the fifth day we reached the river Aegyptus; there I stationed my ships in the river, bidding my men stay by them and keep guard over them while I sent out scouts to reconnoitre from every point of vantage.

"But the men disobeyed my orders, took to their own devices, and ravaged the land of the Egyptians, killing the men, and taking their wives and children captive. The alarm was soon carried to the city, and when they heard the war cry, the people came out at daybreak till the plain was filled with horsemen and foot soldiers and with the gleam of armour. Then Jove spread panic among my men, and they would no longer face the enemy, for they found themselves surrounded. The Egyptians killed many of us, and took the rest alive to do forced labour for them. Jove, however, put it in my mind to do thus- and I wish I had died then and there in Egypt instead, for there was much sorrow in store for me- I took off my helmet and shield and dropped my spear from my hand; then I went straight up to the king's chariot, clasped his knees and kissed them, whereon he spared my life, bade me get into his chariot, and took me weeping to his own home. Many made at me with their ashen spears and tried to kil me in their fury, but the king protected me, for he feared the wrath of Jove the protector of strangers, who punishes those who do evil.

"I stayed there for seven years and got together much money among the Egyptians, for they all gave me something; but when it was now going on for eight years there came a certain Phoenician, a cunning rascal, who had already committed all sorts of villainy, and this man talked me over into going with him to Phoenicia, where his house and his possessions lay. I stayed there for a whole twelve months, but at the end of that time when months and days had gone by till the same season had come round again, he set me on board a ship bound for Libya, on a pretence that I was to take a cargo along with him to that place, but really that he might sell me as a slave and take the money I fetched. I suspected his intention, but went on board with him, for I could not help it.

"The ship ran before a fresh North wind till we had reached the sea that lies between Crete and Libya; there, however, Jove counselled their destruction, for as soon as we were well out from Crete and could see nothing but sea and sky, he raised a black cloud over our ship and the sea grew dark beneath it. Then Jove let fly with his thunderbolts and the ship went round and round and was filled with fire and brimstone as the lightning struck it. The men fell all into the sea; they were carried about in the water round the ship looking like so many sea-gulls, but the god presently deprived them of all chance of getting home again. I was all dismayed; Jove, however, sent the ship's mast within my reach, which saved my life, for I clung to it, and drifted before the fury of the gale. Nine days did I drift but in the darkness of the tenth night a great wave bore me on to the Thesprotian coast. There Pheidon king of the Thesprotians entertained me hospitably without charging me anything at all for his son found me when I was nearly dead with cold and fatigue, whereon he raised me by the hand, took me to his father's house and gave me clothes to wear.

"There it was that I heard news of Ulysses, for the king told me he had entertained him, and shown him much hospitality while he was on his homeward journey. He showed me also the treasure of gold, and wrought iron that Ulysses had got together. There was enough to keep his family for ten generations, so much had he left in the house of king Pheidon. But the king said Ulysses had gone to Dodona that he might learn Jove's mind from the god's high oak tree, and know whether after so long an absence he should return to Ithaca openly, or in secret. Moreover the king swore in my presence, making drink-offerings in his own house as he did so, that the ship was by the water side, and the crew found, that should take him to his own country. He sent me off however before Ulysses returned, for there happened to be a Thesprotian ship sailing for the wheat-growing island of Dulichium, and he told those in charge of her to be sure and take me safely to King Acastus.

"These men hatched a plot against me that would have reduced me to the very extreme of misery, for when the ship had got some way out from land they resolved on selling me as a slave. They stripped me of the shirt and cloak that I was wearing, and gave me instead the tattered old clouts in which you now see me; then, towards nightfall, they reached the tilled lands of Ithaca, and there they bound me with a strong rope fast in the ship, while they went on shore to get supper by the sea side. But the gods soon undid my bonds for me, and having drawn my rags over my head I slid down the rudder into the sea, where I struck out and swam till I was well clear of them, and came ashore near a thick wood in which I lay concealed. They were very angry at my having escaped and went searching about for me, till at last they thought it was no further use and went back to their ship. The gods, having hidden me thus easily, then took me to a good man's door- for it seems that I am not to die yet awhile."

To this you answered, O swineherd Eumaeus, "Poor unhappy stranger, I have found the story of your misfortunes extremely interesting, but that part about Ulysses is not right; and you will never get me to believe it. Why should a man like you go about telling lies in this way? I know all about the return of my master. The gods one and all of them detest him, or they would have taken him before Troy, or let him die with friends around him when the days of his fighting were done; for then the Achaeans would have built a mound over his ashes and his son would have been heir to his renown, but now the storm winds have spirited him away we know not whither.

"As for me I live out of the way here with the pigs, and never go to the town unless when Penelope sends for me on the arrival of some news about Ulysses. Then they all sit round and ask questions, both those who grieve over the king's absence, and those who rejoice at it because they can eat up his property without paying for it. For my own part I have never cared about asking anyone else since the time when I was taken in by an Aetolian, who had killed a man and come a long way till at last he reached my station, and I was very kind to him. He said he had seen Ulysses with Idomeneus among the Cretans, refitting his ships which had been damaged in a gale. He said Ulysses would return in the following summer or autumn with his men, and that he would bring back much wealth. And now you, you unfortunate old man, since fate has brought you to my door, do not try to flatter me in this way with vain hopes. It is not for any such reason that I shall treat you kindly, but only out of respect for Jove the god of hospitality, as fearing him and pitying you."

Ulysses answered, "I see that you are of an unbelieving mind; I have given you my oath, and yet you will not credit me; let us then make a bargain, and call all the gods in heaven to witness it. If your master comes home, give me a cloak and shirt of good wear, and send me to Dulichium where I want to go; but if he does not come as I say he will, set your men on to me, and tell them to throw me from yonder precepice, as a warning to tramps not to go about the country telling lies."

"And a pretty figure I should cut then," replied Eumaeus, both now and hereafter, if I were to kill you after receiving you into my hut and showing you hospitality. I should have to say my prayers in good earnest if I did; but it is just supper time and I hope my men will come in directly, that we may cook something savoury for supper."

Thus did they converse, and presently the swineherds came up with the pigs, which were then shut up for the night in their sties, and a tremendous squealing they made as they were being driven into them. But Eumaeus called to his men and said, "Bring in the best pig you have, that I may sacrifice for this stranger, and we will take toll of him ourselves. We have had trouble enough this long time feeding pigs, while others reap the fruit of our labour."

On this he began chopping firewood, while the others brought in a fine fat five year old boar pig, and set it at the altar. Eumaeus did not forget the gods, for he was a man of good principles, so the first thing he did was to cut bristles from the pig's face and throw them into the fire, praying to all the gods as he did so that Ulysses might return home again. Then he clubbed the pig with a billet of oak which he had kept back when he was chopping the firewood, and stunned it, while the others slaughtered and singed it. Then they cut it up, and Eumaeus began by putting raw pieces from each joint on to some of the fat; these he sprinkled with barley meal, and laid upon the embers; they cut the rest of the meat up small, put the pieces upon the spits and roasted them till they were done; when they had taken them off the spits they threw them on to the dresser in a heap. The swineherd, who was a most equitable man, then stood up to give every one his share. He made seven portions; one of these he set apart for Mercury the son of Maia and the nymphs, praying to them as he did so; the others he dealt out to the men man by man. He gave Ulysses some slices cut lengthways down the loin as a mark of especial honour, and Ulysses was much pleased. "I hope, Eumaeus," said he, "that Jove will be as well disposed towards you as I am, for the respect you are showing to an outcast like myself."

To this you answered, O swineherd Eumaeus, "Eat, my good fellow, and enjoy your supper, such as it is. God grants this, and withholds that, just as he thinks right, for he can do whatever he chooses."

As he spoke he cut off the first piece and offered it as a burnt sacrifice to the immortal gods; then he made them a drink-offering, put the cup in the hands of Ulysses, and sat down to his own portion. Mesaulius brought them their bread; the swineherd had bought this man on his own account from among the Taphians during his master's absence, and had paid for him with his own money without saying anything either to his mistress or Laertes. They then laid their hands upon the good things that were before them, and when they had had enough to eat and drink, Mesaulius took away what was left of the bread, and they all went to bed after having made a hearty supper.

Now the night came on stormy and very dark, for there was no moon. It poured without ceasing, and the wind blew strong from the West, which is a wet quarter, so Ulysses thought he would see whether Eumaeus, in the excellent care he took of him, would take off his own cloak and give it him, or make one of his men give him one. "Listen to me," said he, "Eumaeus and the rest of you; when I have said a prayer I will tell you something. It is the wine that makes me talk in this way; wine will make even a wise man fall to singing; it will make him chuckle and dance and say many a word that he had better leave unspoken; still, as I have begun, I will go on. Would that I were still young and strong as when we got up an ambuscade before Troy. Menelaus and Ulysses were the leaders, but I was in command also, for the other two would have it so. When we had come up to the wall of the city we crouched down beneath our armour and lay there under cover of the reeds and thick brush-wood that grew about the swamp. It came on to freeze with a North wind blowing; the snow fell small and fine like hoar frost, and our shields were coated thick with rime. The others had all got cloaks and shirts, and slept comfortably enough with their shields about their shoulders, but I had carelessly left my cloak behind me, not thinking that I should be too cold, and had gone off in nothing but my shirt and shield. When the night was two-thirds through and the stars had shifted their their places, I nudged Ulysses who was close to me with my elbow, and he at once gave me his ear.

"'Ulysses,' said I, 'this cold will be the death of me, for I have no cloak; some god fooled me into setting off with nothing on but my shirt, and I do not know what to do.'

"Ulysses, who was as crafty as he was valiant, hit upon the following plan:

"'Keep still,' said he in a low voice, 'or the others will hear you.' Then he raised his head on his elbow.

"'My friends,' said he, 'I have had a dream from heaven in my sleep. We are a long way from the ships; I wish some one would go down and tell Agamemnon to send us up more men at once.'

"On this Thoas son of Andraemon threw off his cloak and set out running to the ships, whereon I took the cloak and lay in it comfortably enough till morning. Would that I were still young and strong as I was in those days, for then some one of you swineherds would give me a cloak both out of good will and for the respect due to a brave soldier; but now people look down upon me because my clothes are shabby."

And Eumaeus answered, "Old man, you have told us an excellent story, and have said nothing so far but what is quite satisfactory; for the present, therefore, you shall want neither clothing nor anything else that a stranger in distress may reasonably expect, but to-morrow morning you have to shake your own old rags about your body again, for we have not many spare cloaks nor shirts up here, but every man has only one. When Ulysses' son comes home again he will give you both cloak and shirt, and send you wherever you may want to go."

With this he got up and made a bed for Ulysses by throwing some goatskins and sheepskins on the ground in front of the fire. Here Ulysses lay down, and Eumaeus covered him over with a great heavy cloak that he kept for a change in case of extraordinarily bad weather.

Thus did Ulysses sleep, and the young men slept beside him. But the swineherd did not like sleeping away from his pigs, so he got ready to go and Ulysses was glad to see that he looked after his property during his master's absence. First he slung his sword over his brawny shoulders and put on a thick cloak to keep out the wind. He also took the skin of a large and well fed goat, and a javelin in case of attack from men or dogs. Thus equipped he went to his rest where the pigs were camping under an overhanging rock that gave them shelter from the North wind.

—Translated by Samuel Butler

Agamemnon
Aeschylus
Translated by Ian Johnston

Agamemnon was written by Aeschylus in 458 BCE and centers around the inauspicious homecoming of King Agamemnon who has been away, fighting in the Trojan War for ten years.

The play depicts the assassination of the title character at the hands of his wife, Clytemnestra, as an act of vengeance. Agamemnon had previously sacrificed his daughter, Iphigenia, to gain favorable winds during his journey to Troy.

While it might seem easy enough to label the assassination as the desperate act of one grief-stricken and deeply angered woman, there is also the overriding understanding that the tragic bloodshed is, at least partially, a symptom of a terrible curse that has been plaguing Agamemnon's bloodline for generations.

The curse began with Agamemnon's great grandfather, Tantalus, who killed his son and attempted to feed the human flesh to the gods. The gods discovered this crime and banished Tantalus to the deepest reaches of Hades.

While the fate of Tantalus might be sealed, his bloodline would continue to suffer as a result of his crimes. His family would be curse by the gods; his subsequent children and grandchildren forever plagued with bloodshed and death.

And so it would seem that the death of Agamemnon was not only triggered by his own crimes, but also by the crimes of his father and grandfathers.

The audience would have been acutely aware of these details. It is well known that the family cannot escape the cursed cycle of death propagated by the past.

DRAMATIS PERSONAE

WATCHMAN: servant of Agamemnon and Clytaemnestra.
CHORUS: old men, citizens of Argos.

CLYTAEMNESTRA: Wife of Agamemnon.
HERALD: soldier serving with Agamemnon.
AGAMEMNON: king of Argos, leader of the Greek expedition to Troy.
MESSENGER: a servant in the palace.
CASSANDRA: Daughter of King Priam, prisoner of Agamemnon.
AEGISTHUS: Cousin to Agamemnon, Clytaemnestra's lover.
SOLDIERS and SERVANTS attending on Agamemnon and on
    Clytaemnestra and Aegisthus.

*[The scene is in Argos immediately in front of the steps leading up to the
main doors of the royal palace. In front of the palace there are statues
of gods. At the start of the play, the Watchman is prone on the roof of the
palace resting his head on his arms. It is just before dawn.]*

WATCHMAN
    I pray the gods will give me some relief
    and end this weary job. One long full year
    I've been lying here, on this rooftop,
    the palace of the sons of Atreus,
    resting on my arms, just like a dog.
    I've come to know the night sky, every star,
    the powers we see glittering in the sky,
    bringing winter and summer to us all,
    as the constellations rise and sink.
    I'm still looking for that signal flare,
    the fiery blaze from Troy, announcing
    it's been taken. These are my instructions
    from the queen. She has a fiery heart,
    the determined resolution of a man.
    When I set my damp, restless bed up here,
    I never dream, for I don't fall asleep.
    No. Fear comes instead and stands beside me,
    so I can't shut my eyes and get some rest.
    If I try to sing or hum a tune,
    something to do instead of trying to sleep,
    since I'm always awake, I start to weep,
    as I lament what's happened to this house,
    where things are not being governed well,
    not like they used to be. How I wish
    my watching could end happily tonight,

with good news brought by fire blazing
through this darkness.

*[The signal fire the Watchman has been waiting for suddenly appears.
The Watchman springs to his feet]*

Fire gleaming in the night!
What a welcome sight! Light of a new day—
you'll bring on many dancing choruses
right here in Argos, celebrations
of this joyful news.

[Shouting]

It's over! It's over!
I must call out to wake the queen,
Clytaemnestra, Agamemnon's wife,
to get her out of bed, so she can raise
a shout of joy as soon as possible
inside the palace, welcoming this fire—
if indeed the city of Troy's fallen,
as this signal fire seems to indicate.
For my part, I'll start things off by dancing,
treating my king's good fortune as my own.
I've had a lucky dice roll, triple six,
thanks to this fiery signal . . . .

*[His mood suddenly changes to something much more hesitant and
reserved]*

But I hope
the master of this house may come home soon,
so I can grasp his welcome hand in mine.
As for all the rest, I'm saying nothing.
A great ox stands on my tongue. But this house,
if it could speak, might tell some stories.
I speak to those who know about these things.
For those who don't, there's nothing I remember.

*[The Watchman goes down into the house. Enter the Chorus of Argive
elders, very old men who carry staves to help them stand up. As they
speak, servants come out of the palace and light oil lamps in offering to
the statues of the gods outside the palace doors]*

36

CHORUS
It's now ten years since Menelaus,
Priam's great adversary,
and lord Agamemnon,
two mighty sons of Atreus,
joined by Zeus in double honours—
twin thrones and royal sceptres—
left this country with that fleet,
a thousand Argive ships,
to back their warrior cause with force,
hearts screaming in their battle fury,
two eagles overwhelmed by grief,
crying for their young—wings beating
like oars, they wheel aloft,
high above their home, distressed
because they've lost their work—
their fledglings in the nest are gone!*

Then one of the supreme powers—
Apollo, or Pan, or Zeus—
hears the shrill wailing cry,
hears those screaming birds,
who live within his realm,
and sends a late-avenging Fury
to take revenge on the transgressors.
In just that way, mighty Zeus,
god of hospitality,
sends those sons of Atreus
against Alexander, son of Priam—
for that woman's sake, Helen,
the one who's had so many men,
condemning Trojans and Danaans
to many heartfelt struggles, both alike,
knees splintering as the fighting starts.*

Now things stand as they stand.
What's destined to come will be fulfilled,
and no libation, sacrifice, or human tears
will mitigate the gods' unbending wrath
of sacrifice not blessed by fire.

But as for us, whose old bodies
confer no honour, who were left behind
when the army sailed so long ago,
we wait here, using up our strength
to support ourselves with canes,
like children, whose power,
though growing in their chests,
is not yet fit for Ares, god of war.
And so it is with old men, too,
who, when they reach extreme old age,
wither like leaves, and go their way
three-footed, no better than a child,
as they wander like a daydream.

But you, daughter of Tyndareus,
queen Clytaemnestra,
what's going on? What news?
What reports have you received
that lead you to send your servants out
commanding all this sacrifice?
For every god our city worships—
all-powerful gods above the earth,
and those below, and those in heaven,
and those in the marketplace—
their altars are ablaze with offerings.
Fires rise here and there and everywhere,
right up to heaven, fed by sacred oils
brought from the palace—sweet and holy,
their purity sustains those flames.
Tell us what you can,
tell us what's right for us to hear.
Cure our anxious thoughts.
For now, at one particular moment,
things look grim, but then our hopes,
rising from these sacrificial fires,
make things seem better, soothing
corrosive pains that eat my heart.

I have the power to proclaim
that prophecy made to our kings,

as they were setting on their way,
a happy outcome for their expedition.
My age inspires in me Persuasion still,
the power of song sent from the gods,
to sing how two kings of Achaea's troops,
united in a joint command, led off
the youth of Greece, armed with avenging spears,
marching against Troy, land of Teucer.
They got a happy omen—two eagles,
kings of birds, appeared before the kings of ships.
One bird was black, the other's tail was white,
here, close to the palace, on the right,
in a place where everyone could see.
The eagles were gorging themselves,
devouring a pregnant hare
and all its unborn offspring,
struggling in their death throes still.

Sing out the song of sorrow, song of grief,
but let the good prevail.

Then the army's prophet, Calchas,
observing the twin purposes
in the two warlike sons of Atreus,
saw the twin leaders of the army
in those birds devouring the hare.
He then interpreted the omen, saying,

"In due course this expedition
will capture Priam's city, Troy—
before its towers a violent Fate
will annihilate all public goods.
But may no anger from the gods
cast its dark shadow on our troops,
our great bit forged to curb Troy's mouth.
For goddess Artemis is full of anger
at her father's flying hounds—she pities
the cowering sacrificial creature in distress,
she pities its young, slaughtered
before she's brought them into life.
Artemis abominates the eagles' feast."

Sing out the song of sorrow, song of grief,
but let the good prevail.

"And lovely Artemis—
though you're gentle with the tender cubs
of vicious lions and take special joy
in the suckling young of all wild living beasts,
promise things will work out well,
as this omen of the eagles indicates,
an auspicious sign, but ominous.
And I call Apollo, god of healing,
to stop Artemis delaying the fleet,
by sending hostile winds
to keep the ships from sailing,
in her demand for another sacrifice,
one which violates all human law,
which no feast celebrates—
it shatters families and makes the wife
lose all respect and hate her husband.
For in the home a dreadful anger waits.
It does not forget and cannot be appeased.
Its treachery controls the house,
waiting to avenge a slaughtered child."

Calchas prophesied that fatal destiny,
read from those birds, as the army marched,
speaking by this palace of the kings.

And to confirm all this
sing out the song of sorrow, song of grief,
but let the good prevail. O Zeus, whoever he may be,
if this name please him as invocation,
then that's the name I'll use to call him.
As I try to think all these things through,
I have no words to shape my thoughts,
other than Zeus—if I truly can succeed
in easing my heart of this heavy grief,
this self-defeating weight of sorrow.

As for Uranus, who was once so great,
bursting with arrogance for every fight,
people will talk about that god
as if he'd never even lived.
And his son, Cronos, who came after,
has met his match and is no more.
But whoever with a willing heart
cries his triumphal song to Zeus
will come to understand all things.*

Zeus, who guided mortals to be wise,
has established his fixed law—
wisdom comes through suffering.
Trouble, with its memories of pain,
drips in our hearts as we try to sleep,
so men against their will
learn to practice moderation.
Favours come to us from gods
seated on their solemn thrones—
such grace is harsh and violent.

So then the leader of Achaean ships,
the elder brother, Agamemnon,
did not blame or fault the prophet,
but gave in to fortune's sudden blows.
For Achaea's army, stranded there,
on the shores across from Calchis,
was held up by opposing winds at Aulis,
where tides ebb and flow.
Troops grew weary, as supplies ran low.
Winds blew from the Strymon river,
keeping ships at anchor, harming men
with too much leisure. Troops grew hungry.
They wandered discontent and restless.
The winds corroded ships and cables.
The delay seemed endless, on and on, until
the men, the flower of Argos, began to wilt.
Then Calchas proclaimed the cause of this—
it was Artemis. And he proposed
a further remedy, but something harsh,

41

even worse than the opposing winds,
so painful that the sons of Atreus
struck their canes on the ground and wept.

Then Agamemnon, the older king, spoke up:
"It's harsh not to obey this fate—
but to go through with it is harsh as well,
to kill my child, the glory of my house,
to stain a father's hands before the altar
with streams of virgin's blood.
Which of my options is not evil?
How can I just leave this fleet,
and let my fellow warriors down?
Their passionate demand for sacrifice
to calm the winds lies within their rights—
even the sacrifice of virgin blood.
So be it. All may be well."

But when Agamemnon strapped on
the harsh yoke of necessity,
his spirits changed, and his intentions
became profane, unholy, unsanctified.
He undertook an act beyond all daring.
Troubles come, above all, from delusions
inciting men to rash designs, to evil.
So Agamemnon steeled his heart
to make his own daughter the sacrifice,
an offering for the Achaean fleet,
so he could prosecute the war
waged to avenge that woman Helen.

In their eagerness for war, those leaders
paid no attention to the girl,
her pleas for help, her cries of "Father!"—
any more than to her virgin youth.
Her father offered up a prayer,
then ordered men to seize her
and lift her up—she'd fallen forward
and just lay there in her robes—to raise her,
high above the altar, like a goat,
urging them to keep their spirits up.

42

They gagged her lovely mouth,
with force, just like a horse's bit,
to keep her speechless, to stifle any curse
which she might cry against her family.

As she threw her saffron robe onto the ground,
she glanced at the men, each of them,
those carrying out the sacrifice,
her eyes imploring pity. She looked
just like a painting dying to speak.
She'd often sung before her father's table,
when, as host, he'd entertained his guests,
a virgin using her flawless voice
to honour her dear father with her love,
as he prayed for blessing
at the third libation.

What happened next I did not see.
And I won't say. What Calchas' skill
had prophesied did come to pass.
The scales of Justice move to show
that wisdom comes through suffering.
As for what's to come—you'll know that
when it comes. So let it be.
To know would be to grieve ahead of time.
It's clear whatever is to happen
will happen, like tomorrow's dawn.

[Enter Clytaemnestra through the palace doors]

But I hope whatever follows will be good,
according to the wishes of our queen,
who governs here, our closest guard,
keeping watch all by herself,
protecting Peloponnesian lands.

CHORUS LEADER
Queen Clytaemnestra, we've come here
in deference to your royal authority.
With our king far away, the man's throne
is empty—so it's appropriate for us
to pay allegiance to his wife, the queen.

I'd really like to hear your news,
whether what you've heard is good or not.
Your sacrificial offerings give us hope.
But we won't object if you stay silent.

CLYTAEMNESTRA
It's a welcome message. As the proverb says,
"May Dawn be born from mother Night."
You'll hear great news, greater than all your hopes—
the Argives have captured Priam's city!

CHORUS LEADER
What's that you say? I misheard your words—
what you've just said—it defies belief!

CLYTAEMNESTRA
I say Troy is now in Achaean hands.
Is that clear enough?

CHORUS LEADER
That fills me with joy.
So much so I can't stop crying.

CLYTAEMNESTRA
Then your eyes reveal your faithful loyalty.

CHORUS LEADER
Is this report reliable? Is there proof?

CLYTAEMNESTRA
Of course there is. Unless some god deceives me.

CHORUS LEADER
Has some vision persuaded you of this,
something in a dream, perhaps?

CLYTAEMNESTRA
Not at all.
As if I'd listen to some dozing brain.

CHORUS LEADER:
Perhaps some unfledged rumour raised your hopes?

CLYTAEMNESTRA
Now you're insulting my intelligence,
as if I were a youngster, just a child.

CHORUS LEADER
When exactly was the city captured?

CLYTAEMNESTRA
I'll tell you. It was the very night
that gave birth to this glorious day.

CHORUS LEADER
How could a messenger get here so fast?

CLYTAEMNESTRA
Hephaestos, god of fire, sent his bright blaze
speeding here from Ida, his messenger,
flames racing from one beacon to the next—
from Ida to Hermes' rock in Lemnos.
From that island the great flames sped
to the third fire, on the crest of Athos,
sacred to Zeus, and then, arcing high,
the beacon light sprang across the sea,
exulting in its golden fiery power,
rushing on, like another sun, passing
the message to the look-out towers
at Macistus. The man there was not sleeping,
like some fool. Without a moment's pause,
he relayed the message, so the blazing news
sped on, leaping across Euripus' stream,
to pass the signal to the next watchmen,
at Messapion. Those men, in their turn,
torched a pile of dried-out heather, firing
the message onward. The flaming light
was not diminished—its strength kept growing.
Like a glowing moon, it jumped across
the plain of Asopus, up to the ridges
on mount Cithaeron, where it set alight
the next stage of the relay race of fire.
Those watching there did not neglect their work—
that light which came to them from far away
they passed on with an even greater blaze,

which dashed across the shores of Gorgopus,
to reach mount Aegiplanctus, with orders
for those there to keep the beacon moving.
They lit a fire, a huge flaming pillar,
with unchecked force, speeding the message on—
its light visible even at the headland
by the Saronic Gulf. It swooped down,
once it reached the crest of Arachnaeus,
that look-out near our city—and from there
jumped down onto the roof of Atreus' sons,
flames directly linked to blazing Troy.
I organized these messengers of fire,
setting them up in sequence, one by one.
In that race the first and last both triumph,
the ones who sent the message and received it.
That's the evidence I set before you,
a message from my husband, dispatched
all the way from burning Troy to me.

CHORUS
My queen, I'll offer up to all the gods
my prayers of thanks, but now I'd like to hear
the details of your wonderful report.
Can you tell me the news once more?

CLYTAEMNESTRA
On this very day Achaea's army
has taken Troy. Inside that town, I think,
voices cry out in mass confusion.
If you place oil and vinegar together,
in the same container, you'll observe
they never mix, but separate themselves,
like enemies—well, in Troy the shouting
of conquerors and conquered is like that,
matching their very different situations.
Trojans fall upon their family corpses,
husbands, brothers. The children scream
over dead old men who gave them life.
As captives now, they keep lamenting
all their slaughtered loved ones. But the Argives,
famished after a long night's roaming,

and weary after battle, are set to eat,
to gorge themselves on what the town affords.
They're quartered now in captured Trojan homes,
sheltered from the night sky's frost and dew,
but not according to official rank,
rather as luck determines each man's lot.
They're happy. They'll sleep straight through the night,
without posting a guard. Now, if these troops
fully and piously respect Troy's gods,
a captured country's divinities and shrines,
those who've conquered may not, in their turn,
be conquered. But let no frenzied greed,
no overpowering lust for plunder,
fall upon the army from the start,
so they ravage what they should leave alone.
For to get safely home, the army needs
to make that long journey back again.
But even if the soldiers do reach home
without offending any god, harsh sorrow
for the dead may still be watching for them,
unless some new disaster intervenes.
Well, I've let you hear my woman's words.
May good things now prevail for all to see.
I take this news as cause for common joy.

CHORUS LEADER
You speak wisely, like a prudent man.
But now I've heard that I can trust your news,
we must prepare ourselves to thank the gods,
who've given a blessing worthy of our toil.

[Clytaemnestra goes back into the palace]

CHORUS
O Zeus, my king, and friendly Night,
you've handed us great glories
to keep as our possession.
You cast upon the towers of Troy
your all-encompassing hunting net,
and no one, young or old, escaped
its enslaving fatal mesh
that overpowered them all.

I worship mighty Zeus,
god of hospitality,
who made this happen.
For a long time now
he's aimed his bow at Paris,
making sure his arrow
would not fall short or fly
above the stars and miss.

Men will say it's a blow from Zeus
and trace his presence in all this.
He acts on what he himself decides.
Some people claim that gods
don't really care about those men
who trample underfoot
favours from the pure in heart.
Such people are profane.
For we now clearly see
destruction is the penalty
for those with reckless pride,
who breathe a boastful spirit
greater than is just,
because their homes are full,
stuffed with riches to excess,
beyond what's best for them.
Let men have sufficient wealth
to match good sense, not so much
it piles up their misfortunes.
There's no security in riches
for the insolent man who kicks aside
and pushes from his sight
great altars of righteousness.

Such a man is overpowered
by perverse Persuasion,
insufferable child of scheming Folly.
And there's no remedy.
His evil's not concealed—
it stands out, a lurid glitter,
like false bronze when rubbed.

All men can judge his darkness,
once he's tested by events.
He's like a child chasing a flying bird.
He brands his city with disgrace
which cannot be removed,
for no god hears his prayers.
The man who lives this way,
doing wrong, the gods destroy.
Such a man was Paris. He came
to the home of the sons of Atreus,
and then abused their hospitality,
running off with his host's wife.

But she left her people
the smash of shield and spear,
a fleet well armed for war.
To Troy she carried with her
no dowry but destruction.
Daring what should not be dared,
she glided through Troy's gates.
The prophets in this house cried out,
"Alas, alas for house and home,
and for the royal leaders here.*
Alas, for the marriage bed,
still holding traces of her body,
the one who loved her husband."
As for him, he sits apart,
in pain, silent and dishonoured.

He does not blame her—
no, he aches to be with her,
the woman far across the sea.
Her image seems to rule the house.
Her husband finds no beauty now
in graceful statues, for to his blank eyes
all sexual loveliness has gone.

In his dreams he sees sad images,
with memories of earlier joy—
a vain relief, for when the man
thinks he sees such beauty there,

49

all at once it's gone, slipping
through his hands, flying away
along the paths of sleep.

These are the sorrows in the house,
around the hearth, and pain
much worse than this. For everywhere,
throughout the land of Greece,
in every home where men set out
to gather in that army
there is insufferable grief.
Many disasters pierce the heart.
People know the ones who leave,
but every house gets back
weapons and ash, not living men.

For Ares, god of war, pays gold
for soldier's bodies. In spear fights
he tips the scales, then back from Troy
he ships a heavy freight of ash,
cremated bodies of the dead,
sent home for loved ones to lament.
He trades funeral dust for men,
shiploads of urns filled up with ashes.
Back home the people weep,
praising one man for his battle skill,
another for courageous death.
Some complain about that woman,
how she's to blame for all of this—
but do so quietly. Nonetheless,
this sorrow spreads resentment
against the leaders of the war,
the sons of Atreus. Meanwhile,
over there, across the seas in Troy,
around the city walls, the hostile ground
swallows our beautiful young men,
now hidden in the earth they conquered.

The people's voice, once angered,
can create dissent, ratifying a curse
which now must have its way.

And so, in my anxiety, I wait,
listening for something murky,
something emerging from the gloom.
For gods aren't blind to men who kill.
In time, black agents of revenge,
the Furies, wear down and bring to nothing
the fortunes of a man who prospers
in unjust ways. They wear him out,
reverse his luck, and bring him at last
among the dead. There's no remedy.
To boast too much of one's success
is dangerous—the high mountain peak
is struck by Zeus' lightning bolt.
I'd choose wealth no one could envy.
May I never be the sort of man
who puts whole cities to the sword.
Let me never see myself enslaved,
my life in someone else's power.

CHORUS MEMBER ONE
　　This welcome fiery message has spread fast;
　　it's gone throughout the town. But is it true?
　　Sent from the gods or false? Who knows?

CHORUS MEMBER TWO
　　What man is such a senseless child
　　he lets his heart catch fire at this news,
　　and then is shattered by some fresh report?

CHORUS MEMBER THREE
　　That's just the nature of a woman—
　　to give thanks before the truth appears.

CHORUS MEMBER FOUR
　　Yes, they're far too trusting.
　　The proper order in a woman's mind
　　is easily upset. Rumours women start
　　soon die out, soon come to nothing.

CHORUS LEADER
　　We'll quickly know about these signal fires,
　　flaming beacons passed from place to place.
　　We'll find out if that really did occur

51

or if, just like a dream, this joyful light
has come in order to deceive our hopes.
For I see a herald coming from the shore—
an olive bough of triumph shades his face.
The dry dust on him, all those muddy clothes,
tell me he'll report the facts. Nor will he
light some flaming pile of mountain wood
to pass a signal on with smoke. No—
he'll shout out to us what he has to say,
and we can then rejoice still more,
or else... but I won't think of that. Let's have
good news to add to what we know already.
If anyone is praying for something else
to happen to our city, let him reap
the harvest of his own misguided heart.

[Enter Herald]

HERALD
Greetings to this Argive soil, my father's land.
On this day, ten years later, I've come back.
I've seen many hopes of mine destroyed,
and only one fulfilled—I've made it home.
I never dreamed I'd die here in Argos,
with a burial plot in this land I love.
I bless the land, the bright light of this sun—
and I give thanks to Zeus, our highest god,
and to Apollo, lord of Pytho.
May you never fire your arrows at us
any more. We had enough of those,
my lord, beside Scamander's banks,
when you took your stand against us. But now,
Apollo, may you preserve and heal us.
And I greet all gods assembled here,
including Hermes, whom I honour,
the well-loved herald god, worshipped
as the herald's patron. And next I pray
the heroic spirits who sent us off
will welcome back the remnants of our army,
those spared being slaughtered by the spear.
O you hall of kings, you roof I cherish,
you sacred seats and gods who face the sun,

if your shining eyes in days gone by
have welcomed our king home, then do so now,
after his long absence. He's coming here,
carrying light into this darkness, for you
and all assembled here—our mighty king,
lord Agamemnon. Greet him with full respect.
For he's uprooted Troy—with the pick axe
of avenging Zeus he's reduced her soil.
The altars of the gods and all their shrines
he has obliterated, laying waste
all that country's rich fertility.
Around Troy's neck he's fixed destruction's yoke.
Now he's coming home, king Agamemnon,
the fortunate elder son of Atreus,
among all men he merits the most honour.
For neither Paris nor his accomplice,
the Trojan city, can ever boast again
their deeds were greater than their suffering.
Guilty of rape and theft, he's lost his loot.
He's utterly destroyed his father's house,
the land, too, which sustained his people.
So Priam's sons have paid the price twice over.

CHORUS LEADER
    All joyful greetings to you, herald,
    as you come back from our army.

HERALD
    I, too, rejoice.
    Now I don't fear death—it's as the gods decide.

CHORUS LEADER
    Did your love of this land cause you distress?

HERALD
    Yes. That's why my eyes are filled with tears.

CHORUS LEADER
    It's as if you had some pleasing sickness.

HERALD
    How so? Tell me exactly what you mean.

CHORUS LEADER
You suffered from love for those who loved you.

HERALD
You mean the country and the army
both missed each other?

CHORUS LEADER
Yes, so much so,
often my anxious heart cried out aloud.

HERALD
What caused this gnawing trouble in your heart?

CHORUS LEADER
Long ago I learned to keep my silence—
the best antidote against more trouble.

HERALD
Why's that? Were you afraid of someone,
once the kings were gone?

CHORUS LEADER
Indeed I was.
In fact, as you have said, there'd be great joy
in dying now.

HERALD
It's true we have done well.
As for what happened long ago, you could say
some worked out happily, and some was bad.
But who except the gods avoids all pain
throughout his life? If I told what we went through—
the hardships, wretched quarters, narrow berths,
the harsh conditions—was there anything
we did not complain about? We had our share
of trouble every day. And then on shore
things were even worse. We had to camp
right by the enemy wall. It was wet—
dew from the sky and marshes soaked us.
Our clothes rotted. Our hair grew full of lice.
And it was freezing. The winters there,
beyond endurance, when snows from Ida

froze birds to death. And then the heat,
so hot at noon, the sea, without a ripple,
sank to sleep. ... But why complain about it?
Our work is done. It's over for the dead,
who aren't about to spring to life again.
Why should the living call to mind the dead?
There's no need to relive those blows of fate.
I think it's time to bid a long farewell
to our misfortune. For those still living,
the soldiers left alive, our luck's won out.
No loss can change that now. We've a right,
as we cross land and sea, to boast aloud,
and cry out to the sun, "Argive forces once,
having captured Troy, took their spoils of war
and nailed them up in gods' holy shrines,
all through Greece, glorious tribute from the past!"
So whoever hears the story of these things
must praise our generals—our city, too.
Full honour and thanks to Zeus who did the work.
That's my full report.

CHORUS LEADER
What you say is true.
I was in the wrong—I won't deny that.
But the old can always learn from younger men,
and what you've said enriches all of us.

[Enter Clytaemnestra from the palace]

But your news will have a special interest
for Clytaemnestra and her household.

CLYTAEMNESTRA
Some time ago I cried out in triumph,
rejoicing when that first messenger arrived,
the fiery herald in the night, who told me
Troy was captured and was being destroyed.
Some people criticized me then, saying,
"How come you're so easily persuaded
by signal fires Troy's being demolished?
Isn't that just like a woman's heart,
to get so jubilant?" Insults like these

55

made it appear as if I'd lost my wits.
But I continued with my sacrifice,
and everywhere throughout the city
women kept up their joyful shouting,
as they traditionally do, echoing
their exultation through all holy shrines,
tending sweet-smelling spicy flames,
as they consumed their victims. So now,
why do I need you to go on and on
about all this? I'll hear it from the king.
But, so I can give my honoured husband
the finest welcome home, and with all speed—
for what light gives a woman greater pleasure
than to unbar the gates to her own husband
as he comes home from battle, once the gods
have spared his life in war?—tell him this,
and give him the message to come home
as soon as possible. The citizens
will love to see him, and when he gets back,
in this house he'll find his wife as faithful
as when he left, a watch dog of the home,
loyal to him, hostile to his enemies,
and, for the rest, the same in every way.
In this long time, I've not betrayed our bond—
I've known no pleasure with another man,
no breath of scandal. About such things
I understand as much as tempering bronze.
I'm proud to state this, for it's all true—
nothing a noble lady should feel shame to say.

[Clytaemnestra exits back into the palace]

CHORUS LEADER
She seems to speak as if she really wants
to tell you something, but, in fact,
to those who can interpret her words well
she's only saying what she ought to say.
But tell me, herald, can I learn something
of Menelaus, this country's well-loved king—
did he make it back safe and sound with you?

HERALD
I can't lie with false good news of Menelaus,
so his friends can enjoy themselves for long.

CHORUS LEADER
I wish your news of him was true and good.
It's hard when both of these don't go together.

HERALD
Menelaus disappeared—the army
lost sight of him and his ship. That's the truth.

CHORUS LEADER
Did you see him sail off from Ilion,
or did some storm attack the entire fleet
and cut him off from you?

HERALD
Like a master archer, you hit the mark—
your last question briefly tells the story.

CHORUS LEADER
According to the others in the fleet
what happened? Is he alive or dead?

HERALD
No one knows for certain, except the sun,
moving around the earth sustaining life.

CHORUS LEADER
Tell me how that storm struck the soldiers' ships.
How did the anger of the gods come to an end?

HERALD
It's not right I talk of our misfortunes,
and spoil such an auspicious day as this.
We ought to keep such matters separate
in deference to the gods. When a messenger
arrives distraught, bringing dreadful news
about some slaughtered army, that's one wound
inflicted on the city. Beyond that,
from many houses many men are driven
to their destruction by the double whip

57

which Ares, god of war, so loves—
disaster with two prongs, a bloody pair.
A messenger weighed down with news like this
should report the Furies' song of triumph.
But when he brings good news of men being saved
to a city full of joyful celebrations...
How can I mix the good news and the bad,
telling of the storm which hit Achaeans,
a storm linked to the anger of the gods?
For fire and sea, before now enemies,
swore a common oath and then proclaimed it
by destroying Achaea's helpless forces.
At night malevolent seas rose up,
as winds from Thrace smashed ships together.
Pushed round by the power of that storm,
and driven by great bursts of rain, the ships
scattered, then disappeared, blown apart
by the evil shepherd's whirlwind. Later,
when the sun's bright light appeared again,
we witnessed the Aegean sea in bloom
with corpses of Achaean troops and ships.
As for us, some god saved us in secret
or interceded for us—our boat survived,
its hull intact. That was no human feat.
Some divine hand was on our steering oar,
some stroke of Fortune wanted our ship saved,
not swamped by surf as we rode at anchor
or smashed upon the rocky coast. And then,
once we'd avoided Hades on those seas,
we couldn't believe our luck, as we brooded,
in the bright light of day, on all our troubles,
this new disaster which destroyed our fleet,
dispersing it so badly. So on those ships
if anyone's still breathing, he'll now say
we're the ones who've been destroyed. Why not,
when we say much the same of them?
But let's hope things all turn out for the best.
As for Menelaus, wait for his return—
that should be your first priority.
If some ray of sunlight finds him still alive,
his vision still intact, thanks to Zeus,

whose crafty plans at this point don't include
destruction of the entire race, there's hope
he'll soon come home again. Now you've heard this,
you've listened to the truth.

[Exit Herald]

CHORUS
Whoever came up with that name,
a name so altogether true—
was there some power we can't see
telling that tongue what to say,
the tongue which prophesied our fate—
I mean the man who called her Helen,
that woman wed for warfare,
the object of our strife?
For she's lived up to that name—
a hell for ships, a hell for men,
a hell for cities, too.
From her delicately curtained room
she sailed away, transported
by West Wind, an earth-born giant.
A horde of warriors with shields
went after her, huntsmen
following the vanished track
her oars had left, all the way
to where she'd beached her ship,
on leafy shores of Simois.
Then came bloody war.

And so Troy's destiny's fulfilled—
wrath brings a dreadful wedding day,
late retribution for dishonour
to hospitality and Zeus,
god of guest and host,
on those who celebrated with the bride,
who, on that day, sang aloud
the joyful wedding hymns.
Now Priam's city, in old age,
has learned a different song.
I think I hear loud funeral chants,

lamenting as an evil fate
the marriage Paris brought.
The city's filled with songs of grief.
It must endure all sorrows,
the brutal slaughter of its sons.

So a man once raised a lion cub
in his own home. The beast
lacked milk but craved its mother's teat.
In early life the cub was gentle.
Children loved it, and it brought
the old men great delight.
They gave it many things
and clasped it in their arms,
as if it were a nursing child.
Its fiery eyes fixed on the hands
that fed it, the creature fawned,
a slave to appetite.

But with time the creature grew
and its true nature showed—
the one its parents gave it.
So it paid back those who reared it,
preparing a meal in gratitude,
an unholy slaughter of the flocks,
house awash with blood,
while those who lived inside the home
were powerless against the pain,
against the massive carnage.
By god's will they'd brought up
a priest of doom in their own house.

I'd say she first arrived in Troy
a gentle spirit, like a calming breeze,
a delicate, expensive ornament—
her soft darting eyes a flower
which stings the heart with love.
Then, changing her direction,
she took her marriage to its bitter end,
destroying all those she lived with.
With evil in her train and led by Zeus,

60

god of guest and host, she turned into
a bride of tears, a Fury.

Among men there's a saying,
an old one, from times long past:
A man's prosperity, once fully grown,
has offspring—it never dies
without producing children.
From that man's good fortune
spring up voracious pains
for all his race. But on this
I don't agree with other men.
I stand alone and say
it's the unholy act that breeds
more acts of the same kind.
A truly righteous house is blessed,
its children always fair and good.

Old violent aggression
loves to generate new troubles
among evil men—soon or late,
when it's fated to be born,
new violence springs forth,
a spirit no one can resist or conquer,
unholy recklessness,
dark ruin on the home,
like the destructiveness
from which it sprang.

But Righteousness shines out
from grimy dwellings, honouring
the man who lives in virtue.
She turns her eyes away
from gold-encrusted mansions
where men's hands are black,
and moves towards integrity,
rejecting power and wealth,
which, though praised, are counterfeit.
Righteousness leads all things
to well-deserved fulfillment.

[Enter Agamemnon in a chariot with Cassandra and a large military escort]

CHORUS LEADER
Welcome, son of Atreus, my king,
Troy's destroyer. How shall I address you?
How honour you without extravagance,
without failing to say what's suitable?
For many men value appearances
more than reality—thus they violate
what's right. Everyone's prepared to sigh
over some suffering man, though no sorrow
really eats their hearts, or they can pretend
to join another person's happiness,
forcing their faces into smiling masks.
But a good man discerns true character—
he's not fooled by eyes feigning loyalty,
favouring him with watered-down respect.
Back when you were gathering the army
in Helen's cause—I won't deny the fact—
I saw you in an unflattering light,
an unfit mind steering our ship astray,
trying through that sacrifice to boost the spirits
of dying soldiers. But now, with love,
with a full heart, I welcome your return.
For those who've won final success, the joy
is worth the toil. If you enquire, in time
you'll learn about the men who stayed at home,
those who with justice stood guard for the city
and those who failed to carry out what's right.

AGAMEMNON
First I salute Argos and my native gods,
as is right, the ones who worked with me
for my safe return and for the justice
I brought down on Priam's city. The gods
refused to listen to their urgent pleas,
then cast their ballots—there was no dissent—
into the urn of blood—to kill their men,
to wipe out Ilion. The other urn,
the one for clemency, stood there empty—

only Hope took up her stand beside it.
Even now smoke from the burning city,
an auspicious sign, tells of its capture.
The storms from its destruction still live on.
As fiery embers cool, their dying breaths
give off ripe smells of wealth. For all this,
we must give the gods eternal thanks.
Around Troy we've cast a savage net.
For a woman's sake, the beast from Argos,
born from the belly of that wooden horse,
in the night, as the Pleiades went down,
jumped out with their shields and razed the city.
Leaping over walls, the ravenous lion
gorged itself on blood of royalty.
So much for my long prelude to the gods.
As for your concerns, I've heard your words,
and I'll keep them in mind. I agree with you—
we'll work together. By nature few men
possess the inborn talent to admire
a friend's good fortune without envy.
Poisonous malice seeps into the heart,
doubling the pain of the infected man,
weighing him down with misfortunes of his own,
while he groans to see another's wealth.
I understand too well companionship
no more substantial than pictures in a glass.
From my experience, I'd say those men
who seemed so loyal to me are shadows,
no more than images of true companions.
All except Odysseus—he sailed with me
much against his will, but once in harness,
he was prepared to pull his weight for me.
I say this whether he's alive or dead.
For other issues of the city and our gods,
we'll set up a general assembly,
all of us discussing things together.
We must make sure what's working well
remains that way in future. By contrast,
where we need some healing medicine,
we'll make a well-intentioned effort
to root out all infectious evil,

burning the sores or slicing them away.

[Enter Clytaemnestra with attendants carrying the purple carpet]

Now I'll go inside my palace, my hearth and home,
first, to greet the gods who sent me off
and today bring me back. May victory,
which has been mine, stay with me forever.

[Agamemnon moves to climb out of the chariot but is held up by Clytaemnestra's speech]

CLYTAEMNESTRA
Citizens, you senior men of Argos here,
I'm not ashamed to speak before you all,
to state how much I love my husband. With time,
men's fears diminish. So I'll speak out now.
I don't talk as one who has been taught
by others, so I'll just describe my life,
my oppressive life, all the many years
my husband's been away at Ilion.
First, it's unmitigated trouble
for a woman to sit at home alone,
far from her man. She has to listen to
all sorts of painful rumours. Messengers
arrive, hard on each other's heels, bearing
news of some disaster—and everyone
tells of troubles worse than those before,
shouted throughout the house. If my husband
had had as many wounds as I heard rumours
coming to this house, he'd have more holes in him
than any net. If he'd died as many times
as rumour killed him, he could claim to be
a second Geryon, that triple-bodied beast,
and boast of being covered up with earth
three times, one death for every separate shape.
Because of all these spiteful messages,
others have often had to cut me loose,
a high-hung noose strung tight around my neck.
That's why our son, Orestes, is not standing here,
the most trusted bond linking you and me.
He should be, but there's no cause to worry.

He's being cared for by a friendly ally,
Strophius of Phocis, who warned me twice—
first, of your own danger under Ilion's walls,
second, of people here, how they could rebel,
cry out against being governed, then overthrow
the Council. For it's natural to men,
once someone's down, to trample on him
all the more. That's how I explain myself.
And it's all true. As for me, my eyes are dry—
the welling sources of my tears are parched,
no drop remains. Many long nights I wept
until my eyes were sore, as I kept watching
for that beacon light I'd set up for you,
but always it kept disappointing me.
The faint whirring of a buzzing fly
would often wake me up from dreams of you,
dreams where I saw you endure more suffering
than the hours in which I slept had time for.
But now, after going through all this, my heart
is free of worry. So I would salute my lord—
the watch dog who protects our household,
the mainstay which saves our ship of state,
the lofty pillar which holds our roof beams high,
his father's truly begotten son, for men at sea
a land they glimpse beyond their wildest hopes,
the fairest dawn after a night of storms,
a flowing stream to thirsty travellers.
What joy it is to escape necessity!
In my opinion, these words of greeting
are worthy of him. So let there be no envy,
since in days past we've suffered many ills.
And now, my beloved lord, come to me here,
climb down from that chariot. But, my king,
don't place upon the common ground the foot
which stamped out Troy.

[Clytaemnestra turns to the women attending on her who, on her orders, begin to spread out at Agamemnon's feet the tapestries they have brought out from the house, making a path from the chariot to the palace doors. The tapestries are all a deep red-purple, the colour of blood]

You women, don't just stand there.
I've told you what to do. Spread out those tapestries,
here on the ground, directly in his path. Quickly!
Let his path be covered all in red, so Justice
can lead him back into his home, a place
he never hoped to see. As for the rest,
my unsleeping vigilance will sort it out,
with the help of gods, as fate decrees.

AGAMEMNON
Daughter of Leda, guardian of my home,
your speech was, like my absence, far too long.
Praise that's due to us should come from others.
Then it's worthwhile. All those things you said—
don't puff me up with such female honours,
or grovel there before me babbling tributes,
like some barbarian. Don't invite envy
to cross my path by strewing it with cloth.
That's how we honour gods, not human beings.
For a mortal man to place his foot like this
on rich embroidery is, in my view,
not without some risk. So I'm telling you
honour me as a man, not as a god.
My fame proclaims itself. It does not need
foot mats made out of such embroideries.
Not even to think of doing something bad
is god's greatest gift. When a man's life ends
in great prosperity, only then can we declare
that he's a happy man. Thus, if I act,
in every circumstance, as I ought to now,
there's nothing I need fear.

CLYTAEMNESTRA
Don't say that just to flout what I've arranged.

AGAMEMNON
You should know I'll not go back on what I've said.

CLYTAEMNESTRA
You must fear something, then, to act this way.
You've made some promise to the gods.

AGAMEMNON
> I've said my final word. I fully understand,
> as well as any man, just what I'm doing.

CLYTAEMNESTRA
> What do you think Priam would have done,
> if he'd had your success?

AGAMEMNON
> That's clear—
> he'd have walked across these tapestries.

CLYTAEMNESTRA
> So then why be ashamed by what men say?

AGAMEMNON
> But what people say can have great power.

CLYTAEMNESTRA
> True, but the man whom people do not envy
> is not worth their envy.

AGAMEMNON
> It's not like a woman
> to be so keen on competition.

CLYTAEMNESTRA
> It's fitting that the happy conqueror
> should let himself be overcome.

AGAMEMNON
> And in this contest
> that's the sort of victory you value?

CLYTAEMNESTRA
> Why not agree? Be strong and yield to me,
> of your own consent.

AGAMEMNON
> Well, if it's what you want...
> Quick, someone get these sandals off—
> they've served my feet so well. As I now walk
> on these red tapestries dyed in the sea,
> may no distant god catch sight of me,

and, for envy, strike me down. There's much shame
when my feet squander assets of my house,
wasting wealth and costly woven finery.

[Agamemnon, in bare feet, comes down from the chariot onto the tapestries]

So much for that.

[Agamemnon turns to call attention to Cassandra in the chariot]

Welcome this foreign girl
into our house. And do it graciously.
For god, who sees us from far away,
looks down with favour on a gentle master.
No one freely puts on slavery's yoke,
but this girl, the finest flower of all our loot,
comes with us as my army's gift to me.
And now, since you've talked me into this,
I'll proceed into my palace, treading
on this crimson pathway as I go.

[Agamemnon starts to move slowly along the tapestries towards the palace and up the stairs. Cassandra remains in the chariot]

CLYTAEMNESTRA
There is the sea. Who will drain it dry?
It gives us crimson dye in huge amounts,
as valuable as silver, inexhaustible.
With that we dye our garments. And of these
our house has a full store, thanks to the gods.
We're rich. We have no sense of poverty.
I'd have vowed to tread on many clothes,
to use what we have stored up in our home,
if an oracle had ordered such a payment
to save your life. If the root still lives,
the house can blossom into leaf once more,
growing high-arching shade, protection
against the Dog Star's scorching season.
Your return to your father's hearth and home
brings us the summer's heat in winter time.
It's like when Zeus makes wine from bitter grapes,

the house immediately grows cool, once its lord
strolls through his own halls in complete command.

*[By this time Agamemnon has reached the palace doors and has just
entered the palace]*

O Zeus, Zeus, who accomplishes all things,
answer my prayers. Take care to bring about
all things that reach fulfillment through your will.

[Exit Clytaemnestra into the palace. The doors close behind her]

CHORUS
Why does this sense of dread
hover so unceasingly
around my heart
with such foreboding?
My song of prophecy goes on
unbidden and unpaid.
Why can't some calming confidence
sit on my mind and spurn
my fears as enigmatic dreams?
It was so long ago—
Time has long since buried
deep in sand the mooring cables
cast when the army sailed to Troy.

My own eyes tell me
Agamemnon has returned.
For that I need no further witness.
But still, here, deep in my heart,
the spontaneous song
keeps up its tuneless dirge,
as the avenging Furies chant.
It kills my confidence, my hope.
Everything inside me
beats against my chest,
surging back and forth
in tides of grim foreboding—
something's moving to fulfillment.
But I pray my premonitions

prove false and never come to light.
For, as we know, boundaries
of vigorous health break down—
disease is always pressing hard
the common wall between them.
So with the fate of men.
It holds to a straight course,
then, all at once, can crash
upon a hidden rock of grief.
But if, as a precaution,
men toss overboard
some part of their rich cargo,
and time their throw just right,
the house, though grieving,
will not completely founder,
nor will its hull be swamped.
And Zeus' bountiful rich gifts
reaped from the furrows every year
hold off the plague of famine.

But once a murdered man's dark blood
has soaked the ground, who then
can bring him back through song?
Even Aesculapius, whose skill
could raise men from the dead,
was stopped by Zeus' thunderbolt.
Was that not warning to us all?
If one fate settled by the gods
did not prevent another fate
securing an advantage,
my heart would then outrace my tongue—
I'd speak out loud and clear,
I'd cry out my forebodings.
But now it mutters in the dark,
uneasy, holding little hope
for any resolution.
And still my spirit smoulders.

*[Enter Clytaemnestra from the palace. She addresses Cassandra, who
is still in the chariot]*

CLYTAEMNESTRA
You should go in, too—I mean you up there,
Cassandra. Zeus, in his mercy to you,
has made you member of our household,
one who shares its purification rites.
So you can take your place before the altar
of the god protecting all our wealth,
along with other slaves. So come down.
Leave the chariot. And leave your pride behind.
Men say even Hercules, Alcmene's son,
once long ago was sold in slavery
and had to eat its bitter bread. If Fate
has brought you to the same condition,
be very grateful you serve masters here
who've been rich forever. Certain men,
those who've reaped a harvest of rich goods
beyond their dreams, maltreat their slaves.
They go too far. But here, with us, you'll get
the treatment our traditions say is right.

CHORUS LEADER *[addressing Cassandra]*
Our queen is talking to you. Her meaning's clear.
Fate has caught you in its nets—you'd best obey,
unless such action is beyond your power.

CLYTAEMNESTRA
If she's not like a swallow, with a song
all her own, something barbarously obscure,
I'll speak so she can understand. She must obey.

CHORUS LEADER *[to Cassandra]*
Go with the queen. Of all your options now
what she says is best. Do as she says.
Step down from your chariot seat.

CLYTAEMNESTRA
Come down now.
I don't have time to waste on this girl here.
Inside, by our central hearth, our victims
are already waiting for the sacrifice,
a joyful time beyond our fondest hopes.
So if you want to play your part in this,

71

you'd better come at once. If what I say
means nothing to you, if you can't understand,
at least use your foreign hand to make a sign.

CHORUS LEADER
An interpreter is what this stranger needs.
She's like some wild thing, freshly trapped.

CLYTAEMNESTRA
She's mad, too busy listening to her troubled heart.
She's just left her newly captured city,
then come here, without sufficient time
to learn to stomach the controlling bit.
She will, once her anger's been dissolved
in foaming blood. But I'll waste no more time,
dealing with her contempt outside the house.

[Clytaemnestra turns and exits into the palace. The members of the
Chorus gather around Cassandra]

CHORUS LEADER
I'll not lose my temper. I pity her.
You unhappy creature, why not come down?
Leave the chariot. Why not accept fate's yoke
of your own free will?

CASSANDRA [searching the sky for a sign of Apollo and screaming]
Aieeeee ... earth ... sky ...
Apollo ... Apollo ...

CHORUS MEMBER
Why cry out your distress in Apollo's name?
He's not a god who pays attention
to those who mourn like this.

CASSANDRA
Aieeee ... earth ... sky ...
Apollo ... my destroyer ...

CHORUS MEMBER
She cried out again. Such ominous words—
and to a god who's not the one
to have around at times of grieving.

CASSANDRA
Apollo! Apollo! God of the road...
You're destroying me. Why leave me here
beyond all hope a second time?

CHORUS MEMBER
It looks as if she's going to prophesy,
to say something of her unhappiness.
She may be a slave, but inside her
the god's voice still remains.

CASSANDRA
Apollo!
O Apollo! God of the road...
You're obliterating me! Where am I now?
Where have you led me? What house is this?

CHORUS MEMBER
If you don't know where you are, I'll tell you—
you're at the house of the sons of Atreus.
That's the truth.

CASSANDRA
No...no...a house
that hates the gods... house full of death,
kinsmen butchered... heads chopped off...
a human slaughterhouse awash in blood...

CHORUS MEMBER
This stranger's like a keen hound on the scent.
She's on the trail of blood.

CASSANDRA
...I see evidence I trust—young children
screaming as they're butchered—then their father
eating his own infants' roasted flesh...

CHORUS MEMBER
We've heard about your fame in prophecy.
But here in Argos no one wants a prophet.

CASSANDRA
O god what's this she has in mind?

What new agony inside the house
is she preparing? Something monstrous,
barbaric, evil ... beyond all love,
all remedy. And help is far away.

CHORUS MEMBER

I don't understand what she's saying now.
What she first said, that I understood—
the whole city talks about it.

CASSANDRA

O evil woman, you're going to do it.
Your own husband, the man who shares your bed—
once you've washed him clean ... there in the bath ...
How shall I describe how all this ends?
It's coming soon. She's stretching out her hand ...
and now her other hand is reaching for him ...

CHORUS MEMBER

I still don't understand. What she's saying
is just too confused. Her dark prophecies
leave me bewildered.

CASSANDRA

Look! Look over there!
What's that apparition? Is that death's net?
No, she's the net, the one who sleeps with him,
that woman, murder's willing agent.
Let those Furies insatiably at work
against this clan rise up and scream for joy—
they have another victim fit for stoning.

CHORUS MEMBER

What Fury do you now invoke to shriek
throughout this house? What you've just said
makes me afraid.

CHORUS

Drop by drop the dark blood flows
around my heart—like mortal wounds
when life's sunset comes,
when death is near.

CASSANDRA
Look over there! Look now!
Keep the great bull from his mate.
She's caught him in her robes—
now she gores him with her black horn.
A trap! He's collapsing in the bath!
I'm telling you what's going on—
he's being murdered in there,
while bathing—a plot to kill him!

CHORUS MEMBER
I can't boast of any skill with prophecies,
but these strike me as pointing to disaster.

CHORUS
What good ever comes to men
from prophecies? They talk of evil.
All those skilful words encourage men
to be afraid of what the prophet chants.

CASSANDRA
Alas for me! Alas for my unwelcome fate!
I'm crying out for my own suffering—
my cup of grief is full, brim full...
Why have you brought me here,
so wretched, if not to die,
the second victim? Why else?

CHORUS MEMBER
Your mind's possessed—some god is in control.
And so you wail aloud about your death,
just like some shrill nightingale that sings,
without a pause, of her heart's distress,
lamenting all her life for her dead son,
life rich in sorrow.

CASSANDRA
O to have that—
the fate of the singing nightingale!
Gods gave her body wings and a sweet life.
She does not weep. But murder waits for me—
a two-edged sword hacks me to death.

CHORUS MEMBER
These vain prophetic cries of woe you chant,
where do they start? Why introduce
such horrific fear into your songs?
How do you set some limit to the path
where what you see so ominously leads?

CASSANDRA
Alas for that wedding ... Paris and his bride ...
how it destroyed his loved ones ...
Alas for the Scamander, river of my home!
By your banks I was raised so long ago,
brought up to all this misery ... And now it seems
I must soon chant my prophecies
by Cocytus and banks of Acheron,
twin rivers of the dead.

CHORUS MEMBER
What's that? The words seem clear enough—
any child could understand. Your cruel fate
strikes at me like a bloody fang. It hurts.
My heart breaks to hear you chant your sorrows.

CASSANDRA
Alas for my city's fate—
totally destroyed ...
Alas for my father's sacrifices,
all those grazing herds ...
offerings to save our walls!
In vain ... the city was not spared ...
all that misery it's endured.
Now I, on fire too, must go to ground.

CHORUS MEMBER
You keep repeating what you said before.
Some evil-minded demon, swooping down,
has fallen on you, forcing you to sing,
to chant your songs of death.
Where does this end?
That's what I can't see.

CASSANDRA

> Then my prophecy will veil itself no more,
> like some new bride half-concealed from view.
> Let it now rise as clear as a fresh wind
> blowing toward the rising sun, a wave
> cresting through the dawn and bringing on
> a tide of woe far greater than my own.
> I'll teach you no more in cryptic riddles.
> And you bear witness—run the trail with me,
> as I sniff out the track of ancient crimes.
> Up there on that roof there sits a chorus—
> it never leaves. They sing in harmony,
> but the song is harsh, predicting doom.
> Drinking human blood has made them bold—
> they dance in celebration through the house.
> The family's Furies cannot be dislodged.
> Sitting in the home, they chant their song,
> the madness that began all this, each in turn
> cursing that man who defiled his brother's bed.
> Have I missed the mark? Or like a fine archer
> have I hit the beast? Or am I selling lies,
> a fortune-teller babbling door to door?
> Tell me on your oath how well I know
> these old stories of this family's crimes.

CHORUS LEADER

> How could an oath of ours be any help,
> no matter how sincere, to heal your grief?
> But I'm amazed that you, born overseas,
> can say so much about a foreign city,
> as if you'd lived here.

CASSANDRA

> It was Apollo, god of prophecy, who made me what I am.

CHORUS MEMBER

> Surely the god was not in love with you?

CASSANDRA

> I used to be ashamed to talk of this…

CHORUS MEMBER
When we're doing well, we all have scruples.

CASSANDRA
Apollo was like a mighty wrestler,
panting all over me, in love.

CHORUS MEMBER
Did you go through with it—
bear him a child?

CASSANDRA
I promised to, but then I broke my word.

CHORUS MEMBER
Did you already have prophetic skill,
inspired by the god?

CASSANDRA
At that time
I used to prophesy to all my countrymen.
I'd foretell disasters.

CHORUS MEMBER
How did you escape Apollo's anger?

CASSANDRA
Since I resisted him, no one believes me.

CHORUS MEMBER
But to us, at least, what you prophesy
seems true enough.

CASSANDRA
Aieee ... the pains I feel.
The fearful labour pains of true prophecy
seize me, confuse me, as they start again,
full of foreboding. Look there—see those creatures,
young ones, sitting by the house, dark shapes,
like something from a dream? They're like children
murdered by their loved ones ... their hands are full,
clenching chunks of their own flesh as food,
their guts and inner organs ... it's all so clear ...
that awful meal their own father tasted.

For all that, I say, revenge is on the way,
someone's planning it, a craven lion,
a beast wallowing in bed, keeping watch,
waiting for my master to get back.
Yes, my master—since I must now bear
the yoke of slavery. That lord of war,
who led the fleet and ravaged Ilion,
has no idea what that cur is up to,
what evil plans the hateful bitch is hatching,
as her tongue licks his hands in welcome,
ears perked up for joy, like treacherous Ate,
goddess who destroys. It's outrageous—
the woman kills her man. What shall I call her?
What awful monster suits her? A snake?
An amphisbaena with a head at either end?
Or perhaps a Scylla living in the rocks,
preying on sailors, raging mother of hell,
who breathes relentless war on loved ones.
How that woman, in her audacity,
screamed out in triumph, like a battle cry,
pretending to enjoy his safe return!
Whether you credit what I say or not—
that doesn't really matter. Why should it?
What will come will come. And soon enough,
as you stand here full of pity, you'll say
Cassandra's prophecies were all too true.

CHORUS

I understand about Thyestes' meal,
and tremble thinking how he ate his children's flesh.
Terror grips me as I hear these truths
without embellishment. As for the rest,
hearing that just makes me lose my way.

CASSANDRA

I tell you you'll see Agamemnon dead.

CHORUS MEMBER

Poor girl, calm yourself. Tone down those words.

CASSANDRA

No—no one can heal what my words prophesy.

79

CHORUS
Not if they're true. But may the gods forbid!

CASSANDRA
While you pray here, others move in to kill.

CHORUS LEADER
What man is going to commit such crimes?

CASSANDRA
What man? You've completely missed the point.
You've failed to understand my prophecies.

CHORUS LEADER
Yes I have—
I don't see who has means to do it.

CASSANDRA
Yet I can speak Greek well enough.

CHORUS LEADER
So does the oracle at Delphi,
but understanding what it says is hard.

CASSANDRA
O this fire! His fire comes over me once more!
The pain ... Lycian Apollo ... burning me ...
That two-footed lioness ... crouching there
with a wolf, once the noble lion's gone ...
She's going to kill me ... the agony!
Now she prepares her drugs, and in her rage,
vows I too will be a part of her revenge,
as she whets a sword to kill her king.
He brought me here. Now we both die.
Her retribution. So why do I bear
these ornaments that mock me, this rod,
these prophet's wreaths around my neck?
Let me be rid of you before I die ....

[Cassandra breaks her wand and throws off the insignia of her office as a prophet]

There, an end to you. With you down there,

80

I get revenge. Make some other woman rich.
Let her preach destruction instead of me.

[Cassandra now starts tearing off her clothes]

Look how Apollo now in person strips me,
rips my prophetic robes, the god who watched,
as my friends in their hatred turned on me,
mocked me so savagely in these very clothes—
they thought they knew what they were doing.
But they were wrong. I heard them call me names,
"beggar," "starving wretch"—I endured them all.
And now the prophet god is done with me.
He's led his prophet to her place of death.
No father's altar for me here—instead
a chopping block awaits, slaughtered
in one hot stroke of bloody sacrifice.
But we'll not die without the gods' revenge.
Another man will come and will avenge us,
a son who'll kill his mother, then pay back
his father's death, a wanderer in exile,
a man this country's made a stranger.
He'll come back and, like a coping stone,
bring the ruin of his family to a close.
For gods have made a powerful promise—
his father's stretched out corpse will bring him home.
Why then do I lament so piteously?
Since I'm the one who first saw how Troy
would be wiped out the way it was,
since I see now how those who took the city
are being destroyed in judgment from the gods,
I'll go to meet my fate. I'll dare to die.
I greet this doorway as the gates of Death.
Once the death blow strikes, I pray I'll have
a gentle end—no struggle, as my life blood
drains away. And then I'll close my eyes.

CHORUS LEADER
You poor woman, so much pain and wisdom.
You've said so much. But if you see your death—
see it so clearly—how can you go on

81

so bravely to the altar, like an ox
destined by gods for sacrifice?

CASSANDRA
There's no way out. My friends, the time has come.

CHORUS LEADER
But there's some benefit in going last.

CASSANDRA
This is the day. It makes no sense to run.

CHORUS LEADER
You know, you endure your suffering
with courage I admire.

CASSANDRA
No one hearing that has reason to be glad.

CHORUS LEADER
But to die well
confers some human dignity.

CASSANDRA *[approaching the door then moving back in horror]*
I cry for you, my father, your noble children.

CHORUS LEADER
What's wrong? Why turn around in fear?

CASSANDRA
This house ... It's horrific!

CHORUS
Why call out in horror? Is there some vision
in your mind?

CASSANDRA
It's this house—
it stinks of murder, blood slaughter ...

CHORUS LEADER
No, no—that's the smell of sacrifice,
victims at the hearth.

CASSANDRA
That smell...
it's like an open grave...

CHORUS
Do you mean the splendid Syrian incense?
It's all through the house.

CASSANDRA *[turning back to the palace doors]*
No. But I must go.
I'll lament my death, and Agamemnon's, too,
inside the house. Enough of living!
Alas, my friends, I'm not holding back in fear,
like some bird trapped in bushes. I want you
to witness how I went to meet my death,
when for me another woman will be killed,
a man will die for one who married evil.
This is my last request before I die.

CHORUS LEADER
I pity you, poor creature, and your death,
which you have prophesied.

CASSANDRA
                                          One last time
I feel the urge to speak, not sing a dirge
about my death. I pray to the sun,
here in the light of his most recent day,
that those who carry out revenge for me
will make my enemies pay with their blood
for butchering a slave, an easy victim.
Alas, for human life. When things go well,
a shadow overturns it all. When badly,
a damp sponge wipes away the picture.
Of these two, the second is more pitiful.

*[Cassandra exits slowly and deliberately through the palace doors,
which close behind her]*

CHORUS
To rest unsatisfied amid great wealth
is in the nature of all human beings.
No one can point and order it away

from princely homes by uttering the words
"Dissatisfaction, enter here no more!"
Take Agamemnon. The powers in heaven
permitted him to capture Priam's town,
to return home honoured by the gods.
But now, if he must pay the penalty
for blood which other men before him shed
and die in retribution for the dead
he killed himself, what mortal human being
who hears all this can boast he lives
a life unscarred by fate?

[A scream comes from inside the palace]

AGAMEMNON *[from inside]*
    Help me!
    I'm hit... a deadly blow...

CHORUS LEADER
    Silence!
    Who cried out then? Something about a deadly blow.

AGAMEMNON *[within]*
    Aaagh! I'm hit again... a second blow...

CHORUS LEADER
    That's the king in there. Those cries, I think,
    tell us what's going on. Come now, let's decide
    what's best to do, our safest course of action.

*[At this point the Chorus breaks up in panic, losing its unity as a group.
Individual members speak to each other in great confusion]*

CHORUS MEMBER ONE
    Here's my advice—summon all the people,
    call them to bring help up to the palace.

CHORUS MEMBER TWO
    I say we must attack the house at once,
    catch them at it, swords still wet with blood.

CHORUS MEMBER THREE
    My view is we should do something like that.
    I vote we act. There's no time to delay.

CHORUS MEMBER FOUR
It's all so clear. This is their opening move—
a sign they're going to tyrannize the city.

CHORUS MEMBER FIVE
We're wasting time. They've thrown aside
all sense of hesitation. Their hands won't rest.

CHORUS MEMBER SIX
I don't know what scheme I could propose.
It's up to those who can carry out the plan
to tell us what to do.

CHORUS MEMBER SEVEN
That's my view, too
I don't know how to bring the dead to life
with nothing but our words.

CHORUS MEMBER EIGHT
But just to stay alive,
should we bow down before these tyrants,
who desecrate the house?

CHORUS MEMBER NINE
No. We can't do that.
Death would be preferable, a gentler fate
than such a tyranny.

CHORUS MEMBER TEN
But should we assume,
just on the basis of those groans we heard,
that Agamemnon's dead?

CHORUS MEMBER ELEVEN
Before we act,
we must have clearer evidence. To guess like this
is not really knowing what is true or not.

CHORUS LEADER
That's it then—everyone agrees on this—
we need to know more clearly how things stand
with Agamemnon, son of Atreus.

[The palace doors open, revealing the bodies of Agamemnon and Cassandra. Clytaemnestra stands over them. She is covered in blood]

CLYTAEMNESTRA
  Before this moment I said many things
  to suit my purposes. I'm not ashamed
  to contradict them now. How else could I
  act on my hate for such a hateful man,
  who feigned his love, how else prepare my nets
  of agony so high no one could jump them?
  I've brooded on this struggle many years,
  the old blood feud. My moment's come at last,
  though long delayed. I stand now where I struck,
  where I achieved what I set out to do.
  I did all this. I won't deny the fact.
  Round this man I cast my all-embracing net,
  rich robes of evil, as if catching fish—
  he had no way out, no eluding fate.
  I stabbed him twice. He gave out two groans.
  Then as his limbs went limp, I hit again,
  a third blow, my prayerful dedication
  to Zeus, underground protector of the dead.
  He collapsed, snorting his life away,
  spitting great gobs of blood all over me,
  drenching me in showers of his dark blood.
  And I rejoiced—just as the fecund earth
  rejoices when the heavens send spring rains,
  and new-born flower buds burst into bloom.
  That's how things stand, old men of Argos.
  Be joyful, if that's how you feel. For me,
  this is my triumph. If it were fitting
  to pour libations on this corpse,
  I'd pour my curses out—that would be just.
  He filled the mixing bowls in his own house
  with such destructive misery, and now
  he drinks it to the dregs. He's home at last.

CHORUS LEADER
  What you say I find incredible!
  How can that tongue of yours gloat like this,
  exulting over your dead husband?

CLYTAEMNESTRA
　　You're testing me, as if I were some silly woman.
　　But my heart is fearless. Let me tell you
　　what you already know—then you can praise
　　or criticize me as you like. I don't care.
　　This man is Agamemnon, my husband.
　　He's a corpse, the work of this right hand,
　　a work of justice. That's how matters stand.

CHORUS LEADER
　　Woman, what earth-grown poison have you eaten,
　　what evil drink drawn from the surging sea,
　　that you're so mad to risk the public voice,
　　the curses people mutter? You cast him off.
　　You cut him down. So now you'll be thrown out,
　　exiled from the city—a hateful thing
　　to your own people.

CLYTAEMNESTRA
　　So now you'd sentence me to banishment,
　　send me from the city a thing accursed?
　　Back then you made no accusation
　　against this man lying here. He sacrificed
　　his own child, that dear girl I bore in pain,
　　to charm the winds from Thrace—and didn't care.
　　To him she was a beast for slaughter.
　　He had flocks of them—his farms were full.
　　Shouldn't you have banished him from Argos
　　in punishment for that polluting crime?
　　You're strict enough when you pass judgment
　　on what I've done. So let me caution you—
　　I'm prepared to fight you head to head.
　　If you win, well then, you can govern me.
　　But if god lets me prevail, you old men
　　will learn, old as you are, to behave yourselves.

CHORUS LEADER
　　You're too ambitious, far too arrogant.
　　Blood-drenched murder's made you mad. That's plain.
　　Your eyes are full of blood. Now stroke for stroke
　　you'll pay for what you've done. You've lost your friends,
　　you've lost your honour...

CLYTAEMNESTRA *[interrupting]*
    Then hear this, too, the force behind my oath—
    by that Justice I exacted for my child,
    by Ate, goddess of destruction,
    by the Fury to whom I offered up this man,
    my hopes will never walk these halls in fear,
    so long as Aegisthus stokes the blazing fires
    in my hearth. And he's as loyal to me now
    as always, my shield, no man to trifle with.
    He'll boost my confidence. Here he lies,
    the man who abused his wife, seduced
    by every captive girl at Ilion—
    and here she lies, his concubine, his spear prize,
    the faithful prophetess who shared his bed.
    She also knew the rowing benches
    where sailors sweat. They get what they deserve.
    He's dead. She, like a swan, sang her last song,
    then died. Now she lies there, his sweetheart.
    She'll bring new thrills, fresh pleasures to my bed.

CHORUS
    O that some Fate would soon come,
    free from suffering and quick,
    bringing endless sleep,
    our last eternal sleep,
    now our gracious lord is dead.
    For a woman's sake
    he suffered much, and now
    by a woman's hand he died.

    Alas for you, Helen, frantic woman.
    On your own, beneath Troy's walls,
    you slaughtered many lives,
    and more than many.
    Now you wear your final garland—
    one long remembered for the blood
    which will never wash away.
    Back then in this house
    lived a spirit of strife,
    a power that broke our king.

CLYTAEMNESTRA
Don't torment yourself like this, invoking
death and fate, or redirect your rage
on Helen, as if she killed those men,
all those Danaan lives, all by herself,
and brought us pain past remedy.

CHORUS
O spirit that falls upon this house,
on Menelaus, on Agamemnon,
descendants of Tantalus,
you overpower me
through these two sisters,
each with power like a man.
You consume my heart with grief.
Perched on his corpse
the hateful raven caws her song,
her harsh triumphal tune.

CLYTAEMNESTRA
Now you're talking sense, when you call on
the demon of this house, who's eaten up
three generations, the one who nurtures
bloodlust in our guts. And so new blood
spurts out before the old wound heals.

CHORUS
You appeal to that huge fiend
haunting this house,
whose anger weighs it down,
to that tale of evil fate
insatiably consuming us.
Alas, alas, the will of Zeus,
the cause of everything,
who brings all things about.
What can come to mortal men
except at Zeus' will?
And in what's happened here
what's not caused by the gods?

Alas, my king, my lord—
How shall I weep for you?

How speak of you with love?
To lie entangled in the spider's web,
gasping life away—a sacrilege—
stretched out on this bed of shame,
struck down in treachery,
the two-edged sword
wielded by your wife.

CLYTAEMNESTRA
Are you saying this work is mine? That's not so.
Don't think of me as Agamemnon's wife.
The form of this corpse's wife was taken on
by the ancient savage spirit of revenge.
For that brutal meal prepared by Atreus,
it sacrificed one full-grown man,
payment for two butchered children.

CHORUS
Who would ever say
you bear no guilt
for Agamemnon's murder?
How could they? How?
Yet that avenging spirit
acting on his father's crime
could well have egged you on.
Black Ruin moves ahead with force
through streams of family blood
granting vengeance for the young
served up as chunks of meat.

Alas, my king, my lord—
How shall I weep for you?
How speak of you with love?
To lie entangled in the spider's web,
gasping life away—a sacrilege—
stretched out on this bed of shame,
struck down in treachery,
the two-edged sword
wielded by your wife.

CLYTAEMNESTRA
I don't think the man died wretchedly,

like some poor slave. Surely his own deceit
brought ruin on this house? His suffering
matches exactly what he did himself.
Remember my own Iphigeneia,
his daughter, that sweet flower whom we mourn.
So let him not boast out loud in Hades.
He was the first to draw his sword,
and by the sword he's been repaid.

CHORUS

There's no clear way, and now
this family's falling. I'm afraid.
It's not just bloody drops. No,
storms of blood rain batter down,
destroying the house, while fate
on yet another whetstone,
hones the edge of Justice,
for the next act, one more crime.

O Earth, my Earth—
how I wish you'd swallowed me
before I ever saw my king
lying low on such bed,
a silver-plated bath.
Who will now bury him?
Who will lament for him?
Will you dare to do this,
a woman mourning for the spirit
of the husband she's just killed,
complete the injustices you've done
with wretched favours to the dead
to expiate your monstrous crimes?
As people stand around the grave
to praise this god-like man, in tears,
whose sad heart will be sincere?

CLYTAEMNESTRA

That business is none of your concern.
At our hands he collapsed in death.
We'll bury him. But this house will not weep.
No. Iphigeneia will meet him down there,
as is fitting—the daughter greets her father

happily by that swift stream of sorrow.
Then she'll embrace the man with love.

CHORUS

One disgrace exchanged for yet another,
the struggle to decide is hard.
The man who sins is sinned against,
the killer pays the price.
Yet while Zeus sits upon his throne
this decree from god remains—
the man who acts will suffer.
Who can then cast from this house
its self-perpetuating curse?
This race is wedded to destruction.

CLYTAEMNESTRA

Now you're close to getting at the truth.
For my part, I'm prepared to swear an oath
to the demon of the House of Atreus—
I'll rest content with what's been done,
hard though that is, if he'll leave this house alone,
transferring family murder somewhere else,
to some other clan. I don't need much,
a small part of our wealth, if I can free
these halls entirely of this madness,
the urge we have to kill each other.

*[Enter Aegisthus with armed attendants. The situation now grows
increasingly tense, with the soldiers menacing the members of the
Chorus, who begin to coalesce as a political unit, rediscovering their
strength. This sense of a major irreconcilable political division and the
threat of civil war grows increasingly acute until the end of the play]*

AEGISTHUS

What a glorious day of retribution!
Now I can say that once again the gods
looking down on men avenge their crimes.
How it fills my heart with joy to see this man
stretched out here in a robe the Furies wove,
full payment for deceitful treachery
his father's hand devised. For Atreus,
king of Argos, was this man's father.
To set the record straight, my father,

Thyestes, brother to Atreus,
challenged his authority. So Atreus
expelled him from his home and city.
But Thyestes in his misery returned,
a suppliant at his own hearth, praying
Fate would save him, he would not be killed,
his own blood would not stain his native ground.
Atreus, the godless father of this man,
welcomed him effusively, but not with love.
He set up what seemed a celebration—
a feast day with lots of meat, but served
my father flesh of his own children.
He sliced their toes and fingers off. Over these
he diced the other parts, then passed this dish
to Thyestes, where he sat beside him.
My father then, in total ignorance,
took the food he didn't recognize,
and ate the meal which, as you've witnessed,
destroyed the race. When Thyestes learns
the abominable thing he's done, he screams,
staggers back, vomits up the butchered flesh.
Then, kicking down the banquet table
to underscore his cry for justice,
he calls down on the House of Atreus
a curse no one can bear, "Let them all die,
the race of Pleisthenes—all die like this."*
That's why you see this man lying here.
This murder was my plan for justice.
For Atreus threw my broken father out,
and me as well, his third son, still a child,
an infant wrapped in swaddling clothes.
But I grew up. And Justice brought me back.
I seized the man who'd banished me.
I planned each detail of this murderous scheme.
Now I see him in the nets of Justice,
I can face even my own death with joy.

CHORUS LEADER
To me you're contemptible, Aegisthus,
getting pleasure from all this agony.
You say you killed the king deliberately,
and planned the cowardly slaughter on your own.

93

I tell you—remember this—when justice comes,
your head will not escape the people's cursing
or death by stoning at their hands.

AEGISTHUS

So you say—but you man the lower oars.
Your masters on the higher tiers control the ship.
You may be old, but you'll learn how painful
it is at your age to be taught your place.
Hunger pangs and chains, two worthy teachers,
make excellent cures for teaching wisdom,
even with old men. Surely you have eyes.
Can't you see this? You shouldn't kick at thorns.
You'll only hurt yourselves.

CHORUS MEMBER ONE

You womanly creature!
You stayed at home, waiting out the war,
until the men came back. You soiled a real man's bed,
then planned to kill our king.

AEGISTHUS

This talk of yours
will soon give you sufficient cause to weep.
The tongue of Orpheus was not like yours—
the pleasure of his voice drew all things to him.
Your puny squawking merely irritates.
But once I chain you up, my force has ways
to make you more compliant.

CHORUS MEMBER TWO

As if you rule in Argos!
You, the one who plotted Agamemnon's death,
but weren't brave enough to kill the man yourself!

AEGISTHUS

Clearly it was the woman's role to trick him.
I was not a man whom he would trust.
After all, I'm an old enemy of his.
But with his wealth I'll try to rule the people.
Those who resist I'll strap under the yoke.
It won't be light—not like a well-fed trace horse.

No. Miserable starvation in the dark—
then we'll see how docile they can be.

CHORUS MEMBER THREE
You coward!
Why not kill the man yourself? Why rely
upon that woman for the murder,
a disgrace to her own country and its gods?
O can Orestes still see the light of day?
If his good fortune holds, will he come home,
win out, and kill the two of them up there?

AEGISTHUS
If that's the way you want to act and speak,
you'll get your lesson fast. Men, stand ready.
My trusty guard, your work's in front of you.

[The soldiers place their weapons at the ready and move into menace the Chorus. The Chorus stands its ground, raising their staves as weapons]

CHORUS LEADER
Don't give way. Each of you, get your weapons ready.

AEGISTHUS *[half drawing his sword]*
My hand is on my sword, as well.
I'm not afraid to die.

CHORUS LEADER
You say you'll welcome death. That's good to hear.
We're happy to oblige.

[Clytaemnestra, alarmed at the way in which the conflict has grown, moves quickly between the guards led by Aegisthus and the Chorus]

CLYTAEMNESTRA
Stop this, my dearest.
Let's not act to bring on further trouble.
Our wretched harvest is bountiful enough—
we've reaped sufficient pain. No more bloodshed.
You honourable old men, go home. Yield to fate,
before you hurt yourselves. What we've done here
we had to do. Let our troubles end right now.
That we'll allow, even though our fate

has struck a heavy blow. That's my advice,
what a woman ought to say, if any here
will act on it.

AEGISTHUS
What about these men
who let their tongues prattle on against me,
hurling insults in my face, testing fate?
They throw aside all moderate restraint
to abuse their master.

CHORUS LEADER
Men of Argos will never cringe before an evil man.

AEGISTHUS
I'll get my own back soon enough.

CHORUS LEADER
Not if fate brings Orestes home again.

AEGISTHUS
I understand how exiles feed on hope.

CHORUS LEADER
Go on. Fatten yourself up. While you still can,
pollute all Justice.

AEGISTHUS
You must know you'll pay
for all this insolence to me.

CHORUS
Keep on bragging—
just like a cock beside his hen.

CLYTAEMNESTRA *[pulling Aegisthus towards the palace doors]*
Leave them their feeble yelping. You and I
control the house. We'll put things in order.

*[Clytaemnestra and Aegisthus back slowly into the palace and close the
doors, leaving the guards and Chorus still facing each other. Slowly the
Chorus disintegrates and its members walk off one by one. The guards
form up in front of the palace, an armed defence before the doors].*

—*Translated by Ian Johnston*

Ajax
Sophocles
Translated by Ian Johnston

The play **Ajax** *was written by Sophocles sometime between 450 and 430* BCE *and centers around the play's namesake who has been struck with a type of madness after being denied the honor of wearing the armor of Achilles.*

Taking place after the siege of Troy, the hero Achilles has died and the fate of his armor is uncertain; which of the Achaeans will be granted the honor of wearing the armor of their most fearsome warrior?

The decision comes down to either Ajax or Odysseus, who each contend for the right to claim the armor. Ultimately, Odysseus is victorious of Ajax.

By being denied the armor, Ajax believes that he has been greatly dishonored and is thrown into a fit of madness. He slaughters the sheep of the Achaeans believing they are Greek soldiers.

Eventually, the shame that is placed upon him will become too great. Ajax takes his own life, throwing himself onto his sword as retribution for this great injustice.

The play deals heavily with the themes of honor and the heroes to which it is owed. Moreover the tragedy tells us of the sorrow and anger that can be bred as a result of heroes being denied the glory that they so desperately need.

DRAMATIS PERSONAE

ATHENA: goddess of war and wisdom
ODYSSEUS: king of Ithaca, a leader in the Argive forces at Troy
AJAX: king of Salamis
CHORUS: sailors from Salamis
TECMESSA: daughter of the king of Phrygia, concubine of Ajax
MESSENGER: a soldier
TEUCER: a Greek warrior, half brother of Ajax
MENELAUS: one of the commanders of the Argive forces at Troy
AGAMEMNON: brother of Menelaus, commander of the Greek army

EURYSACES: young son of Ajax and Tecmessa.
ATTENDANTS, SERVANTS, SOLDIERS

*[The action takes place during the last year of the Trojan War. The
scene is one end of the Argive camp beside the sea, outside Ajax's hut.
The hut is a substantial building with main doors facing the audience
and some side doors. There are steps leading up to a platform outside
the main doors. It is early in the morning, without very much light yet.
ODYSSEUS enters slowly, tracking footprints in the sand and trying to
look through the partially open door into the hut. The goddess ATHENA
appears and speaks to ODYSSEUS.]*

ATHENA
    Odysseus, I keep seeing you prowl around,
    seeking by stealth to gain the upper hand
    against your enemies. And now, by these huts
    at one end of the army, where Ajax
    has his camp beside the ships, for some time
    I've been observing as you track him down,
    keeping your eyes fixed on his fresh-made trail,
    to find out whether he's inside or not.1
    Like a keen-nosed Spartan hunting dog,
    your path is taking you straight to your goal—
    the man has just gone in, his head and arms
    dripping with sweat after the butchery
    he's just carried out with his own sword.
    So you don't need to peer inside the doors.
    What are you so eager to discover here?
    Why not tell me? You could learn the answer
    from someone who knows.

ODYSSEUS *[looking up but he cannot see Athena]*
    Ah, Athena's voice, of the gods
    the one I cherish most. How clear you sound.
    I can't see you, but I do hear your words—
    my mind can grasp their sense, like the bronze call
    of an Etruscan trumpet.2And you are right.
    You see me circling around, tracking down
    that man who hates me, shield-bearing Ajax.
    I've been following his trail a long time now—
    just him, no one else. During the night
    he's done something inconceivable to us,

if he's the one who did it. We're not sure.
We don't know anything for certain.
So I volunteered to find out what's gone on.
We've just discovered all our livestock killed—
our plunder butchered by some human hand,
and with them the men who guard the herd.
Everyone blames Ajax for the slaughter.
What's more, an eyewitness who saw him
striding by himself across the plain, his sword
dripping with fresh blood, informed me of it
and told me what he saw. I ran off at once
to pick up his trail. I'm following the tracks.
But it's confusing—sometimes I don't know
whose prints they are. So you've come just in time,
for in the past and in the days to come
your hand has been and will remain my guide.

ATHENA
I am aware of that, Odysseus, that's why
for some time I've been keen to come to you
as a watchman on your hunt.

ODYSSEUS
Well then, dear lady,will what I'm doing here have good results?

ATHENA
I'll tell you this: Ajax did those killings,
as you suspected.

ODYSSEUS
Why would he do that?
Why turn his hands to such a senseless act?

ATHENA
The weapons—that armour from Achilles—
it made him insanely angry.

ODYSSEUS
But then why would he slaughter all the animals?

ATHENA
He thought he was staining both his hands with blood from you.

ODYSSEUS
 You mean this was his planagainst the Argives?

ATHENA
 Yes—and it would have worked,
 if I had not been paying attention.

ODYSSEUS
 How could he have done something so reckless?
 How could his mind have been so rash?

ATHENA
 At nightin secret he crept out alone after you.

ODYSSEUS
 How close was he? Did he get to his target?

ATHENA
 He reached the camp of both commanders—
 he made it right up to their double gates.

ODYSSEUS
 If he was so insanely keen for slaughter,
 how could he prevent his hands from killing?

ATHENA
 I stopped him. I threw down into his eyes
 an overwhelming sense of murderous joy
 and turned his rage against the sheep and cattle
 and those protecting them—the common herd
 which so far has not been divided up.5
 He launched his attack against those animals
 and kept on chopping down and slaughtering
 the ones with horns by slicing through their spines,
 until they made a circle all around him.
 At one point he thought he was butchering
 both sons of Atreus—he had them in his hands.6
 Then he went at some other general
 and then another. As he charged around
 in his sick frenzy, I kept encouraging him,
 kept pushing him into those fatal nets.
 And then, when he took a rest from killing,
 he tied up the sheep and cattle still alive

and led them home, as if he had captured
human prisoners and not just animals.
Now he keeps them tied up in his hut
and tortures them. I'll let you see his madness—
in plain view here—so you can witness it
and then report to all the Argives. Be brave.
Do not back off or look upon this man
as any threat to you. I will avert his eyes,
so he will never see your face.

[Calling to Ajax inside the hut]

You in there—
the one who's tying up his prisoner's arms—
I'm calling you! I'm shouting now for Ajax!
Come on out here! Outside the hut! In front!

ODYSSEUS
Athena! What are you doing? Don't call him!
Don't bring him out here!

ATHENA
Just be patient.
Don't run the risk of being called a coward.

ODYSSEUS
For the gods' sake, don't do it! Leave him be!
Let him stay inside!

ATHENA
What's the matter with you?
He was just a man before this, wasn't he?

ODYSSEUS
Yes, and in the past unfriendly to me,
and especially now.

ATHENA
But the sweetest laughter comes from mocking enemies.
Is that not true?

ODYSSEUS
Still, I'd prefer he stayed inside his hut.

ATHENA
> You hesitate to see before your eyes
> someone in a raving fit?

ODYSSEUS
> Yes, I do-if he were fully sane I'd not avoid him
> or hesitate...

ATHENA
> But he won't see you now,not even if you stand beside him.

ODYSSEUS
> How will that occur, if he still can seewith his own eyes?

ATHENA
> His eyes see very well, but I will make them dark.

ODYSSEUS
> Well, it is true
> a god's work can make all things possible.

ATHENA
> Stand here, then, and stay quiet.

ODYSSEUS
> I'd better stay,
> although I'd have preferred to keep my distance.

ATHENA
> You in there, Ajax! I'm calling you again!
> Why show your ally so much disrespect?

[AJAX enters from the hut. He is carrying a bloody whip with which he has been lashing the cattle]

AJAX
> Welcome Athena! Welcome child of Zeus!
> You have given me so much assistance!
> In gratitude for those I've captured
> I'll offer you a crown, presents of pure gold.

ATHENA
> That's nobly spoken. But tell me this—
> did that sword of yours slake itself on blood
> when you attacked the Argive army?

AJAX
　　Yes. That I can boast about. I don't deny it.

ATHENA
　　You went after the two sons of Atreus
　　with that weapon in your fist?

AJAX
　　Indeed I did.
　　They'll not dishonour Ajax any more.

ATHENA
　　So, as I understand you, those men are dead.

AJAX
　　Yes, dead. Let them rob me of my weapons now!

ATHENA
　　I see. Well, what about Laertes' son?
　　As far as you're concerned, where does he stand?
　　Did he escape you?

AJAX
　　That damned slimy fox!
　　You ask me where he is?

ATHENA
　　Yes, I'm asking.
　　I mean that enemy of yours Odysseus.

AJAX
　　My favourite prisoner, lady, sits inside.
　　I don't want him to die just yet.

ATHENA
　　But when?
　　What further actions do you have to do?
　　Or what advantage will you gain by that?

AJAX
　　Not before he's tied up to a pillar,
　　the main one holding up the roof in there.

ATHENA
    What harm will you inflict on the poor man?

AJAX
    I'll whip his back blood red. Then I'll kill him.

ATHENA
    Don't abuse the poor man so viciously.

AJAX
    You can follow your desires, Athena,
    in all other things. That I will concede.
    But this is the penalty he's going to pay—
    not something else.

ATHENA
    All right, since it pleases you,
    give that arm of yours some exercise. Don't stop.
    Do what you've planned.

AJAX
    Then I'll get back to work.
    And I'll leave you with this request from me—
    always stand beside me as my ally
    the way you did today.

[AJAX goes back into the hut]

ATHENA
    Do you see,
    Odysseus, how powerful the gods can be?
    Could you find anyone more sensible
    than Ajax, a man with more ability
    to carry out in every situation
    the most appropriate action?

ODYSSEUS
    No one I know.
    All the same, although he despises me,
    I pity his misfortune under that yoke
    of catastrophic madness. It makes me think
    not just of his fate but my own as well.
    I see that in our lives we are no more
    than phantoms, insubstantial shadows.

104

ATHENA
Well then, now you've seen his arrogance,
make sure you never speak against the gods,
or give yourself ideas of your own grandeur,
if your strength of hand or heaped-up riches
should outweigh some other man's. A single day
pulls down any human's scale of fortune
or raises it once more. But the gods love
men who possess good sense and self-control
and despise the ones who are unjust.

*[ATHENA and ODYSSEUS leave. Enter the CHORUS, sailors from
Salamis and followers of Ajax]*

CHORUS LEADER
Son of Telamon, who holds the throne
on wave-washed Salamis beside the sea,
I rejoice with you when things go well,
but when a blow from Zeus or angry words
from slanderous Danaans are aimed at you,
then I hold back in fear and shake with terror,
like the fluttering eye on a feathered dove.8
I'm like that now. In the night that's passing,
there were noisy rumours thrown against us,
against our honour, saying that you went off
into that meadow where our horses range
and massacred Danaan animals,
together with the spoils their spears had captured,
prizes which had not yet been allotted.
With that bright sword of yours you butchered them.
Such slanderous reports Odysseus shapes
and whispers into every soldier's ear.
Many men believe him. For he now speaks
persuasively about you, and everyone
who listens is filled with spite and pleased
that you have come to grief, even more
than is the man who told them. Throw a spear
at some great soul, and you will never miss,
but if someone said things like that of me,
he'd never be believed. Envy creeps up
against the man of wealth and power.

And yet without the great, we lesser men
are fragile ramparts in our own defence.
It's best for small men to ally themselves
with greatness, and for the powerful
to be supported by the lesser men.
But teaching foolish people such good sense
ahead of time is just not possible.
So men like this are now denouncing you,
and we do not possess sufficient power
to deflect these charges, not without you,
not without our king. With you out of their sight,
they keep on chattering like flocks of birds.
But if you unexpectedly appeared,
they would be terrified, as if they faced
a mighty eagle, and soon would cower there,
and hold their tongues in silence.

CHORUS
    Was it that goddess Artemis,
    bull-tending child of Zeus,
    who drove you on,
    drove you at the common herd?
    O mighty Rumour, mother of my shame!
    Was it perhaps in retribution for a victory
    where she received no tribute,
    splendid weapons she was cheated of?
    Or did some hunter kill a stag
    and set no gifts aside for her?
    Or has Enyalios, bronze-plated god of war,
    with reason to complain about an armed alliance,
    taken his revenge for such an insult
    by a devious stratagem at night?
    For with your own mind, O son of Telamon,
    you'd never go so far along the path to ruin
    as to attack the flocks.But nothing can prevent
    a sickness which the gods implant.
    I pray that Zeus, that Phoebus Apollo
    will stave off this catastrophe,
    this disastrous rumour of the Argives.
    And if great kings are slandering you now
    with stories full of lies, or if it is that man

born from the worthless line of Sisyphus,
do not, my lord, take on the grievous weight
of a dishonoured reputation by remaining here,
hiding your presence in this hut beside the sea.
Up now, get up from where you sit,
wherever you've been settled for so long
in your pause from battle. You are fuelling
a fire of disaster blazing up to heaven.
Your enemies' insolence keeps charging on
quite fearlessly, whipped up by favouring winds
through forest thickets, while every soldier
wags his tongue and laughs and jeers.
They bring us grief and reinforce our sorrow.

[Enter TECMESSA]

TECMESSA
You men, shipmates of Ajax, sons of the race
of earth-born Erechtheus, all of us
who love the distant house of Telamon
are in despair. For now our master Ajax,
our great and terrifying and forceful king,
lies suffering from tempestuous disease.

CHORUS LEADER
What heavy grief has come during the night
to change the troubles we had yesterday?
Daughter of the Phrygian Teleutas,
speak to us—though bold Ajax won you
fighting with his spear, he still maintains
a strong affection for you, so you may know
and offer us an answer.

TECMESSA
How can I tell
a story much too terrifying for words?
You will hear of suffering as harsh as death.
Last night madness seized our glorious Ajax,
and now he has been totally disgraced.
You can see everything inside his hut,
the blood-soaked butchered victims who were killed
as sacrifices at his very hands.

107

CHORUS

    The news you tell us of our fiery king
    we cannot bear, and yet there's no escape.
    It's what the powerful Danaans say,
    what their great story-telling spreads around.
    O, how I fear what's coming next. This man
    is going to die—and in full public view—
    with a black sword in those mad hands of his
    he massacred the herd and herdsmen, too,
    the ones who ride to guard our animals.

TECMESSA

    Alas! From those fields he came to me
    right after that, leading his captive beasts.
    On the floor in there he slit some of their throats,
    struck others in the ribs, tore them apart.
    He grabbed two rams—the legs on both were white—
    cut off the head on one and sliced its tongue,
    right at the tip, then threw the parts away,
    and lashed the other upright on the pillar.
    He seized a thick strap from a horse's harness
    and flogged it with a whistling double lash.
    He was cursing with an awful violence,
    not human words—ones a god had taught him.

CHORUS LEADER

    The time has come for us to hide our heads
    and steal away on foot—or take our seats,
    each man at his swift oar, and let our ship
    sail out on her seaworthy way. Those threats
    our two commanders, sons of Atreus,
    keep hurling at us are so serious,
    I am afraid of savage death by stoning,
    sharing the suffering of the man in there,
    struck down with him now in the grip of fate,
    his own inexorable doom.

TECMESSA

    No, no.
    He is no longer like that. He's grown calm.
    Like a sharp south wind that rushes past
    without a lightning flash, he's easing off.

Now he's sane again, but in new agonies.
To look at self-inflicted suffering
when no one else played any part in it
brings on great anguish.

CHORUS LEADER
If he's no longer mad,
I'm confident that things may be all right.
For when disaster has already passed
it doesn't have as much significance.

TECMESSA
But if you had the choice of causing grief
to your own friends while feeling good yourself
or of grieving too, a suffering man
among a common sorrow, which would you choose?

CHORUS LEADER
The double grieving, lady, is far worse.

TECMESSA
So at this moment we, although not sick,
are facing disaster.

CHORUS LEADER
What does that mean?
I don't understand what you are saying.

TECMESSA
That man in there, when he was still so ill,
enjoyed himself while savage fantasies
held him in their grip, but we were sane,
and, since he was one of us, we suffered.
But now there is a pause in his disease,
he can recuperate and understand
the full extremity of bitter grief,
yet everything for us remains the same—
our anguish is no milder than before.
This is surely not a single sorrow,
but a double grief?

CHORUS LEADER
I think that's true.

I fear a blow sent from a god has struck him.
How else could this take place, if his spirit
is no more hopeful now that he's been cured
than when he was sick?

TECMESSA

That's how things stand.
You must see that.

CHORUS LEADER

How did his illness start?
How did this trouble first swoop down on him?
Since we share your grief, tell us what happened.

TECMESSA

You are all involved in this, and so you'll hear
the entire story. At some point in the night,
when the evening torches had stopped burning,
Ajax took up his two-edged sword, resolved
to set off on a senseless expedition.
I challenged him and said, "What are you doing?
Ajax, why are you going out like this?
There's been no summons, no messenger,
nor any trumpet call. All the army
is now sleeping."His reply to me was brief,
that old refrain, "Woman, the finest thing
that females do is hold their tongues."So I,
taking my cue from that, did not respond,
and he charged out alone. I cannot say
what went on out there, but he came back
and took his chained-up prisoners inside,
all linked together—bulls and herding dogs
and captured sheep. He cut the heads off some.
He twisted back the skulls of other beasts
and cut their throats or chopped their spines.
Others, whom he kept tied up, he tortured,
as if they were human beings, even though
it was only beasts he was attacking.
At last, he charged out through the doorway
and forced out some words of conversation
with a shadow. Sometimes he'd talk about
the sons of Atreus, at other times

about Odysseus, with manic laughter
at how by going out he had avenged
all their arrogance in full. After that,
he rushed back in the hut again and there
he gradually regained his sense somehow,
though not without an effort. Once he saw
his room filled up with that deluded slaughter,
he struck his head and howled. Then he collapsed,
a ruined man among so many ruins,
carcasses of butchered sheep. He sat there,
fists gripping his hair with nails clenched tight.
For a long time he remained quite silent.
Then he made some dreadful threats against me
if I would not tell him every detail
of what had taken place. He questioned me—
What on earth had he become involved with?
My friends, I was afraid. So I told him
everything that had gone on, all the things
I knew were true. He at once began to groan,
doleful sounds I'd never heard from him before.
He's always claimed that wailing cries like that
were only fit for gloomy men and cowards.
He used to grieve, but never wail aloud—
just a deep moan, like from a lowing bull.
But now, overwhelmed by his misfortune,
he takes no food, no drink, sprawled in silence
where he fell down among dead animals
his own sword killed. It seems clear enough
he will do something bad. The words he speaks
and his laments show that intent somehow.
My friends, you should come in and help him,
if that's possible. That's why I came out here.
For words from friends can cure a man like him.

CHORUS LEADER
    Tecmessa, daughter of Teleutas,
    what you've described to us about the man
    being driven mad with sorrow—that's dreadful.

AJAX *[crying out from inside the hut]*
    Aaaiiii ... Alas for me!

TECMESSA
It looks as if his fit could soon be worse.
Did you not hear that loud cry from Ajax?

AJAX
Aaaiiii! ... Alas!

CHORUS LEADER
I think the man is sick or still suffering
the effects of that disease he had before—
they're all around him where he sits.

AJAX
My child!My son!

TECMESSA
How miserable I feel!
Eurysaces, he's calling you. But why?
What does he have in mind? Where are you?
I'm overwhelmed.

AJAX
I call on Teucer!
Where is Teucer? Will that fighting raid he's on
keep going forever, with me dying here?

CHORUS LEADER
I think the man may have his wits again.
Open the door. Perhaps when he sees me
he'll quickly feel a sense of self-respect.

TECMESSA *[opening the door of the hut]*
There. It's open. Now you can take a look
at what he's done and see the state he's in.

[AJAX is revealed sitting among the dead animals]

AJAX
Ah, my cherished sailors, of all my friends
the only ones who still observe true loyalty.
You see how great a wave has just rolled over me,
a crashing surge lashed on by murderous winds.

CHORUS LEADER *[to Tecmessa]*
It looks as if what you told us is true—
his condition clearly shows his madness.

AJAX
Ah, you race of master mariners,
who crossed the sea and with your oars sped out
across the salty ocean, I see in you,
and in you alone, the one support
in my despair. Come, help me kill myself.

CHORUS LEADER
No more of that! Speak words of hope.
Don't seek to cure one bad thing with another
or make this mad disaster any worse.

AJAX
Do you see how this bold and valiant heart,
this warrior so fearless in those wars
against his enemies, has turned his hands,
these awesome hands, against tame animals?
Ah, the mockery! How I have been abused!

TECMESSA
I beg you, my lord Ajax, don't say that.

AJAX
Just go away. Why not turn your feet around
and wander off somewhere?Aaaaiiii ....

CHORUS LEADER
By the gods, concede. Use your common sense.

AJAX
It's my bad luck I let slip from my grasp
those criminals deserving punishment.
Instead I went at bulls with twisted horns,
fine herds of goats, and made their dark blood flow.

CHORUS LEADER
Why lament those deeds which have been done
and cannot be recalled? Such final acts
will never be anything but what they are.

AJAX
> O you who keeps prying into everything,
> you nasty instrument for every crime,
> Odysseus, the filthiest degenerate
> in all the army, you must be laughing now,
> taking great delight in this.

CHORUS LEADER
> Divine will
> determines if each man laughs and cries.

AJAX
> But still I'd like to face him, though I'm injured. Ahhhh ....

CHORUS LEADER
> Don't make boasts like that. Do you not see
> the catastrophe you face?

AJAX
> O Zeus,
> you ancestral father of my father,
> if only I could die after I had killed
> that wheedling scoundrel enemy of mine
> and those twin-reigning kings.

TECMESSA
> When you make that prayer,
> pray also that I die as well. With you gone,
> why should I continue living?

AJAX
> O darkness, now my daylight,
> O gloom of Erebus, for me
> the brightest light there is,
> take me, take me now
> to live with you.13Take me,
> a man no longer worthy to seek help
> from families of gods or men,
> those creatures of a day.
> For Zeus' daughter, brave Athena,
> abuses and destroys me.
> Where can one escape?
> Where could I go and rest?

If my past fame has been cut down,
along with these dead beasts beside me,
then, my friends, if I now seek
a madman's triumphs, all the army,
with repeated blows from their own swords
will cut me down as well.

TECMESSA
How hard it is for me to hear this man,
this worthy man, say things he'd never say
before this happened!

AJAX
O you paths of the resounding sea!
You tidal caves and coastal pastures,
for a long time now, for far too long,
you have detained me here in Troy.
But that you will no longer do, no,
not while I am breathing still.
Let men of sense be sure of that.
O you streams of the Scamander,
my neighbour, so friendly to the Argives,
you no longer will be seeing Ajax,
a man whose equal as a warrior—
and I can make this boast—
Troy never saw arriving here from Greece.
But now I lie among this heap, dishonoured.

CHORUS LEADER
I don't have the strength to stop your words
or to let you go on saying such things—
you've fallen into such calamity.

AJAX
Alas! Who would ever think my name
would suit my troubles so poetically?
For I could well cry out two or three times
"Alas for Ajax!"—that shows the magnitude
of the disaster I am going through.
I am the man whose father's excellence
won supreme respect from all the army.
He took the fairest prize and carried home

every glory from the land of Ida.
I am his son, who journeyed after him
to this same land of Troy. I'm just as strong,
with the work of my own hands I have attained
achievements just as great, but, as you see,
these Argive insults have quite ruined me.
And yet I think I can affirm this much—
had Achilles lived and been about to judge
the man who should receive his weapons,
the prize for being the finest man in war,
no soldier would have put his hand on them
before I did. But now the sons of Atreus
have dealt them to a fellow whose spirit
will stoop to anything, and pushed aside
all those triumphant victories of Ajax.
If with my distorted mind and eyes,
I had not abandoned what I planned,
they would not have had what's mine by right
put to the vote against another man.
But then that goddess with the glaring eyes,
implacable Athena, Zeus' daughter,
threw me over at the very instant
I was steadying my hand against them.
She hurled in me a frenzied sickness,
so blood from grazing beasts would stain my hands,
and those men now can laugh at their escape,
something I did not want. But when a god
commits an injury, the unworthy man
escapes someone more powerful. And now,
what do I do, when I am obviously
hated by the gods, when the Greek army
despises me, and everyone in Troy
and on the plain holds me an enemy?
Should I give up my station in the fleet,
leaving the sons of Atreus alone,
and sail for home across the Aegean Sea?
How could I face my father, Telamon,
when I arrive back there? How could he bear
to see me showing up with nothing,
without the prize for highest excellence
with which he won his own great crown of fame?

116

That's not a thing I could endure to do.
Well, then, should I charge out there on my own
against the Trojan wall, a lone attack,
fight single combats, do something valiant,
and then at last be killed? But that would please
the sons of Atreus. It must not happen.
I must seek out some act which will reveal
to my old father how, at least by nature,
his own son has not become a coward.
It is dishonourable for any man
to crave a lengthy life, once he discovers
the troubles he is in will never change.
What joy is there for him when every day
just follows on another, pulling him away
or pushing him toward death? I would not pay
for any sort of mortal man who's warmed
by futile hopes. A man of noble birth
lives on with honour, or he dies in glory.
Now you've heard everything I have to say.

CHORUS LEADER
No one will ever claim that you, Ajax,
have said a word that's illegitimate,
for what you say is born in your own heart.
But you should stop. Get rid of thoughts like these.
Let friends overrule what you're suggesting.

TECMESSA
O my lord Ajax, for human beings
the worst of evils is what they endure
when they're compelled to. Consider me.
I was the daughter of a free-born father,
a wealthy man, if anyone in Phrygia
could be accounted rich. Now I'm a slave,
a circumstance the gods somehow made happen—
yes, the gods and especially your strong limbs.
And thus, since I have come into your bed,
I want the best for you. So I beg you,
by Zeus who guards our home, by that bed
where you had sex with me, do not leave me
to the savage insults of your enemies.

117

Do not abandon me to some strange hand.
For if you die and leave me all alone,
that day you may be sure the Argive men
will take me by force, as well as your own son.
We will then both lead the lives of slaves.
One of our lords will speak these biting words,
shooting insults at me, "Look here at this,
a bed mate of Ajax, the strongest man
in all our army. What menial chores she does!
How she's changed from such an enviable state!"
Men will talk that way, and then my fate
will wear me down. Those shameful words will stain
you and your family. Respect your father,
whom you will leave a miserable old man.
Respect your mother, too, who shares his years.
She keeps begging the gods that you're alive,
that you'll return back home. And, my lord,
have pity for your son. For if you die,
consider how, whenever that day comes,
both he and I will face desolation.
He will lack the nurturing a young lad needs
if you leave and he becomes an orphan,
in the care of people who are not friends
or from his family. And I have nothing
I can look to except you. It was you
who killed my homeland for me with your spear.
My mother and my father were destroyed
by a different fate which led them down
to make their home in Hades after death.
What country could I have except with you?
What wealth? My safety, all security,
that rests with you. So remember me as well.
A genuine man should cherish memory,
if he gets pleasure still from anything.
Kindness always engenders gratitude.
A man who gives up his good memories
will no longer be a noble, worthy man.

CHORUS LEADER

Ajax, I wish that pity touched your heart,
as it does mine. Then you'd approve her words.

AJAX
So far as I'm concerned, she'll win approval
only if she keeps being obedient
and carries out my orders properly.

TECMESSA
Yes, beloved Ajax, I will obey
in everything.

AJAX
Then bring me my son,
so I may see him.

TECMESSA
I sent him away,
out of my care. I was so terrified.

AJAX
Afraid because I was in trouble?
What do you mean?

TECMESSA
Yes, that's it. I feared
that the unlucky boy might bother you
and then somehow get killed.

AJAX
Yes, such a thing
the god who watches me would think fitting.

TECMESSA
At least I took a suitable precaution
to stop that happening.

AJAX
I approve of that.
The steps you took were quite correct.

TECMESSA
And so, as things are now, how can I best serve you?

AJAX
Let me talk to him, see him face to face.

TECMESSA
Yes. He's close by, with servants watching him.

AJAX
Why then this delay? Why is he not here?

TECMESSA *[calling to the side]*
My son, your father is calling for you.
Whichever of you servants has his hand,
bring the boy out here.

AJAX
Is he coming, the one you called?
Or did he not hear?

TECMESSA
The servant's on his way.
He's bringing Eurysaces with him.

[Enter the SERVANT leading EURYSACES]

AJAX
Lift him up. Hand the boy to me up here.
He'll have no fear of fresh-spilt blood, no,
not if he's a true-bred son of mine
who shares his father's nature. It is time
he was broken in to that harsh code
his father follows and his nature shaped
to something like my own. O my boy,
may you have better fortunes than your father,
although remain like him in other ways,
for then you'll never be dishonoured.
Now I envy you, and with good reason—
for you have no idea of any troubles.
The sweetest life comes when one senses nothing—
to lack all feeling is a painless evil—
until you learn what joy and sorrow mean.
Once you reach that stage, you must reveal
the kind of man you are, your ancestry,
to those who were your father's enemies.
Meanwhile, you should feed on gentle breezes,
fostering your young life so as to bring
your mother joy. I know that no Achaean

120

will go at you with insults and contempt,
even when I'm gone. For I am leaving Teucer
here with you as guardian of your gates.
He will not falter in his care for you,
although he now is busy far away,
chasing his enemies. But my warriors,
my people of the sea, I charge you now
with the same joyful duty I give Teucer.
Report to him what I have ordered here—
he is to take this boy back to my home,
show him to Telamon and Eriboea,
my mother, so he may always comfort them
in their old age, until the time they reach
the yawning caverns of the gods below.
And none of those who judge our competitions
nor the man who ruined me will offer
my weapons as a prize for the Achaeans.
No, my son, for my sake you will have to take
that broad shield from which you get your name.
Hold it up high. Shift it by its well-stitched grip,
my impenetrable seven-layered shield.
My other weapons you will bury with me.
Come, take the boy, and quickly. Close the hut.
And don't keep on weeping here in front.
How these women really love their wailing!
Quick now, close up the hut. A skilful healer
does not howl incantations when a wound
is crying for the knife.

CHORUS LEADER
    When I hear
    that you're in such a rush, I get afraid.
    The sharp edge on your tongue brings me no joy.

TECMESSA
    O lord Ajax, what are you going to do?

AJAX
    Don't keep on asking me! No more questions!
    The best thing now is self-restraint.

TECMESSA
> But I'm desperate!
> By the gods, by your own son, I beg you—
> do not become a man who now betrays us!

AJAX
> You pester me too much. Do you not see
> that I no longer owe the gods my service?

TECMESSA
> You must not utter such impieties.

AJAX
> Speak to those who listen.

TECMESSA
> You will not hear me?

AJAX
> You have already chatted far too much.

TECMESSA
> Yes, my lord, because I'm so afraid.

AJAX *[to the servants]*
> Shut the doors. Do it now!

TECMESSA
> By all the gods, concede!

AJAX
> It looks as though you're thinking like a fool,
> if, at this late date, you still believe
> that what you teach will shape my character.

*[The SERVANTS close the main door of the hut, leavingAJAX inside.
TECMESSA, EURYSACES, and the SERVANTS go into the hut through
the side door from which Eurysaces emerged earlier]*

CHORUS
> O splendid Salamis,
> you, I know, lie in the sea,
> whose waves beat on your happy shores,
> a famous place among all men forever.

I have been held back a long time here
in misery, for countless months
still camped out in the fields of Ida,
consumed by time and my anxiety,
expecting to complete my journey
to implacably destructive Hades.
And now my troubles multiply,
a situation hard to remedy,
for I must wrestle now with Ajax,
share my life with that insanity
sent from the gods. Alas for me!
Once, long ago, you sent him out
filled with the frenzied power of war.
But now his spirit feeds in isolation,
and his friends acquire from him
a heavy sorrow. His earlier deeds,
those acts of highest excellence,
have fallen, fallen where he has no friends,
among the wretched hostile sons of Atreus.
The years have changed his mother's hair to white,
and given her old age for company.
When she learns of his disease,
that maddening infection of his mind,
she'll start to wail forth her laments.
She will not chant out melodies
sung by the plaintive nightingale.
No. In her mood of desolation
the sharp-toned music of her grief
will scream abroad her anguish.
Her beating hands will thud down on her breasts,
and she'll keep tearing out her old gray hair.
A man brain sick with mad delusions
is better off concealed in Hades,
a man who by his ancestry
is ranked the best of the Achaeans,
who have endured so much. But now,
no longer following his inbred character,
he wanders far beyond himself.
O you unhappy father Telamon,
you have yet to hear the heavy curse
laid on your son, a curse which up to now

has never played a part in any life
nurtured by the sons of Aeacus.

[Enter AJAX through the main doors of the hut, carrying a sword.
TECMESSA enters after him.]

AJAX
    The long succession of the countless years
    reveals what's hidden, then hides it once again,
    and there is nothing we should not anticipate.
    The solemn oath and the most stubborn heart
    are overcome. In this way, even I,
    who used to be so marvellously strong,
    like tempered iron, felt my sharp edge dissolve
    at what this woman said. I now feel pity
    leaving her a widow and my son an orphan
    among my enemies. And so I'll go
    to the bathing waters by the sea shore
    and wash off my defilement. I will deflect
    the weighty anger of the goddess there.
    When I leave, I'll find some isolated place
    and then inter my sword, of all my weapons
    the one I most despise. I'll dig the earth
    where no one else will see. Then let Night
    and Hades keep it there below the ground.
    For ever since I've held it in my grip,
    this gift from Hector, my greatest enemy,
    I've won no prizes from the Argives.
    That old human saying is true: gifts men get
    from enemies—they are no gifts at all
    and bring them no advantages. And so,
    from this day forward I shall understand
    how to revere the gods. And I will learn
    how to respect the sons of Atreus.
    They are our rulers, so we must obey.
    Why not? Things of the greatest power and awe
    give way to privileged authorities.
    Snow-footed Winter yields to fruitful Summer,
    and Night's dark vault withdraws the moment Day
    with her white-footed horses fires up the sky;
    the blasts of fearful Winds at last bring rest

which calms the groaning seas. All-powerful Sleep
lets go the one he holds tied up in chains;
his grasp does not go on forever. As for us,
how can we mortals not learn self-control?
I, at least, am only now discovering
that we should hate our enemies as much
as suits a man who will become a friend.
And when I help a friend, then I will give
only what is due a man who'll not remain
a friend forever. For common mortals
see that the shelter comradeship affords
is treacherous. Thus, my situation
will turn out for the best. And so, woman,
go inside now. Keep praying to the gods
my heart's desires will reach fulfilment
and be carried out to their conclusion.

[TECMESSA return into the hut through the side door. AJAX turns to address the CHORUS]

AJAX
    My comrades, you, too, honour this request.
    Tell Teucer, when he comes, to care for me
    and also to protect your interests.
    I am now going where I have to go.
    As for you, carry out what I have said,
    and very soon, perhaps, you will find out
    that, though I'm suffering now, I am at peace.

[AJAX leaves, heading for the sea shore.]

CHORUS
    I feel a sudden thrill of passionate delight,
    which makes me soar aloft with happiness
    and cry with joy to Pan—
    O Pan, Pan—
    appear to us, sea rover—
    come down from your stony ridge
    on snow-beat Mount Cyllene,
    you dancing master of the gods—
    come, O king,
    begin your self-taught dancing steps

from Mysia and Cnossos,
or what I want now is to dance.
And may Apollo, lord of Delos,
race across the Icarian Sea
and manifest himself to me,
show his benevolence in everything.
From our eyes Ares has removed
those terrifying agonies.
What joy! O joy!
For now, O Zeus, now
the dazzling light of brighter days
can come to our swift ships
which speed across the seas,
for Ajax is free of pain once more
and, in a transformed state of mind,
has carried out appropriate sacrifice
to all the gods in full, showing them
due reverence and strictly following
our most important laws.
The power of time extinguishes all things,
so I can't say that anything
lies beyond all expectation—
since, in contrast to what we were waiting for,
now Ajax's mind has changed again
away from actions done in anger
and his great fight with Atreus' sons.

[Enter the MESSENGER]

MESSENGER
Friends, the first thing I have to report is this—
Teucer has just come from the Mysian heights.
He's now in the middle of our line of ships,
in the generals' camp. All the Argives
are shouting insults at him, all at once.
They saw him coming and, as he approached,
surrounded him, hurling accusations
from all directions—everyone joined in—
calling him the brother ofthat maniac
who had conspired against the army
and saying he could not escape his death—

their stones would cut him down completely.
Things reached the point where men had pulled their swords
out of their scabbards and held them fully drawn.
Then, as the fight was getting out of hand,
some elders intervened. Their words stopped it.
But where can I find Ajax to tell him this?
I must provide our king a full report.

CHORUS LEADER
He's not inside. He has just gone away,
with new intentions yoked to his changed mood.

MESSENGER
O no! No! Then the man who sent me here
did so too late, or I have been too slow.

CHORUS LEADER
What's so urgent? What's been overlooked?

MESSENGER
Teucer said that Ajax had to stay inside
and not leave his hut until he gets here.

CHORUS LEADER
Well, as I told you, Ajax has gone off.
He intends to follow now what's best for him,
to cleanse away his anger at the gods.

MESSENGER
Your words reveal your complete foolishness,
if what Calchas prophesies has any merit.

CHORUS LEADER
What do you mean? What information
do you have about what's happening here?

MESSENGER
Well I was there, so I know this much—
I witnessed it. Calchas left the leaders
sitting in their royal council circle,
moving off from the sons of Atreus.
In a friendly gesture he placed his right hand
in Teucer's palm. Then he spoke to him,

giving him strict orders to use every means
to keep Ajax in his hut while this day lasts
and to prevent him moving anywhere
if he ever wished to see him still alive.
For divine Athena's rage would whip Ajax
only for that day. That's what Calchas said.
Then the prophet added, "Those living things
which become too large and thus unwieldy
fall into harsh disasters from the gods—
the sort of man who, born from human stock,
forgets and thinks beyond his mortal state.
Take Ajax. As soon as he set out from home,
he revealed his folly, though his father
had passed on good advice. For Telamon
commanded him, 'My son, with that spear of yours
you must seek victory, but always fight
with some god at your side.' But then Ajax,
in a lofty boast, thoughtlessly replied,
'Father, with god's help even a worthless man
can be victorious. But I believe
I'll win glory on my own without them.'
Such was his arrogance. Another time,
with divine Athena, as she was rousing him
and telling him to turn his deadly hands
against the enemy, he answered her
with a fearful and sacrilegious speech,
'Lady, stand there with the other Argives.
The fight will never break the line through Ajax.'
It was with words like these that he provoked
the unremitting anger of the goddess,
because he does not think as humans should.
But if he remains alive all day today,
with god's help we might be his saviours."
That's what Calchas said. From where he sat
Teucer sent me off at once with orders
which you were meant to follow. If we fail,
Ajax is done for—that is, if Calchas
has any skill in prophecy.

CHORUS LEADER *[calling into the side door of the hut]*
Tecmessa, unfortunate lady born for sorrow,

128

come out and see this man. Hear his news.
The razor's slicing closer. I feel its pain.

[Enter TECMESSA through the side door of the hut]

TECMESSA
Why are you making me come out once more
and leave the chair where I was getting
some relief from these unending troubles?

CHORUS LEADER
Listen to this man—he's come with news
about what's happening with Ajax,
and it's disturbing.

TECMESSA
O no! You there,
tell me what you have to say. Does this mean
we're finished?

MESSENGER
I have no idea how things stand with you. As for Ajax,
if he is not inside, then I've lost hope.

TECMESSA
He's gone away. So I'm in agony
about just what you mean.

MESSENGER
Teucer gave orders
that you keep Ajax safely in his hut
and do not let him leave all by himself.

TECMESSA
But where is Teucer? Why did he say that?

MESSENGER
He has only just returned. He suspects
if Ajax goes somewhere he'll be destroyed.

TECMESSA
That's horrible! What man told him this?

MESSENGER
Thestor's son, the prophet, whose words proclaimed
this very day would bring life or death for Ajax.

TECMESSA
O my friends, protect me from this destiny!
Some of you, get Teucer here more quickly,
while others go off to the western cove
and to the east, as well, to investigate—
find out where Ajax went, when he set off
on that ill-fated path. For now I know
I have, in fact, been totally deceived,
and Ajax has finally cast away
all that affection he once had for me.
Alas, my son, what am I going to do?
I can't stay idle. So I'll go out there,
as far as I have strength to go. Let's leave—
and hurry! This is no time to sit around,
if we want to save a man who's eager
for destruction.

CHORUS LEADER
I'm prepared to help,
not just with words, as I will demonstrate.
If we move fast, we can do this quickly.

[They all exit in various directions, leaving the stage empty. The scene now changes to a deserted part of the seashore. AJAX enters, carrying his sword, which he sets upright in the sand, with the blade sticking upward.]

AJAX
The sacrificial killer is in place,
so it will now cut most effectively.
If a man had time, he might reflect on this.
It is a gift from Hector, a warrior
who was a friend most hateful to me,
the one I looked on as my greatest foe.
Then, this sword is firmly set in Trojan soil,
land of my enemy, freshly whetted
on the iron-eating sharpening stone.
And I have fixed it in the ground with care,

so it will kill me quickly and be kind.
Thus, we are well prepared. So, O Zeus,
in this situation, be the first to help,
as is appropriate. I'm not asking you
to give me a grand prize, but for my sake
send a messenger to carry this bad news
to Teucer, so he may be the first
to raise me, once I've fallen on the sword
and covered it with fresh-spilt blood. Don't let
the first to spot me be some enemy,
who'll throw me out, exposed as carrion food
for dogs and birds. I appeal to you, O Zeus.
Grant me this much. I also call on Hermes,
guide to the world below, to let me sleep
without convulsions, when by one quick leap
I break my bones apart on this sharp blade.
And I summon those immortal maidens
to my aid, those who always see all things
of human suffering, the dread, far-striding Furies,
to witness how, in my wretchedness,
the sons of Atreus worked my destruction.
May they seize on them and destroy them, too,
with deaths as vile as their disgusting selves.
Just as they see me killed by my own hand,
so let them perish, killed by their own kindred,
the children they love most. Come, you Furies,
you swift punishers, devour the army,
all of them, sparing no one. And you, Helios,
whose chariot wheels climb that steep path to heaven,
when you look down over my father's land,
pull back those reins of yours, which flash with gold,
then tell the story of my miseries,
my destiny, to my old father
and to the unhappy one who nursed me.
That poor lady, when she hears this news,
will, I think, sing out a huge lamenting dirge
throughout the city. But for me to weep
is useless. It's time to start the final act.
O Death, Death, come now and watch in person.
Yet I'll be seeing you on the other side,
and there we can converse. And so to you,

the radiant light of this bright shining day,
I make my final call, and to the Sun—
I'll never see that chariot any more.
O light, O sacred land of Salamis,
my home, my father's sturdy hearth,
and glorious Athens, whose race was bred
related to my own—and you rivers,
you streams, you plains of Troy, I call on you.
Farewell, you who have nurtured me—to you
Ajax now speaks his final words. The rest
I'll say to those below in Hades.

*[Ajax falls on his sword. Enter the CHORUS in two separate groups
from two different directions. Each has a separate leader. They do not
see Ajax's body until Tecmessa finds it.]*

CHORAL GROUP 1
We work and work,
and that brings on more work.
Where have I not walked? Where?
No place where I have searched
has revealed to me where Ajax is.
What's that? Listen! I heard a noise.

CHORAL GROUP 2 LEADER
It's us—the crew that shares the ships with you.

CHORAL GROUP 1 LEADER
What can you report?

CHORAL GROUP 2 LEADER
We've searched everywhere
on the west side of the ships.

CHORAL GROUP 1 LEADER
Did you come up with anything?

CHORAL GROUP 2 LEADER
Just lots of work. There's nothing there to see.

CHORAL GROUP 1 LEADER
Well, we haven't seen him either—
not on the path facing the rising sun.

CHORUS
> Who then can lead me on,
> what toiling sons of the sea,
> sleepless in their shacks?
> What nymph on high Olympus
> or from the streams that flow
> into the Bosphorus
> could say if she has seen somewhere
> fierce-hearted Ajax wandering around?
> It is not fair that after a long search
> and so much effort I can't find
> the proper path to him. I cannot see
> where that elusive man might be.

[Enter TECMESSA behind the Chorus. As she moves on, she stumbles across the corpse of Ajax]

TECMESSA
> Ahhh ....

CHORUS LEADER
> Who cried out? It sounded close,
> from that group of trees.

TECMESSA
> O how horrible ....

CHORUS LEADER
> I see her, the unfortunate young bride,
> Tecmessa, a prize won with his spear—
> she's lying there, prostrate with grief, in pain...

TECMESSA
> I'm lost ... destroyed ... my life is over.
> O my friends....

CHORUS LEADER
> What's happened?

TECMESSA
> It's our Ajax—
> he's lying here ... he's just been murdered,
> his body's wrapped around a buried sword.

CHORUS LEADER
O no! Our dreams of getting home are gone.
Alas, my king, you have destroyed me, too,
the one who sailed across the seas with you....
you poor, unhappy man... heart-sick lady...

TECMESSA
With Ajax dead like this, we have good cause
to wail out our grief.

CHORUS LEADER
Who did this?
With whose help could ill-fated Ajax
have gone through with this?

TECMESSA
He did it by himself.
That's clear. This sword fixed upright in the ground
indicates he fell down on top of it.

CHORUS LEADER
Alas, for my own foolishness!
You bled to death alone, with no friends there
to keep an eye on you. I was so stupid,
so blind to everything. I took no care.
And now, now where does stubborn Ajax lie,
a man whose very name suggests misfortune.

TECMESSA
He's not a spectacle to gaze upon!
With this cloak I will cover him completely,
tuck it all around him—for nobody,
at least no one who was a friend of his,
could bear to see him, as he spurts blood
up his nostrils and from that dark red wound,
his self-inflicted slaughter. Alas!
What shall I do? What friend of yours'
will lift you up for burial? Where's Teucer?
How I wish that he would come right now,
when we need him—if he ever comes
to care for the body of his brother.
O ill-fated Ajax, how could a man like you

end up like this? Even your enemies
must find you worthy of a funeral song.

CHORUS
O you unhappy man, how you were doomed,
with that unbending heart of yours,
fated to live out an evil destiny
of endless suffering.
I know you groaned such hostile words
against the sons of Atreus
all night long and in the morning light,
the fatal passion of a stubborn heart.
It's obvious that when those weapons
were made the prizes in the competition
for the finest of our battle warriors, 1110
that was a potent source of trouble.

TECMESSA
Alas! Alas for me!

CHORUS LEADER
Your heart, I know,
is truly filled with grief.

TECMESSA
Such misery for me!

CHORUS LEADER
It's no surprise to me, my lady,
you wail and wail again, for you've just lost
a man you loved so much.

TECMESSA
You only guess
how it must feel, but I experience it,
and to the limit.

CHORUS LEADER
That's true enough.

TECMESSA
Alas, my son, what kind of slavery
will yoke us now as we move on from here,
what sort of taskmasters stand over us?

CHORUS LEADER
Ah, now you've given voice to your concerns
about unspeakable actions by those men,
the two unfeeling sons of Atreus,
in this our present grief. May god restrain them!

TECMESSA
But these events would not have taken place
without the gods' consent.

CHORUS LEADER
Yes—they have set
a burden too heavy for us to bear.

TECMESSA
It's Athena, Zeus' savage daughter.
What miseries that goddess has produced,
and for Odysseus' sake.

CHORUS LEADER
I'm sure that man,
who has endured so much, in his black heart
exults and laughs with lofty arrogance
at these insane disasters. Such mockery!
Such a disgrace! And when they hear of this,
those two royal sons of Atreus
will join his merriment.

TECMESSA
Then let them laugh!
Let them get their joy from this man's agony.
Although they did not sense their need of him
while he was living, perhaps they'll mourn his death
when they need him in war. Men with brutal minds
have no idea what fine things they possess
until they throw them out. Ajax's death—
to me so bitter and to them so sweet—
at least has brought him joy, for he has got
what he desired, the death he yearned for.
So why should these men make fun of him?
His death is the gods' concern, not theirs. No!
So let Odysseus vaunt his empty jests.

For them Ajax is dead—for me he's gone,
abandoning me to grief and mourning.

TEUCER *[heard offstage]*
No, no ... No!

CHORUS LEADER
Be quiet. I think I hear Teucer's voice.
His shouts send out a tone which penetrates
the heart of this disaster.

[Enter TEUCER]

TEUCER *[moving up to Ajax's body]*
O dearest Ajax,
my bright source of joy, my brother,
what's happened to you. Is the rumour true?

CHORUS LEADER
He's dead, Teucer. That's the truth.

TEUCER
Alas! Then I bear a heavy destiny!

CHORUS LEADER
Given how things stand....

TEUCER
This is too sad.

CHORUS LEADER
... you have good cause to grieve.

TEUCER
This act of his,
so rash and passionate....

CHORUS LEADER
Yes, Teucer, passion in excess.

TEUCER
This is disastrous.
What about his son? Where on Trojan soil
can I find him?

CHORUS LEADER
He's in the hut—all by himself.

TEUCER*[To Tecmessa]*
You—bring him here as soon as possible,
in case he gets snatched by an enemy,
the way a hunter grabs a lion cub
and leaves its mother childless. Go quickly!
We need your help. For it's a fact all men
love to laugh in triumph above the dead,
when they're stretched out before them.

[Exit TECMESSA]

CHORUS LEADER
Teucer,when Ajax was alive, he said that you
should look after his son, as you're now doing.

TEUCER
O this is surely the most painful sight
of anything my eyes have ever seen.
And, of all the roads I've travelled, the worst,
the one most deeply painful to my heart,
is that pathway I've just walked along,
while trying to track you down, dearest Ajax,
once I'd learned your fate. There was some gossip,
some tale to do with you. It spread quickly,
as if sent by a god, to all the Argives.
It said that you had wandered off and died.
I heard the details far away from here
and there I groaned with sorrow. Now I'm here,
I see it for myself. It breaks my heart.
It's dreadful. Come, take off this covering,
so I get a full view of this horror.

[Attendants remove the cloak covering Ajax's body]

O that face—it's so painful to see now,
so full of bitter daring. How many sorrows
you have sown for me by this destruction!
Where can I go? What sort of people
will take me in, when I was no use to you
in times of trouble? No doubt Telamon,

who fathered you and me, will welcome me,
perhaps with smiles and words of kindness,
when I reach home without you. Of course he will!
For he's the kind of man who never smiles,
not cheerfully, even when things go well.
A man like that—what will he not say?
What sort of insult will he not hurl at me—
a bastard spawned by some battle-prize of his,
who, because of his unmanly cowardice,
betrayed you, dearest Ajax, or by treachery
tried to seize your power and your home,
once you were dead. That's what Telamon will say.
He's a bad-tempered man, and his old age
has made him harsh—his anger likes to argue
over nothing. Hell end up banishing me,
throw me from the land. What he'll say of me
will make me seem a slave instead of free.
That's what will happen if I go back home.
Here in Troy I have many enemies,
and few ways of getting help. All this
has happened to me because you've been killed.
It's a disaster. What am I to do?
How do I raise you up, you sad corpse,
from the sharp bite of this glittering sword,
your murderer, on which you breathed your last?
You've come to sense how, in good time, Hector,
though dead, was going to slaughter you. Look here,
by the gods—see the fate of these two men.
First, Hector was lashed tight to that chariot rail
with the very belt Ajax had given him,
and underwent continual mutilation
until he gasped his life away.Then Ajax
took Hector's gift in hand and used it
to kill himself in that death-dealing fall.
Surely a vengeful Fury forged this blade,
and that harsh craftsman Hades made that belt?
For my part, I would assert that gods
have plotted these events—they always do
in everything that mortal men go through.
If someone finds this view objectionable,
let him love his own beliefs, as I do mine.

139

CHORUS LEADER
Don't stay too long. You need to think
how we can bury Ajax. And what to say.
It's urgent. For someone coming here,
a man who is our enemy. It could be
he comes to mock at our misfortunes, a man
who thrives on harm.

TEUCER
Who is it—the man you see?
What member of the army?

CHORUS LEADER
It's Menelaus,
the one for whom we launched this expedition.

TEUCER
I see him. He's not hard to recognize
when he's so close.

[Enter MENELAUS, with a small escort of soldiers]

MENELAUS
You there—I order you
not to take up that corpse for burial.
Leave it where it is.

TEUCER
Why waste your wordswith such an order?

MENELAUS
I think it's fitting,as does the commander of our army.

TEUCER
Then would it bother you to tell me whyyou issue this command?

MENELAUS
The reason's this:
we hoped that we were leading Ajax here,
away from home, so he'd be our ally,
someone friendly to the Argives, but instead,
when we saw him more closely, we found out
he was more hostile than the Phrygians.
He planned to destroy our entire army

140

and set off at night to take us with his spear.
If some god had not frustrated his attempt,
we would have met the same fate he did—
we'd be dead and lying there, struck down
by shameful fate, and he'd be still alive.
But now, it's clear a god changed these events,
and so the violence in his heart fell elsewhere,
on sheep and cattle. And that's the reason
there's no one powerful enough right now
to take his corpse and set it in a grave.
Instead it will be tossed away somewhere
on the yellow sand, food for shore birds.
Remember that. Curb the anger in your heart.
If we could not control him when he lived,
at least he will obey us now he's dead.
Even if you don't agree, our forceful hands
will take charge of him. When he was alive,
Ajax never listened to a word I said.
And it's a fact that when a common man
thinks it's appropriate to disobey
those in command, he truly demonstrates
his worthless character. Within the city
the laws could never foster benefits
if there was no established place for fear.
Nor can one lead the troops with wise restraint
where there is neither fear or reverence
to act in their defence. So any man,
no matter how powerful his body grows,
must realize he'll fall, even when
the harm to him seems trivial. A man
who has in him a sense of fear and shame
is quite secure—you can be sure of that—
but where there's room for hostile arrogance
and men do what they want, consider how
a state like that, though it has raced ahead
with favouring winds, will, in the course of time,
sink in the ocean depths eventually.
And so for me let fear be set in place
where it's appropriate. Let's not believe
we can just do whatever we desire
and not pay the painful consequence.

These matters fluctuate—Ajax was once
a man of fiery insolence, but now
it's time for me to manifest my power.
And thus I warn you not to bury him.
If you do, you just might fall yourself
into your grave.

CHORUS LEADER
Menelaus,after setting out such well-thought precepts,
do not become too arrogant yourself in dealing with the dead.

TEUCER
Fellow soldiers,
never again will I be much surprised
if someone born a nobody goes wrong,
since those apparently of noble birth
can make so many errors when they speak.
Come, tell me once more from the beginning—
do you really think it was you personally
who led Ajax here an Argive ally?
Did he not sail to Troy all on his own,
under his own command? In what respect
are you this man's superior? On what ground
do you have any right to rule those men
whom he led here from home? You came to Troy
as king of Sparta. You do not govern us.
Under no circumstance did some right to rule
or give him orders lie within your power,
just as he possessed no right to order you.
You sailed here a subordinate to others,
not as commander of the entire force
who could at any time tell Ajax what to do.
Go, be king of those you rule by right—
use those proud words of yours to punish them.
But I will set this body in a grave,
as justice says I should, even though you
or any other general forbids it.
I am not afraid of your pronouncements.
Ajax did not join the expedition
because that woman was a wife of yours,
as did those toiling Spartan drudges—no—
but because he'd sworn an oath to do it.

142

You were no part of it. He never valued
men worth nothing. And so when you return,
come back here and bring more heralds with you,
as well as the commander. Your vain chat
is not something that really bothers me,
not while you stay the kind of man you are.

CHORUS LEADER
When things go badly, I don't like to hear
a tone like that. Even when it's justified,
harsh language stings.

MENELAUS
This mere archer seems to entertain some big ideas.

TEUCER
Indeed I do. My skill is not something to underrate.

MENELAUS
My, my—if only you possessed a shield,
how grand your boasts would be.

TEUCER
Even with no shield,
I'd get the better of you fully armed.

MENELAUS
That tongue of yours, how it likes to feed
the savage spirit inside!

TEUCER
When a man is right,
he's entitled to make impressive claims.

MENELAUS
Do you mean to tell me it is just
for someone to be treated generously
when he's killed me?

TEUCER
Killed you? Your words sound odd,
if, after being killed, you are now alive.

MENELAUS
Some god saved me. As far as Ajax knows,
I'm dead and gone.

TEUCER
Since the gods rescued you,
you should not dishonour them.

MENELAUS
You mean I could be violating sacred laws?

TEUCER
Yes, if you personally intervened
to prevent the burial of the dead.

MENELAUS
That's not so with a personal enemy.
To bury him would not be right.

TEUCER
What's that?
Did Ajax ever march ahead in battle
as your enemy?

MENELAUS
He hated me, and I hated him. But you knew that.

TEUCER
Yes, he did, because you were found out—
you tampered with the vote which robbed him.

MENELAUS
The judges beat him in that competition, not me.

TEUCER
With your deceitful secrecy
you can conceal so many crimes.

MENELAUS
Words like that
could well prove painful to someone I know.

TEUCER
Well, I don't think they will bring more pain
than we'll inflict.

MENELAUS

Once and for all, then,
I tell you this: that man will not be buried.

TEUCER

Then hear my answer: Ajax's corpse
will have a burial.

MENELAUS

I have already seen a man
with a bold tongue urging sailors on
to launch a voyage during winter storms.
But you could hear no sound from him at all
once the storm got nasty. He hid himself
under a cloak and then let the sailors
step on him at will. You're just like him,
you and your braggart mouth—a mighty squall,
even from a tiny cloud, in no time
will snuff out your constant shouting.

TEUCER

And I have seen a man stuffed with stupidity,
whose pride delighted in his neighbours' grief.
Then someone like me, with my temperament,
faced up to him and said something like this,
"Hey, you there, don't harm the dead. If you do,
you can be sure you'll find yourself in trouble."
So he warned the paltry fellow face to face.
I see him now, and it appears to me
he is none other than yourself. I trust
I haven't talked too much in riddles?

MENELAUS

I'm leaving. It would be a great disgrace
if men found out I've started arguing
when I could use my power.

TEUCER

Be off with you!
It would be a great disgrace to me
to listen to such silly chattering
from some fool.

[MENELAUS and his escort leave the way they came]

CHORUS LEADER
We're going to see
a major altercation from this argument.
As quickly as you can, Teucer, you should make
a hollow grave for Ajax, where he'll rest
in a dark tomb, and people for all time
will keep him in their memory.

[Enter TECMESSA and EURYSACES]

TEUCER
Ah, just in time—
his woman and his son have now arrived
to perform a funeral for this sad corpse.
Come, lad, move over here. Stand there by him.
Set your hand in supplication on him,
on your father, from whom you were born.
Kneel down in prayer—hold firmly in your hand
locks of hair from me, from her, from you—
the three of us. These give the suppliant strength.
If any member of the army tries
to remove you from this corpse by force,
then may that wicked man become an exile,
tossed out from his own land in misery,
and remain unburied, his roots severed
from his whole race, just as I cut this hair.
Take this, my boy, and guard it. And don't let
any man push you away. Stay kneeling here,
and hang on tight. You sailors over there,
don't stand around the place like women.
You're men. Stand on guard here, and protect him,
till I get back, once I've set up the grave.
I don't care who has forbidden it.

[Exit TEUCER]

CHORUS
When will our last year here arrive?
When will the number of those wandering years
come to an end—and my interminable fate

to go on carrying this toiling spear
across the wide expanse of Troy,
a sorrow and a shame for Greeks?
How I wish that man had been swept off
high into the great sky or into Hades,
the home that all men share,
before he'd introduced the Greeks
to that war mood which sucks up everyone,
those weapons of the god of war,
which every man detests.
O those toils which just produce more toil!
That man has wiped out our humanity.
He gave me as my portion no delight
in garlands or full cups of wine,
no sweet tunes from flutes around me,
that ill-fated wretch, or in the night
the joys of sleep. And as for love—alas!—
he has denied me love. I lie here
forgotten, my hair always drenched
from thickly falling dew, ah yes,
my memories from desolate Troy.
Bold Ajax used to be my rampart once,
my constant wall against night fears
and flying weapons aimed at me.
But he has now become a sacrifice
to some malevolent deity.
What pleasure, then, what joy
now lies in store for me?
O how I wish I were back there,
where the wooded wave-washed headland
juts out, our guard against the open sea,
below the high flat rock of Sunium,
and we could then greet sacred Athens.

[Enter TEUCER, in a hurry]

TEUCER

I've just seen commander Agamemnon.
He coming here, and quickly. So I ran back.
He's clearly going to give his blundering mouth
some exercise.

[Enter AGAMEMNON with an armed escort]

AGAMEMNON
>You there—I've been told
>you've dared to mouth foul threats against us
>with impunity. I'm talking about you,
>the son of a mere slave, a battle trophy.
>If some well-bred lady were your mother,
>no doubt your boasts would soar high in the sky,
>and you would strut around on tip toe.
>You are a nobody, and here you act
>the champion for this nonentity.
>In all seriousness you made the claim
>we voyaged here with no authority,
>as commanders of the troops or of the fleet,
>to give orders to Achaeans or to you,
>since Ajax sailed under his own command.
>Is it not shameful that I have to hear
>such monstrous insults from the mouths of slaves?
>This man you shout about with so much pride,
>what sort of man was he? Where did he go
>or stand and fight, where I was not there, too?
>Do the Achaeans have no man but him?
>It seems it was a painful thing we did
>when we announced to all Achaeans
>that competition for Achilles' weapons,
>if in every quarter we appear corrupt,
>thanks to Teucer, and if you people here
>never will be satisfied, not even
>after you have been put down, and yield
>to what most of the judges thought was fair.
>Instead you will no doubt keep hurling at us
>these constant gibes, or from your station in the rear
>treacherously lash out at us. In places
>where such conditions hold you'll never find
>a settled order based on rule of law,
>not if we discard the men who justly win
>and put in front the ones who lag behind.
>No. We must prevent such tendencies.
>It's not the big, broad-shouldered warriors
>who make the most reliable allies—
>it's men who think—they win out every time.

One guides a broad-backed ox straight down the path
with only a small whip. And I can see
you'll soon receive some of that medicine,
unless you get yourself some common sense.
That man is no longer living—by this time
he has become a shade, and here you are
rashly insulting us, letting your mouth
run on and on. You should control yourself.
Do you not realize who you are by birth?
Why not let another man step forward,
someone free born, to state your case to us
instead of you? For when you're speaking,
I'm not prepared to listen any more.
To me your barbarian way of speaking
is quite impossible to understand.

CHORUS LEADER
I wish you two were sensible enough
to show some self-restraint. Nothing I say
would be more useful to the both of you.

TEUCER [addressing the corpse of Ajax]
Well now, how quickly among mortal men
grateful thoughts about the dead are gone
and turn into betrayal. This man here
can't even manage a few words, Ajax,
to celebrate your memory, and yet
you often risked your life protecting him,
hefting that spear of yours in battle.
But now, as you can see, all those great deeds
are dead and gone, all thrown aside.

[Teucer turns to address Agamemnon]

And you, you talk a lot of a utter foolishness.
Have you no longer any memory
of the time when you were all bunched up
inside the rampart, almost done for
in that spear fight—then Ajax showed up,
all on his own, and kept protecting you,
with flames already blazing on your ships,
spreading across the decks right at the stern,

and Hector leaping high across the ditch,
heading for our fleet? Who held him back?
Was Ajax not the one who managed that,
the man you claim never went any place
where you did not go, too? Do you concede
his actions then, as far as you're concerned,
set a high standard? And then another time,
when he faced up to Hector by himself
in single combat. No one ordered him.
He was picked out by lot, and his marker,
the one he threw in among the others,
was not designed to help him not get picked.
It was no lump of moistened clay, no,
but a light one which would be the first
out of the crested helmet. Yes, Ajax
was the one who did these things, and I,
the slave whose mother was a foreigner,
was there beside him. You miserable man,
where are your eyes when you go on like this?
Do you not realize your father's father,
ancient Pelops, was a barbarian,
who came from Phrygia? And Atreus,
the man who spawned you, wasn't he the one
who prepared that sacrilegious dinner,
and served up his own brother's children as a meal
for him to eat? And then, as for yourself,
the mother who bore you came from Crete.
And her own father caught her having sex,
screwing some stranger. He abandoned her
to be killed in silence by a bunch of fish.
That's the kind of man you are. How can you
insult a man like me about my origins?
I am a son of Telamon, who won
my mother as his consort, his own prize
for being the army's finest warrior.
She was of royal blood, Laomedon's daughter,
the most desirable of all the battle spoils.
Alcmene's son gave her to Telamon.
Since I am nobly born and my parents
are both noble, too, how could I disgrace
my own flesh and blood? Ajax is lying here,

overcome by all his troubles, and you—
aren't you ashamed to say you'll toss him out
without a burial? Well, think of this—
if you just throw him out, along with him
you'll be casting off three more as well.
It's a finer thing for men to see me die
while labouring hard on his behalf
than fighting for your woman—or should I say
your brother's wife? Given what I've said,
don't think about my safety; look to your own.
For if you make things difficult for me,
you're going to wish you had been more afraid
and not quite so bold when you confronted me.

[Enter ODYSSEUS alone]

CHORUS LEADER
Lord Odysseus, you've come just in time,
if you're here to calm things, not make them worse.

ODYSSEUS
My friends, what's going on? From a long way off
I heard the sons of Atreus shouting out
over this brave man's body.

AGAMEMNON
Lord Odysseus,
we have had to listen for far too long
to the most shameful language from this man.
Is that not reason enough?

ODYSSEUS
Well, let's see—
I could forgive a man who had been listening
to someone else who was abusing him
and who then joined in a war of insults.

AGAMEMNON
I did insult him, because his actions
were a direct affront to me.

ODYSSEUS
What did he do to injure you?

AGAMEMNON

He says he will not let
this corpse remain without a burial.
He'll set it in a grave, no matter what I do.

ODYSSEUS

Well, may someone who's a friend of yours
speak his mind and still remain a colleague
the way he was before?

AGAMEMNON

You should speak out.
I would scarcely be thinking properly
if I said no. Among the Argives
I consider you my greatest friend.

ODYSSEUS

Then listen. In deference to the gods
don't be so unyielding you throw Ajax out
without a burial. You should not let
that spirit of violence at any time
seize control of you, not to the extent
that you then trample justice underfoot.
This man became my greatest enemy
in all our army on that very day
I beat him for the armour of Achilles.
But for all the man's hostility to me,
I would not disgrace him. Nor would I deny
that in my view he was the finest warrior
among the Argive men who came to Troy,
after Achilles. So if you dishonour him,
you would be unjust. It would not harm him,
but you'd be contravening all those laws
the gods established. When a good man dies,
it is not right to harm him, even though
he may be someone you hate.

AGAMEMNON

Odysseus, you mean you're arguing against me,
on his behalf?

ODYSSEUS

Yes, that's what I mean.
I did hate him, when it was all right to hate.

AGAMEMNON

Why would you not walk all over him,
now that he's dead?

ODYSSEUS

Son of Atreus,
do not take pleasure in advantages
which are dishonourable.

AGAMEMNON

An all-powerful king
does not show reverence all that easily.

ODYSSEUS

But he can give out honourable rewards
to friends when they advise him prudently.

AGAMEMNON

A good man should obey those in command.

ODYSSEUS

Why not concede? You'll still be in control,
although you let your friends prevail against you.

AGAMEMNON

Just remember the kind of man he was,
the one for whom you want to do this favour.

ODYSSEUS

The man was an enemy of mine, that's true.
But he was once a noble warrior.

AGAMEMNON

Why are you doing this? Why such respect
for the dead body of an enemy?

ODYSSEUS

His excellence moves me to do it,
far more than his hostility to me.

AGAMEMNON
　Men who act the way you're doing now
　are unreliable.

ODYSSEUS
　Let me assure you,
　among human beings most are changeable,
　sometimes friendly, then sometimes bitter.

AGAMEMNON
　Are those the sort of men you'd recommend
　that we accept as friends?

ODYSSEUS
　Well, I wouldn't recommend
　we choose someone inflexible.

AGAMEMNON
　All right,
　but now you'll make us look like cowards.

ODYSSEUS
　No. Every Greek will think we're being just.

AGAMEMNON
　So you would urge me to give my permission,
　and let this corpse receive a burial?

ODYSSEUS
　I would. For I myself will someday reach
　the state he's in, as well.

AGAMEMNON
　There we have it.
　All men work to benefit themselves.

ODYSSEUS
　For whom should I make such an effort
　if not for myself?

AGAMEMNON
　We'll have to announce
　that you're the one responsible for this,
　not me.

ODYSSEUS
>However you do it, it will serve
>to bring you all kinds of advantages.

AGAMEMNON
>Well, in any case, you can rest assured
>I would grant you a greater favour
>than this burial. As for this man here,
>down in the underworld he is my enemy,
>just as he was on earth. But you can do
>whatever you think is appropriate.

[AGAMEMNON and his escort leave]

CHORUS LEADER
>Given how you have acted here today,
>Odysseus, any man who now asserts
>that you are not by nature wise is stupid.

ODYSSEUS
>I now proclaim that from this moment on
>I am Teucer's friend, as much as earlier
>I was his enemy. And I am willing
>to join with him in burying the dead,
>working with you and omitting nothing
>human beings may need to honour and respect
>their finest warriors.

TEUCER
>Noble Odysseus,
>I have nothing but praise for what you've said.
>You have done so much to disprove my fears.
>Of all the Argives, you were the one
>who was his greatest enemy, and yet
>you are the only one to stand by him,
>to lend a helping hand. For when he died
>and you were still alive, you could not bear
>to see such injuries inflicted on him,
>not like that frantic general who was here.
>He and his brother wanted their revenge
>by casting Ajax off without a grave.
>And so may our all-ruling father Zeus,

high on Olympus, the unforgiving Furies,
and Justice, too, who fulfils all things,
destroy those evil men with evil deaths,
just as they tried to rid themselves of Ajax,
outrageous treatment he did not deserve.
But you, child of venerable Laertes,
I hesitate to let you touch the corpse
in these funeral rites, for that may well offend
the man who died. But as for all the rest,
join in with us. If you wish, bring someone,
any soldier in the army will be welcome.
I must get all things ready. Odysseus,
you must know you've acted nobly for us.

ODYSSEUS

That's what I wished. But if you object
to my participation here with you,
I'll defer to what you want and leave.

[ODYSSEUS leaves]

TEUCER

Enough. Too much time has passed already.
Hurry now. Some of you scoop out a hollow grave,
others set the cauldron high up on the stand,
with fire all around, so we can start
the ritual cleansing promptly. One of you,
bring from his hut the armour he would wear
behind his shield. And you, too, my child,
since he's your father, use those loving arms
with all the strength you have and help me lift him.
His windpipe is still warm, and from it flows
his own dark spirit. Come then, come all of you
who say your are our friends, come quickly,
move out, and with your efforts honour Ajax.
There was no one to match his excellence.34
No nobler man has received such honour.

CHORUS

I know of many things which mortal men
can see and learn from. But until he meets it,
no one sees what is to come or his own fate.

[They all leave, bearing the body of Ajax.]

—*Translated By Ian Johnston*

Electra
Euripides
Translated by Ian Johnston

Written by Euripides sometime between 420 and 410 BCE, Electra takes place years after the murder of Agamemnon at the hands of is wife, Clytemnestra and her new lover, Aegisthus.

Following the death of the king, Agamemnon's children are effectively banished from the kingdom. The son, Orestes, was sent away to live under the care of the king of Phocis, while Electra was married off to a poor farmer in the countryside.

The play opens with Electra lamenting her fate and mourning the loss of her father. It is at this time that Orestes, who has traveled back to Mycenae, comes upon his sister crying.

Electra does not recognize Orestes, as she last saw him when he was very young, and so retells her story to the man whom she believes to be a stranger.

Eventually, Orestes' identity is revealed and brother and sister are reunited at last. It is at this point that the play truly begins, as the two begin to hatch their plan for vengeance against those responsible for the death of their father.

DRAMATIS PERSONAE

PEASANT: a poor farmer in the countryside
ELECTRA: daughter of Agamemnon and Clytaemnestra, married to the
    Peasant
ORESTES: son of Agamemnon and Clytaemnestra, brother of Electra
PYLADES: a friend of Orestes
CHORUS: Argive country women
OLD MAN: an old servant of Agamemnon's who rescued Orestes
MESSENGER: one of Orestes' servants
CLYTAEMNESTRA: mother of Orestes and Electra.
DIOSCOURI (Castor and Polydeuces): divine twin brothers of Helen
    and Clytaemnestra
SERVANTS: attendants for Orestes, Pylades, and Clytaemnestra

[The scene is set in the countryside of Argos, in front of the Peasant's hut. It is just before dawn.]

PEASANT

    O this old land, these streams of Inachus,
    the place from where king Agamemnon once
    set out with a thousand ships on his campaign
    and sailed off over to the land of Troy.
    He killed Priam, who ruled in Ilionk
    and took the famous town of Dardanus.
    Then he returned home, back here to Argos,
    and set up in high temples piles of loot
    from those barbarians.Yes, over there
    things went well for him.But then he was killed
    in his own home, thanks to the treachery
    of his wife, Clytaemnestra, at the hand
    of Thyestes' son Aegisthus.So he died,
    leaving behind Tantalus' ancient sceptre.
    Aegisthus rules this country now.He wed
    Tyndareus' daughter, the dead king's wife.
    As for those he left at home behind him
    when he sailed to Troy, his son Orestes
    and his daughter, too, Electra—well, now,
    Aegisthus was about to kill Orestes,
    but an old servant of his father's took him
    and handed him to Strophius to bring up
    in the land of Phocis.But Electra
    stayed on in her father's house.When she reached
    her young maturity, the suitors came,
    the foremost ones throughout the land of Greece,
    seeking marriage.Aegisthus was afraid
    she'd bear a child to some important man,
    who'd then seek revenge for Agamemnon.
    So he wouldn't give her to a bridegroom,
    but kept her in his home.Even this choice
    filled him with fear, in case she'd give birth
    to a noble child in secret.So he planned
    to kill her.But though her heart is savage,
    her mother saved her from Aegisthus' hands.
    She'd an excuse for murdering her husband,
    but she feared that if she killed her children

she'd be totally disgraced.And that's why
Aegisthus came up with the following scheme—
he offered gold to anyone who'd kill
Agamemnon's son, who'd left the country
as an exile, and he gave Electra
to me to be my wife.My ancestors
were from Mycenae, so in this matter
at least I don't bear any of the blame.
My family was a good one but not rich,
and that destroys one's noble ancestry.
He gave her to a man who had no power.
In that way his fear could be diminished.
If some important fellow married her,
he might have woken up the sleeping blood
of Agamemnon, and then at some point
justice would have come here for Aegisthus.
But I've never had sex with her in bed—
and Cypris knows I'm right in this—and so
Electra's still a virgin. I'd be ashamed
to take the daughter of a wealthy man
and violate the girl, when I'm not born
her equal.As for unfortunate Orestes,
who's now, according to what people say,
a relative of mine, I'm sorry for him,
if he should ever come back to Argos
and see his sister's wretched marriage.
Any man who says I'm just an idiot
to bring a young girl here into my home
and then not touch her should know he's a fool,
measuring wisdom with a useless standard.

[Electra enters from the hut. She is carrying a water jug]

ELECTRA
O pitch black night, nurse of golden stars,
Through you I walk towards the river streams,
holding up this jar I carry on my head.
This is not a task I am compelled to do,
but I will manifest to all the gods
Aegisthus' insolence, and I will send
into this great sky my sorrowing cries

out to my father.For my own mother,
that murderous daughter of Tyndareus,
in her desire to please her husband,
has cast me from my home.With Aegisthus
she's given birth to other children and thinks
Orestes and myself of no account
inside her house.

PEASANT

You unfortunate girl,
why do you work like this to give me help,
carrying out these chores?In earlier days,
you were nobly raised.Why don't you stop,
especially when I mention this to you?

ELECTRA

You're kind to me, and I consider you
the equal of the gods in that.For now,
when I'm in trouble, you don't demean me.
When human beings discover someone there
to soothe their miseries, as I have you,
then fate is doing something great for them.
So I should help you carry out the work
and give you some relief, to the extent
my strength permits, without you asking me,
so you can bear the load more easily.
There's work enough for you to do outside.
I should take care of things within the house.
It's nice when someone working out of doors
comes back in and finds things neat and tidy.

PEASANT

Well, if you think you should do it, then go.
The springs are no great distance from the house.
Once daylight comes, I'll drive the oxen out,
go to the farmlands, and then sow the fields.
No matter how much his mouth talks of gods,
a lazy man can never gather up
the stuff he needs to live without hard work.

*[Electra leaves for the spring, and the Peasant goes back to the house.
Enter Orestes and Pylades, with two servants]*

ORESTES

    Pylades, among men I think of you
    as a loving host, foremost in my trust.
    For you're the only one of all my friends
    who has dealt honourably with Orestes,
    as I've been coping with these dreadful things
    I've had to put up with from Aegisthus,
    who killed my father... he and my mother,
    that destructive woman.I've come here,
    from god's mysterious shrine to Argive lands,
    to avenge the killing of my father,
    by murdering the ones who butchered him.
    Last night I visited my father's tomb.
    where I wept and started sacrificing
    by cutting off a lock of hair.And then,
    on the altar I made an offering of blood
    from a sheep I slaughtered.Butthe tyrants
    who control this land don't know I'm here.
    I've not set foot within the city walls.
    No.I've come out to these border regions
    for two reasons which act on me as one—
    so I may run off to another land
    if someone sees me and knows who I am
    and to find my sister, who's living here,
    so they say, joined in marriage to a man,
    no virgin any more.I could meet her,
    make her my accomplice in the murder,
    and in this way get clear information
    about what's happening inside the walls.
    But now that Dawn is raising her bright eyes,
    let's move aside to some place off the path.
    We'll see a ploughman or a servant woman,
    then ask them if my sister lives near here.
    In fact, I can see a household servant—
    her shaven head holds up a water jug.
    Let sit and ask this female slave some questions,
    Pylades—see if we can get some word
    about the business which has brought us here.

[Orestes and Pylades move back. Electra enters, on her way back from the spring. She does not see them at first. She starts to go through her ritual of mourning]

ELECTRA

You must step quickly now—
it's time to move—
keep going, lamenting as you go.
Alas for me! Yes, for me!
I am Agamemnon's child.
I was born from Clytaemnestra,
Tyndareus' detested daughter.
Miserable Electra—that's the name
the citizens have given me.
Alas, alas! My wretched work
and this detested way of life!
O father, you now lie in Hades,
Agamemnon, thanks to that murder
committed by Aegisthus and your wife.
Come now, raise the same lament,
seize the joy of prolonged weeping.
You must step quickly now—
it's time to move—
keep going, lamenting as you go.
Alas for me! Yes, for me!
O my poor brother, in what town,
in what household are you roaming,
abandoning your abject sister
to such painful circumstance
in her ancestral home? Come to me,
in my unhappy wretchedness.
Be my deliverer from pain—
ah Zeus, Zeus—
be an avenger for my father,
the hateful shedding of his blood,
once the wanderer sets foot in Argos.
Take this water pitcher from my head
and set it down, so I may wail
my night laments, cries for my father,
wild shrieks, a song of death,
your death, my father. For you

beneath the earth, I cry out
chants of sorrow—day after day
I keep up this constant grieving,
ripping my dear skin with my fingernails,
while my hand beats my shaven head—
all this because you're dead.
Ah yes, mutilate your face,
and, just as a swan sings out
beside the streaming river,
crying to its beloved father
who died ensnared within the web
of a deceitful net, so I cry out
for you, unhappy father,
your body bathing in that final bath,
your most pitiable couch of death.6
Ah me... ah me!
that bitter axe that hacked you,
father, the bitter scheme
of your return from Troy!
Your wife failed to welcome you
with victor's wreath and ribbons.
No. Instead she gave you up
to that disgraceful mutilation
by Aegisthus' two-edged sword
and got herself a treacherous mate.

[Enter the Chorus of Argive women]

CHORUS

O Electra, daughter of Agamemnon,
I've come here to your rural dwelling place.
A man's arrived, a milk-drinking man—
he's come here from Mycenae,
a man who walks the mountains.
He says the Argives have proclaimed
a sacrifice two days from now,
and every young bride has to go
to Hera's shrine in the procession.

ELECTRA

My sad heart is beating fast, my friends,
but not for festive ornaments

or necklaces made out of gold.
I won't stand with the Argive girls
in choruses or beat my foot
as I whirl in the dance.
I pass my days in tears—
in my unhappiness my care
day after day is with my tears.
See if this filthy hair and tattered clothes
suit Agamemnon's royal child
or Troy, which bears the memory
of how my father seized the place.

CHORUS

The goddess is great.So come,
borrow thick woven clothes from me
and put them on, with gold as well,
graceful ornaments—to favour me.
Do you think that with your tears
you can control your enemies
if you have no respect for gods?
My child, you'll find yourself a gentler life
by honouring the gods with prayers,
and not with sorrowful laments.

ELECTRA

No god is listening to the cries
of this ill-fated girl or to the murder
of my father all that time ago.
Alas for that slaughtered man
and for the wanderer still alive
dwelling somewhere in a foreign land,
a wretched vagabond at a slave's hearth,
son of such a famous father.
And I am living in a peasant's house,
wasting my soul up on the mountain tops
in exile from my father's house.
My mother, married to another man,
lives in a bed all stained with blood.

CHORUS LEADER

Your mother's sister, Helen, brought the Greeks
so many troublesandyour house, as well.7

[Orestes and Pylades begin to move forward. Electra catches sight of them]

ELECTRA

    Alas, women, I'll end my lamentation.
    Some strangers hiding there beside the house,
    at the altar, are rising up from ambush.
    Let's run off—escape these trouble makers.
    You run along the path.I'll go in the house.

ORESTES

    Stay here, poor girl.Don't fear my hand.

ELECTRA

    O Phoebus Apollo, I beseech you—
    don't let me die!

ORESTES

    And let me cut down others I hate much more than you.

ELECTRA

    Leave now!
    Don't put your hands on those you should not touch.

ORESTES

    There's no one I have more right to touch.

ELECTRA

    Then why wait beside my house in ambush,
    with your sword drawn?

ORESTES

    Stay here and listen.
    Soon you'll be agreeing with me.

ELECTRA

    I'll stand here.
    I'm yours, anyway, since you're the stronger.

ORESTES

    I've come to bring you news about your brother.

ELECTRA

    Dearest of friends—is he alive or dead?

ORESTES
Alive.I'd like you to have good news first.

ELECTRA
My you find happiness as your reward
for those most welcome words.

ORESTES
That's a blessing
I'd like to give to both of us together.

ELECTRA
My unhappy brother—in what country
does he live in wretched exile?

ORESTES
He drifts around, not settling for a single city's customs.

ELECTRA
He's not lacking daily necessities?

ORESTES
No, those he has.But a man in exile
is truly powerless.

ELECTRA
What's the message you've come here to bring from him?

ORESTES
I'm here to see if you're alive and, if you are,
what your life is like.

ELECTRA
Surely you can see,
first of all, how my body's shrivelled?

ORESTES
So worn with pain it makes me pity you.

ELECTRA
And my hair cut off, shorn with a razor?

ORESTES
Perhaps your dead father and your brother
are tearing at you.

ELECTRA
>Alas! Who is there
>whom I love more than those two men?

ORESTES
>Ah yes, and what do you think you are
>to your own brother?

ELECTRA
>He's not here,
>and so no present friend to me.

ORESTES
>Why live here, so distant from the city?

ELECTRA
>I'm married—it's a deadly state.

ORESTES
>I pity your brother.
>Did you marry someone from Mycenae?

ELECTRA
>No one my father ever hoped to give me.

ORESTES
>Tell me. I'll listen and inform your brother.

ELECTRA
>I live in his house, far from the city.

ORESTES
>This is a house fit for a ditch digger or for a herdsman.

ELECTRA
>He's poor but decent, and he respects me.

ORESTES
>Your husband's respect—what does that mean?

ELECTRA
>Never once has he dared to fondle me in bed.

ORESTES
Does he hold back from some religious scruple, or does he think
you're unworthy of him?

ELECTRA
No.He believes it's not right to insult my ancestors.

ORESTES
But how could he not be overjoyed
at making such a marriage?

ELECTRA
Well, stranger,
he thinks the person who gave me away
had no right to do it.

ORESTES
I understand.
He fears that someday he'll be punished
by Orestes.

ELECTRA
He is afraid of that,
but he's a virtuous man, as well.

ORESTES
Ah yes,
you've been talking of a noble man
who must be treated well.

ELECTRA
Yes, if the man
who's far away from here right now comes back.

ORESTES
And your mother, the one who bore you,
how did she take this?

ELECTRA
Women give their love
to their husbands, stranger, not their children.

ORESTES
Why did Aegisthus shame you in this way?

ELECTRA

By giving me to such a man, he planned
the children I produced would not be strong.

ORESTES

Clearly so that you would not bear children
who could take revenge?

ELECTRA

Yes, that's his plan. I hope he'll have to make that up to me!

ORESTES

You're a virgin—does your mother's husband know?

ELECTRA

No. We hide that from him with our silence.

ORESTES

These women listening to what we're saying
are friends of yours?

ELECTRA

Yes. They'll keep well concealed my words and yours.

ORESTES

If he came to Argos what could Orestes do in all of this?

ELECTRA

You have to ask? What a shameful question!
Isn't now a crucial time?

ORESTES

When he comes, how should he kill his father's murderers?

ELECTRA

By daring what my father's enemies
dared to do to him.

ORESTES

And would you dare to help him kill your mother?

ELECTRA

Yes, I would—with the very axe that killed our father!

ORESTES
Shall I tell him this? Are you quite certain?

ELECTRA
Once I've shed my mother's blood, let me die!

ORESTES
Ah, if only Orestes were close by
and could hear this!

ELECTRA
Stranger, if I saw him,
I would not know him.

ORESTES
That's not surprising.
You were youngsters when you separated.

ELECTRA
Only one of my friends would recognize him.

ORESTES
The man who they say saved him from murder
by stealing him away?

ELECTRA
Yes. An old man—
my father's servant long ago.

ORESTES
Your father—when he died, did he get a burial tomb?

ELECTRA
Once he'd been thrown out of the house,
he found what he could find.

ORESTES
Alas! Those words of yours...
Awareness even of a stranger's pains
gnaws away at mortal men. Tell me this—
once I know, I can carry to your brother
the joyless story which he has to hear.
Pity does not exist with ignorance,

171

only with those who know.Too much knowledge
is not without its dangers for wise men.

CHORUS LEADER

My heart's desires are the same as his.
Out here, far from the city, I don't know
the troubles there.Now I want to hear them.

ELECTRA

I will speak out, if that's acceptable—
and it is appropriate to talk with friends
about the burden of my situation
and my father's.And I beg you, stranger,
since you've the one who prompted me to speak,
tell Orestes of our troubles, mine and his.
First of all, there's the sort of clothes I wear,
kept here in a stall, weighed down with filth.
Then there's the style of house I'm living in,
now I've been thrown out of my royal home.
I have to work hard at the loom myself
to make my clothes or else I'd have to go
with my body naked—just do without,
bringing water from the springs all by myself,
with no share in the ritual festivals,
no place in the dance.Since I'm a virgin,
I keep married women at a distance
and felt shamed by Castor, who courted me,
his relative, before he joined the gods.
Meanwhile my mother sits there on her throne,
with loot from Phrygia and Asian slaves,
my father's plunder, standing by her chair,
their Trojan dresses pinned with golden brooches.
My father's blood still stains the palace walls—
it's rotted black—while the man who killed him
climbs in my father's chariot and drives out,
proud to brandish in his blood-stained hands
the very sceptre which my father used
to rule the Greeks.Agamemnon's grave
has not been honoured.It's had no libations,
no myrtle branch, its altar unadorned.
But this splendid husband of my mother,

so they say, when he's soaking wet with drink,
jumps on the grave and starts pelting pebbles
at the stone memorial to my father,
and dares to cry out these words against us:
"Where's your son Orestes?Is he present
to fight well for you and defend this tomb?"
And so absent Orestes is insulted.
But I beg you, stranger, take back this news.
Many are summoning him—I speak for them—
my hands and tongue, my grief-stricken heart,
my shaven head, and Agamemnon, too.
It would be disgraceful if his father
could destroy the Phrygians and yet he,
one against one, could not destroy a man,
when he's young and from a nobler father.

[Enter the Peasant, returning from the fields]

CHORUS LEADER
Look!I see a man—I mean your husband—
he's left his work.He's coming to the house.

PEASANT
Hold on.Who are these strangers I see there,
at the door?And why have they come here,
to a farmer's gate?What do they want from me?
It's shameful for a woman to be standing
with young men.

ELECTRA
My dear friend, don't suspect me.
You'll hear what's going on.These strangers
have come here from Orestes—they're messengers
with news for me.But forgive him, strangers,
for those words he said.

PEASANT
What are they saying?
Is the man still gazing at the daylight?

ELECTRA
That's what they say, and I believe their news.

173

PEASANT

    Does he still recall your father's troubles
    and your own?

ELECTRA

    We can hope about those things,
    but a man in exile has no power.

PEASANT

    What message from Orestes did they bring
    when they came here?

ELECTRA

    He sent them out as spies to look into my troubles.

PEASANT

    They're seeing some, and I suppose you're telling them the rest.

ELECTRA

    They know—there's no shortage of them.

PEASANT

    Surely we should have opened up our doors
    long before this point.Go inside the house.
    In exchange for your good news, you'll find
    the hospitality my house affords.
    You servants, take the stuff inside the house.
    Do not refuse me—you arefriends of ours
    and you've come from someone who's a friend.
    Even if I'm poor, I will not behave
    like someone with an ill-bred character.

ORESTES

    By the gods, is this the man pretending
    you and he are married, who does not wish
    to bring dishonour to Orestes?

ELECTRA

    He is—
    he's the one who in my miserable state
    they call my husband.

ORESTES
> Well, nothing is precise
> when it comes to how a man is valued—
> men's natures are confusing.Before this,
> I've seen a man worth nothing, yet he had
> a noble father, and evil parents
> with outstanding children.I've seen famine
> in a rich man's thinking and great spirit
> in a poor man's body.So how can we
> sort out these things and judge correctly?
> By riches?That would be a wretched test.
> By those who have nothing?But poverty
> is a disease.Through need it teaches men
> to act in evil ways.So should I turn
> to warfare?But when facing hostile spears,
> who can testify which men are virtuous?
> Best to dismiss such things, leave them to chance.
> This man is not great among the Argives,
> nor puffed up by his family's reputation.
> He's one of the crowd, yet has proved himself
> an excellent man.So stop your foolishness,
> those of you who keep wandering around
> full of misguided ways of measuring worth.
> Why not judge how valuable men are
> by their behaviour and their company?
> Men like this one govern homes and cities well,
> while those with muscles and with vacant minds
> are mere decorations in the market place.
> In fights with spears the strong arm holds its ground
> no better than the weak one does—such things
> depend on a man's nature and his courage.
> But because the man who is both absent
> and yet present here is worthy of it—
> I mean Agamemnon's son, for whose sake
> we've come here—let's accept the lodging
> in this home.You slaves, go inside the house.
> May a poor but willing man be my host
> rather than a man with wealth.I applaud
> how this man has received me in his home,
> although I could have hoped your brother,
> enjoying prosperity, might lead me in

to a successful house.Perhaps he'll come.
The oracles of Loxias are strong.
But I dismiss mere human prophecy.

[Pylades, Orestes, and their servants go into the house]

CHORUS LEADER
Now, Electra, our hearts are warm with joy—
more than they were before.Your fortunes
may perhaps advance, although that's difficult,
and end up standing in a better place.

ELECTRA
Reckless man, you know how poor your house is—
why did you offer your hospitality
to people so much greater than yourself?

PEASANT
What's wrong?If they're as well bred as they seem,
won't they be just as happy with small men
as with the great?

ELECTRA
Well, you're one of the small—
and since you've now committed this mistake,
go to that dear old servant of my father's.
He's been expelled from town and tends his flocks
by the Tanaus river, which cuts a line
between lands of Argos and of Sparta.
Tell him this—now these people have arrived,
he must come and provide our guests some food.
He'll be happy to do that and offer
prayers up to the gods, after he finds out
the child he rescued once is still alive.
From my mother and my ancestral home
we'd get nothing—we'd bring them bitter news
if that cruel-hearted woman were to learn
Orestes is still living.

PEASANT
All right then,
I'll take that message to the old man,
if that's what you think.But you should go

inside the house as soon as possible
to get things ready there.If she want to,
surely a woman can find many things
to make into a meal. Within the house
there's still enough to fill them up with food
for one day at least.It's at times like this
when my thoughts can't sort out how to manage,
I think of the great power money has
for giving things to strangers and paying
to save a body whenever it falls sick.
The food we need each day doesn't come to much,
and, rich or poor, all men eat their fill
with the same amount of food.

*[The Peasant and Electra move into the house, leaving the Chorus
alone on stage]*

CHORUS
Youfamous ships which once sailed off to Troy
to the beat of countless oars,
leading the Nereids in their dance,
while the flute-loving dolphin leapt
and rolled around your dark-nosed prows,
conveying Achilles, Thetis's son,
whose feet had such a nimble spring,
and Agamemnon, too, off to Troy,
to the river banks of the Simois.
Leaving Euboea's headland points,
Nereids carried from Hephaestus' forge
his labours on the golden shield and armour,
up to Pelion, along the wooded slopes
of sacred Ossa, where the nymphs keep watch,
and searched those maidens out,
in places the old horseman trained
sea-dwelling Thetis' son
to be a shining light for Hellas,
swift runner for the sons of Atreus.
I heard from a man who'd come from Troy
and reached the harbour in Nauplia
that on the circle of your splendid shield,
O son of Thetis, were these images,
a terror to the Phyrgians—

on the rim around the edge
was Perseus in his flying sandals
holding up above the sea
the Gorgon's head and severed throat,
accompanied by Zeus' messenger
Hermes, Maia's country child.
In the centre of the shield
the circle of the sun shone out
with his team of winged horses.
In the heavens stars were dancing,
the Pleides and Hyades,
a dreadful sight for Hector's eyes.
On his helmet made of hammered gold
in their talons sphinxes clutched
their prey seduced by song.
And on the breastplate breathing fire
a lioness with claws raced at top speed
eying a young horse of Pirene.13
And on his murderous sword
four horses galloped—above their backs
clouds of black dust billowed.
Evil-minded daughter of Tyndareus,
your bed mate killed the king
of spear-bearing warriors like these.
And for that death the heavenly gods
will one day pay you back with death.
Yes, one day I will see your blood,
a lethal flow beneath your throat,
sliced through with sword of iron.

[Enter the Old Man. Electra comes out of the house during his speech]

OLD MAN
So where is she?Where is my young lady,
my mistress—the child of Agamemnon,
whom I once raised?How steep this path is
up to her place for a withered old man
going uphill on foot!Still, they are my friends,
so I must drag my doubled-over spine
and tottering legs up here.O my daughter—
now I can see you there before the house—

I've come bringing here from my own livestock
this newborn lamb taken from its mother,
garlands, cheeses I got from the barrel,
and this ancient treasure from Dionysus—
it smells so rich!There's not much of it,
but still it's sweet to add a tankard of it
to a weaker drink.Go now.Let someone
take these things for guests inside the house.
I want to use a rag, a piece of clothing,
to wipe my eyes. I've drenched them with weeping.

ELECTRA

Why are your eyes so soaking wet, old man?
I'm not reminding you about our troubles
after all this time?Or are you moaning
about Orestes in his wretched exile
and about my father, whom you once held
in your arms and raised, though your friends and you
derived no benefits from it?

OLD MAN

That's right—
it didn't help us.But still, there's one thing
I could not endure.So I went to his tomb,
a detour on the road.I was alone,
so I fell down and wept, then opened up
the bag of wine I'm bringing for the guests,
poured a libation, and spread out there
some myrtle sprigs around the monument.
But then I saw an offering on the altar,
a black-fleeced sheep—there was blood as well,
shed not long before, and some sliced off curls,
locks of yellow hair.My child, I wondered
what man would ever dare approach that tomb.
It surelywasn't any man from Argos.
Perhaps you brother has come back somehow,
in secret, and as he came, paid tribute
to his father's tomb.You should go inspect
the lock of hair, set it against your own—
see if the colour of the severed hair
matches yours.Those sharing common blood

179

from the same father will by nature have
many features which are very similar.

ELECTRA

What you've just said, old man, is not worth much.
You've no sense at all, if you think my brother,
a brave man, would sneak into this country
in secret, because he fears Aegisthus.
And how can two locks of hair look alike,
when one comes from a well-bred man and grew
in wrestling schools, whereas the other one
was shaped by woman's combing?That's useless.
Old man, with many people you could find
hair which looked alike, although by birth
they're not the same.

OLD MAN

Then stand in the footprint,
my child, and see if the impression there
is the same size as your foot.

ELECTRA

How could a foot
make any imprint on such stony ground?
Andeven if it could, a brother's print
would not match his sister's foot in size.
The man's is bigger.

OLD MAN

If your brother's come,
isn't there a piece of weaving from your loom
by which you might know his identity?
What about the weaving he was wrapped in
when I rescued him from death?

ELECTRA

Don't you know
at the time Orestes left this country
I was still young?And if I'd made his clothes
when he was just a child, how could he have
the same ones now, unless the robes he wore
increased in size as his body grew?No.

Either some stranger, pitying the grave,
cut his hair, or someone slipped past the guard.14

OLD MAN
Where are your guests?I'd like to see them
and ask about your brother.

[Orestes and Pylades come out of the house]

ELECTRA
Here they are—coming outside in a hurry.

OLD MAN
They're well born,
but that may be misleading.Many men
of noble parentage are a bad lot.
But still I'll say welcome to these strangers.

ORESTES
Welcome to you, old man.So, Electra,
this ancient remnant of a man—to whom
among your friends does he belong?

ELECTRA
Stranger, this man is the one who raised my father.

ORESTES
What are you saying?Is this the man
who stole away your brother?

ELECTRA
He's the one who rescued him, if he's still alive.

ORESTES
Wait!
Why's he inspecting me, as if checking
some clear mark stamped on a piece of silver?
Is he comparing me with someone?

ELECTRA
It could be he's happy looking at you
as someone who's a comrade of Orestes.

ORESTES
> Well, yes, Orestes is a friend of mine,
> but why's he going in circles round me?

ELECTRA
> Stranger, as I watch him, I'm surprised as well.

OLD MAN
> O my daughter Electra, my lady—
> pray to the gods.

ELECTRA
> What should I pray for,
> something here or something far away?

OLD MAN
> To get yourself a treasure which you love,
> something the god is making manifest.

ELECTRA
> Watch this then.I'm summoning the gods.
> Is that what you mean, old man?

OLD MAN
> Now, my child, look at this man, the one you love the most.

ELECTRA
> I've been observing for a long time now
> to see if your mind is working as it should.

OLD MAN
> I'm not thinking straight if I see your brother?

ELECTRA
> What are you talking about, old man,
> making such an unexpected claim?

OLD MAN
> I'm looking at Orestes, Agamemnon's son.

ELECTRA
> What mark do you see which will convince me?

OLD MAN

> A scar along his eyebrow.He fell one day
> and drew blood.He was in his father's house
> chasing down a fawn with you.

ELECTRA

> What are you saying?
> I do see the mark of that fall....

OLD MAN

> Then why deny embracing the one you love the most?

ELECTRA

> No.I'll no longer hesitate—my heart
> has been won over by that sign of yours.

[Electra moves over to Orestes and they embrace]

ELECTRA

> You've appeared at last.I'm holding you...
> beyond my hopes.

ORESTES

> After all this time, I'm embracing you.

ELECTRA

> I never expected this.

ORESTES

> This was something I, too, could not hope for.

ELECTRA

> Are you really him?

ORESTES

> Yes.Your sole ally.
> If in my net I can catch the prey I'm after...
> But I'm confident.For if wrongful acts
> overpower justice, then no longer
> should we put any faith in gods.

CHORUS

> You've come, ah, you've come,
> this day we've waited for so long.

You've shone out and lit a beacon
for the city, the man who long ago
went out in exile from his father's house
to roam around in misery.
Now a god, my friend, some god
brings victory.Lift up your hands,
lift up your words, send prayers
up to the gods for your success,
good fortune for your brother
as he goes in the city.

ORESTES

Well, I've had the loving joys of welcome.
In time I'll give them back to you again.
You, old man, you've come at a good time.
Tell me this—what should I do to repay
my father's murderer and my mother,
his partner in this sacrilegious marriage?
Do I have any friends who'll help in Argos?
Or are they all gone, just like my fortune?
Who can I make my ally?Do we meet
during the day or at night?What pathway
do I turn towards to fight my enemies?

OLD MAN

My child, in your bad times you've got no friends.
It's a great benefit to find someone
who'll share with you the good times and the bad.
But since, as far as your friends can see,
you and the foundations of your house
have been wiped out completely and you've left
no hope for them, then pay attention to me.
Know this—the only things which you possess
to win back your father's home and city
are your own hands and your good fortune.

ORESTES

What then should I do to succeed in this?

OLD MAN

Kill Thyestes' son and your own mother.

ORESTES
That's the crown of victory I'm after.
But how do I get my hands on it?

OLD MAN
Well, even if you want to try it,
don't go inside the walls.

ORESTES
Is he well supplied
with garrison troops and bodyguards?

OLD MAN
Yes, he is.
He's afraid of you and does not sleep well.

ORESTES
Well, old man, you must give me some advice
about what happens next.

OLD MAN
Then listen to me.
A thought has just occurred to me.

ORESTES
I hope you come up with something good
which I can understand.

OLD MAN
While coming here,
I saw Aegisthus.

ORESTES
I'll accept those words.
Where was he?

OLD MAN
In the fields close to his stables.

ORESTES
What was he doing?I can see some hope
emerging from our desperate circumstances.

OLD MAN

He was setting up a banquet for the Nymphs—
that's what it seemed to me.

ORESTES

But was it for a child that's now being raised or some new birth?

OLD MAN

I only know one thing—there was an ox.
He was preparing it for sacrifice.

ORESTES

How many men did he have there with him?
Or was he by himself with his attendants?

OLD MAN

No Argives, only a group of servants.

ORESTES

Old man, there isn't anybody there
who'll know me if he sees me, is there?

OLD MAN

They're slaves who have never set eyes on you.

ORESTES

If we prevail, will they be on our side?

OLD MAN

Yes. That's what slaves are like. You're lucky.

ORESTES

How do I get close to him?

OLD MAN

You should walk where he can see you as he sacrifices.

ORESTES

So apparently his fields are by the road?

OLD MAN

Yes. When he catches sight of you from there,
he'll summon you to join the feast.

ORESTES
> With god's will,
> I'll make a bitter fellow banqueter.

OLD MAN
> From there on you must sort things out yourself,
> whatever happens.

ORESTES
> A shrewd observation.
> What about my mother?Where is she?

OLD MAN
> In Argos.She'll join her husband at the feast.

ORESTES
> Why did my mother not leave with her husband?

OLD MAN
> She stayed behind because she was afraid
> the citizens would criticize her.

ORESTES
> I see.
> She knows the city is suspicious of her.

OLD MAN
> That's right.People hate a profane woman.

ORESTES
> How do I kill them both at the same time?

ELECTRA
> I'll set up mother's murder on my own.

ORESTES
> Good fortune will bring us success in this.

ELECTRA
> Let the old man give both of us some help.

ORESTES
> All right.But how will you devise a way
> to kill our mother?

ELECTRA

> Old man, you must go
> and report this news to Clytaemnestra—
> say I have given birth, and to a son.

OLD MAN

> Born some time ago or quite recently?

ELECTRA

> Before my quarantine, ten days ago.

OLD MAN

> How does this advance your mother's murder?

ELECTRA

> When she learns I've been through birthing pains,
> she'll come here.

OLD MAN

> Why would she do that?My child,
> do you think she cares for you?

ELECTRA

> Yes.And she'll weep
> because my child is born so common.

OLD MAN

> Perhaps.
> But come back to the point of what you're saying.

ELECTRA

> If she comes, then clearly she'll be killed.

OLD MAN

> Well, she'll come to your house, right to the door.

ELECTRA

> So it won't take much for her to turn aside
> and go to Hades, will it?

OLD MAN

> Once I see that,then let me die!

ELECTRA
> But first of all, old man,
> you must lead my brother ... .

OLD MAN
> To where Aegisthus is now offering gods his sacrifice.

ELECTRA
> ... then go to my mother. Tell her my news.

OLD MAN
> I'll do it so the very words will seem
> as if they came from your own mouth.

ELECTRA *[to Orestes]*
> Now it's up to you. You've drawn first lot
> in this murder sweepstakes.

ORESTES
> Then I'll be off,
> if someone will lead me to the road.

OLD MAN
> I'm quite willing to take you there myself.

ORESTES
> O Father Zeus, scatter my enemies ... .

ELECTRA
> Pity us—we've suffered pitifully.

OLD MAN
> Yes, have pity on them, your descendants.

ELECTRA
> And Hera, who rules Mycenae's altars ...

ORESTES
> Give us victory, if what we seek is just.

OLD MAN
> Yes, give them justice to avenge their father.

ORESTES
You, too, father, living beneath the earth
through an unholy slaughter.

ELECTRA
And lady Earth, whom I strike with my hands.

OLD MAN
Defend these two.
Defend these children whom you love the most.

ORESTES
Come now, with all the dead as allies.

ELECTRA
Those who in that war and by your side
destroyed the Phrygians.

OLD MAN
And all those
who hate the sacrilegious and profane.

ELECTRA
Are you listening, those of you who suffered
such terrors at the hand of my own mother?

OLD MAN
Your father hears it all, I know.Time to go.

ELECTRA *[to Orestes]*
He knows everything.You must be a man.
And I'll tell you this—Aegisthus has to die.
If in the struggle with him you fall dead,
then I die as well.Do not think of me
as still alive.I'll take my two-edged sword
and slice into my heart.I'll go inside
and get things ready.If you send good news
the whole house will ring with cries of triumph.
But if you die, things will be different.
These are my words to you.

[Orestes, Pylades, the Old Man, and the attendants leave. Electra turns to face the Chorus]

ELECTRA
> And you women,
> give a good shout to signal this encounter.
> I'll be ready waiting, gripping a sword.
> If I'm defeated, I'll never submit,
> surrendering to my enemies the right
> to violate my body.

[Electra goes back into the house]

CHORUS
> Among our ancient stories,
> there remains a tale how Pan,
> keeper of the country side,
> breathing sweet-toned music
> on his harmonious flute,
> once led a golden lamb
> with the fairest fleece of all
> from its tender mother
> in the hills of Argos.
> Standing on the platform stone
> a herald with a loud voice cried,
> "Assemble now, you Mycenaeans,
> move into assembly, and see there
> the terrifying and marvelous things
> belonging to your blessed kings."
> So choruses gave out their tributes
> to the House of Atreus.
> Altars of hammered gold were dressed,
> while in the city fires blazed
> with Argive sacrifice—a flute,
> the Muses' servant, piped graceful notes,
> and seductive melodies arose
> in honour of the golden lamb,
> which now belonged to Thyestes.
> He'd secretly talked into bed
> the well-loved wife of Atreus.
> then carries home the marvellous prize,
> and, going to the assembly, says
> he now possesses in his house
> the horned sheep with its fleece of gold.

But then, at that very moment,
Zeus changed the paths
of all the shining stars,
the radiant glory of the sun,
and dawn's bright shining face.
Across the western reaches of the sky
he drove hot flames from heaven.
Rain clouds moved up to the north,
so Ammon's lands were dry—
all withered up, deprived by Zeus
of his most lovely showers of rain.
People speak about these tales,
but in such things my faith is small—
that the sun's hot throne of gold
turned round, to punish human beings,
in a cause involving mortal men.
But tales which terrify mankind
are profitable and serve the gods.
When you destroyed your husband
your mind was unconcerned with them,
you sister of such glorious brothers.

CHORUS LEADER

Wait!Hold on! Did you hear a shout, my friends?
Or has some vain notion overtaken me,
like Zeus' rumbling underneath the ground?
Look, breezes are coming up—that's a sign.
My lady, come out of the house! Electra!

[Electra comes out of the house]

ELECTRA

What is it, my friends?How are we faring
in the struggle?

CHORUS LEADER

There's only one thing I know—
I heard the scream of murder.

ELECTRA

I heard it, too.
It came from far away, but I could hear it.

CHORUS LEADER
Yes, a long way off, but it was clear.

ELECTRA
Was it someone from Argos moaning,
or some of my friends?

CHORUS LEADER
I've no idea.
People are shouting.Things are all confused.

ELECTRA
What you say means my death.Why do I delay?

CHORUS LEADER
Hold on until you clearly know your fate.

ELECTRA
No.We're beaten. Where are the messengers?

CHORUS LEADER
They'll be here.It's no trivial matter
to assassinate a king.

[Enter a Messenger on the run]

MESSENGER
O you victorious daughters of Mycenae,
I can report to all Orestes' friends
that he has triumphed, and now Aegisthus,
Agamemnon's murderer, has fallen.
But we must offer prayers up to the gods.

ELECTRA
Who are you?How can I trust what you've just said?

MESSENGER
Don't you know me on sight—your brother's servant.

ELECTRA
You best of friends!I was too full of fear
to recognize your face.But now I know you.
What are you saying?Has that hateful man,
my father's murderer, been killed?

MESSENGER
  He's dead.
  I've given you the same report twice now.
  Obviously you like the sound of it.

ELECTRA
  O you gods, and all-seeing Justice,
  you've come at last. How did Orestes kill
  Thyestes' son? What was the murder like?
  I want to know.

MESSENGER
  After we'd left this house,
  we walked along the two-tracked wagon path
  to where Mycenae's famous king might be.
  He happened to be walking in his garden,
  a well-watered place, cutting soft myrtle shoots
  to place in his own hair. When he saw us,
  he called out, "Greetings, strangers. Who are you?
  Where are you from? What country is your home?"
  Orestes said, "We are from Thessaly,
  on our way to the Alpheus river,
  to offer sacrifice to Olympian Zeus."
  After hearing that, Aegisthus answered,
  "You must be my guests, share this feast with us.
  It so happens I'm now offering an ox,
  sacrificing to the Nymphs. If you get up
  out of bed at dawn, you'll be no worse off.
  So come, let's go inside the house." Saying this,
  he grabbed our arms and led us off the road,
  insisting that we must not turn him down.
  Once we were inside the house, he said,
  "Let someone bring in water right away,
  so these guests can stand around the altar
  by the basin where they purify their hands."
  But Orestes said, "We've just cleansed ourselves
  in pure water from a flowing river.
  If strangers must join with the citizens
  in making sacrifice, then, Aegisthus,
  we are ready and will not refuse, my lord."
  Those were the words they spoke in public.
  The slaves guarding my master with their spears

set them aside, and they all lent a hand
to do the work, some bringing in the bowl
to catch the blood, others fetching baskets,
still others kindling fire and setting basins
around the hearth.The whole house echoed.
Then your mother's consort took barley grain,
sprinkled it across the altar, and said,
"Nymphs of the rocks, may I and my wife,
Tyndareus' daughter, in our home
offer frequent sacrifice, enjoying success,
as we do now, and may my enemies
do badly"—he meant you and Orestes.
My master prayed for quite the opposite,
not saying the words aloud, so he might win
his ancestral home.Then from a basket
Aegisthus took a sacrificial knife,
sliced off some of the calf's hair, and set it
with his right hand on the sacred fire.
His servants raised the calf onto their shoulders,
he cut its throat and spoke out to your brother,
"People claim this about men from Thessaly—
they're exceptional at butchering bulls
as well as taming horses.So, stranger,
take this knife and demonstrate to us
if that report about Thessalians is true."
Orestes gripped the well-made Dorian knife,
tossed from his shoulders his fine-looking cloak,
and chose Pylades to help him in the work.
Pushing slaves aside, he took the calf's hoof,
and, stretching out his arms, cut open
the beast's white flesh and then stripped off the hide
faster than any runner could complete
two circuits on a track for racing horses.
He opened up the flanks, and Aegisthus
picked up the sacred entrails in his hands
to have a look at them.But on the liver
the lobe was missing.There were signs of damage
which the man inspecting them could see
close to the gall bladder and the portal vein.
Aegisthus was upset.My master asked,
"Why are you upset?" "Stranger," he replied,

"what I'm afraid of is foreign treachery.
Most of all I hate Agamemnon's son,
an enemy of my house."My master said,
"Do you really fear an exile's trickery,
you, lord of the city?Let someone bring me,
a Phthian axe to replace this Doric knife
and let me split apart the breast bone,
so we can feast upon the inner organs."
He took the axe and struck.Then Aegisthus
picked up and separated out the innards
and peered at them.As he was bending down,
your brother, standing on tip toe, hit him
on the spine and cut through his vertebrae.
His whole body went into convulsions,
shaking up and down, and he kept screaming,
he was dying in his own blood, a brutal death.
The servants saw and rushed to get their spears
for a fight of many men against just two.
But Pylades and Orestes stood there,
brandishing their weapons with great courage.
Then my master said, "I have not come here
as an enemy, not to the city
or my servants, but to avenge myself
on the man who murdered my own father.
I am unfortunate Orestes.You men,
old servants of my father, don't kill me."
After the servants heard Orestes' words,
they pulled back their spears.Then an old man
who'd been a long time in the household
recognized him.At once they placed a wreath
on your brother's head, shouting and rejoicing,
and he's coming here carrying a head
to show it to you—not the Gorgon's head,
but from the person you so hate, Aegisthus.
So the bitter debt of murderous bloodshed
is paid by the man who's just been slaughtered.

[The Messenger leaves]

CHORUS
    O my friend, set your feet to dancing,

leaping nimbly up to heaven with joy.
Your brother has emerged victorious
and now he's won himself a crown,
in a competition surpassing those
which happen by Alpheus' streams.
Come, as I perform my dance
sing out a song of glorious victory.

ELECTRA

O light! O blazing chariot of the sun!
O earth and night whom I gazed at before!
I've freedom now to open up my eyes—
Aegisthus, the man who killed my father,
is fallen.Come, my friends, let's bring out
whatever I keep stored up in the house
as decorations for my brother's hair.
I'll make a crown for his triumphant head.

CHORUS

Bring on your decorations for his head.
and we'll keep up the dance the Muses love.
Now those dear kings we had before
will rule this land of ours with justice.
They've cast down those who broke our laws.
So let's sing out in joyful harmony.

[Orestes and Pylades enter with their attendants, who are carrying the
body of Aegisthus]

ELECTRA

O Orestes, you glorious conqueror,
born from a father who was victorious
in the war at Troy.Take these ribbons
for your locks of hair.You've come back home,
and your run around the stadium racetrack
has not been in vain.You've killed Aegisthus,
the man who killed our father, yours and mine,
our enemy.And you, who stood by him,
Pylades, reared by a pious father,
receive from my own hand this wreath.Your share
in this competition matched Orestes.
I hope I see you always prospering.

ORESTES

> First of all, Electra, you must believe
> the gods were leaders in what's happened here.
> Then praise me as a servant of the gods
> and circumstance.I have returned back home
> and killed Aegisthus, not in word but deed.
> To underscore the truth of what I've said,
> I've carried out the dead man's corpse for you.
> If it's what you want, lay him out as prey
> for wild beasts or impale him on a stake,
> a prize for birds, those children of the sky.
> In earlier days he was called your master,
> and now he is your slave.

ELECTRA

> I feel ashamed,
> but nonetheless I wish to speak.

ORESTES

> What is it?
> Speak up.There's nothing you need to fear.

ELECTRA

> To insult the dead—in case someone
> might heap reproaches on me.

ORESTES

> But no one would blame you in the slightest.

ELECTRA

> But the city
> is hard to please and loves to criticize.

ORESTES

> Speak, sister, if you want to say something.
> We are his enemies—there are no rules
> in our relationship with him.

ELECTRA *[to the corpse of Aegisthus]*

> Well, then,
> how shall I first begin to speak about
> the evil you have done?Where do I end?
> What words shall I use for the central part?

It's true that in the dawn I never stopped
rehearsing what I wished to say to you,
right to your face, if I were ever free
from my old fears.Well, now I am free.
So I will pay you back, abusing you
the way I wanted to when you were living.
You ruined me, taking away from me
and from this man here our dear father,
although we hadn't done you any wrong.
You made a shameful marriage with my mother,
then killed her husband, who was the general
who led the Greeks.You never went to Troy.
And you were so idiotic you believed
that with my mother you would get a wife
who was not evil, though she was betraying
my father's bed.But you must know this—
when any man corrupts another's wife,
having sex with her in secret, and then
is compelled to take her as his wife,
such a man is foolish if he believes
that, though she was not virtuous before,
she will be now with him.You were living
an agonizing life, although it seemed
as if the way you lived was not so bad.
You knew well you'd made a profane marriage.
My mother realized she had in you
a sacrilegious man.You are both evil,
and so you both acquired each other's traits.
She shares your wickedness, and you share hers.
You heard these words from all the Argives—
"That woman's husband," not "that man's wife."
And this is truly shameful—when the wife
controls the home rather than the husband.
I hate those offspring whom the city calls
children of their mother instead of saying
sons of their father.Still, when any man
makes a distinguished marriage well above
his station, no one talks of him,
but only of his wife.But most of all,
you were so ignorant you were deceived
in claiming to be someone because your strength

was in your wealth.But that's not worth a thing—
its presence is short lived.What stays secure
is nature, not possessions.It stands there,
beside you, and takes away your troubles.
But when riches live with fools unjustly,
they bloom a little while, then flee the house.
As for your women, I will say nothing—
it's not good a virgin speak about such things.
But I'll provide a hint, a simple riddle.
You were abusive, with your royal home,
your seductive looks. May I never have
a husband with the face of a young girl,
but one who has the look of a real man.
His children hold onto a life of war.
The pretty ones are only ornaments
to decorate the dancing choruses.
So get out of here, and stay ignorant
how you were found in time and punished.
And let no man committing wicked acts
believe that, if he runs the first lap well,
he is defeating justice, not before
he get to the finish, when he completes
the last turn in his life.

CHORUS LEADER
What this man's done
is dreadful, and he's paid a dreadful price
to you and to Orestes.For Justice
has a power that's enormous.

ELECTRA
Well, you servants must take up the body
and hide it inside, somewhere in the dark,
so when my mother comes over here
she won't see his corpse before she's killed.

[Pylades and the attendants take Aegisthus' body into the house]

ORESTES *[looking off stage]*
Wait a moment.Here's another thing
we need to deal with.

ELECTRA
What? Are those men I see
reinforcements coming from Mycenae?

ORESTES
No.That's the mother who gave birth to me.

ELECTRA
She's moving neatly right into our net.
How splendid she looks in that carriage,
such fine clothes.

ORESTES
What are we going to do?
Kill our mother?

ELECTRA
You're not overcome with pity
now you've seen our mother in the flesh?

ORESTES
Ah, how can I kill her?She gave birth to me.
She raised me.

ELECTRA
Just as she killed our father,
yours and mine.

ORESTES
O Phoebus Apollo,
that prophecy of yours was so foolish.

ELECTRA
Where Apollo is a fool, what men are wise?

ORESTES
You instructed me to kill my mother,
but killing her is wrong.

ELECTRA
On the other hand,
if you're avenging your own father
how can you be harmed?

ORESTES
I'll be prosecuted
for slaughtering my mother.Before now
I've been free of all impiety.

ELECTRA
But if you don't defend your father,
you're a guilty man.

ORESTES
But my mother?
If I kill her, how will I be punished?

ELECTRA
What will happen to you if you give up
avenging your own father?

ORESTES
Could it have been a demon in the likeness of a god
who spoke?

ELECTRA
Sitting on the sacred tripod?
I don't think so.

ORESTES
I cannot believe this prophecy was good.

ELECTRA
You must be a man.
Don't give way to cowardice.Set for her
the same trap you used to kill her husband,
when you destroyed Aegisthus.

ORESTES
I'll go in.
I'm about to launch a terrible act
and do dreadful things.Well, so be it,
if the gods approve of this.But to me
this contest is a bitter one, not sweet.

[Orestes goes into the house. Clytaemnestra arrives in a chariot with attendants]

CHORUS
>Greetings lady, child of Tyndareus,
>queen of this country of the Argives,
>sister of those noble twins,
>Zeus' sons, who live in heaven
>among the fiery constellations
>and have the honourable task
>of saving mortals in the roaring waves.
>Welcome!I worship you
>no less than I revere the gods
>for your great wealth and happiness.
>My queen, it's now appropriate
>that we attend to your good fortunes.

CLYTAEMNESTRA
>Get down from the carriage, women of Troy,
>and take my hand, so I, too, may step down
>out of this wagon.The houses of the gods
>may be adorned with Phrygian trophies,
>but I obtained these female slaves from Troy,
>the finest in the land, as ornaments
>within my household, small compensation
>for the child I lost.

ELECTRA
>Mother, is it all right
>for me to take that blessed hand of yours,
>given I live in this decrepit house,
>just like a slave, now I've been cast out
>of my ancestral home?

CLYTAEMNESTRA
>The slaves are here.
>Don't exert yourself on my behalf.

ELECTRA
>Why not?After all, I'm a captive, too,
>you sent away from home.Like these women,
>I was taken when my house was seized
>and left without a father.

CLYTAEMNESTRA
Well, your father
brought that about with plots against the ones
he should have loved the most, his own family.
I'll describe it to you, though when a woman
gets an evil name, her tongue grows bitter,
and that, it seems to me, is no bad thing.
But you should learn the facts of what's gone on
and then despise it, if it's worth your hate.
If not, why hate at all?Tyndareus
gave me to your father, not intending
that I or any children I might bear
should die.But that man, when he left his home,
convinced my daughter to accompany him,
by promising a marriage with Achilles,
and took her to the anchored fleet at Aulis.
There he had Iphigeneia stretched out
and slit her pale white throat above the fire.
If he'd killed one girl for the sake of many,
to protect the city from being taken,
or to help his house or save his family,
I'd have pardoned him.But he killed my child
because of Helen's lust, because the man
who'd taken her as wife had no idea
how to keep his treacherous mate controlled.
For all of that, although I had been wronged,
I'd not have grown enraged or killed my husband.
But he came back to me with some mad girl—
possessed by gods—and put her in his bed,
so he could have two brides in the same house.
Women are foolish.I'll concede the point.
But given that, when a husband goes astray,
rejecting his domestic bed, his wife
may well wish to follow his example
and find another man to love.And then
the blame makes us notorious—the men
who caused it all are never criticized.
If someone had carried Menelaus
away from home in secret, should I then
have killed Orestes to save Menelaus,
my sister's husband?How would your father

have put up with that?So is it not right
for him to die?He slaughtered my own child.
I would've kept on suffering at his hands.
I killed him. The road lay open to me,
and so I turned towards his enemies.
After all, which one of your father's friends
would have joined me to commit the murder?
Speak up, if you wish, and answer frankly.
In what way was your father's death unjust?

CHORUS LEADER
There's justice in your words, but that justice
is disgraceful.If she has any sense,
a woman should give way in everything
to her own husband.Those who disagree
I don't take into account in things I say.

ELECTRA
Bear in mind, mother, the last thing you said,
offering me a chance to be frank with you.

CLYTAEMNESTRA
Yes, my child.And I won't take that back.
I'll repeat it now.

ELECTRA
You'll hear me out, mother,
and won't punish me?

CLYTAEMNESTRA
No, I won't,
not if I'm giving pleasure to your heart.

ELECTRA
Then I'll speak, starting with an opening comment.
O mother, I do wish you had more sense.
Your beauty brings you praise that's well deserved—
the same is true for Helen—but you two
were born twin sisters, both very silly,
quite unworthy of your brother Castor.
She was willing to be carried off and ruined,
and you destroyed the finest man in Greece,
using the excuse you killed your husband

for your child, since people do not know you
the way I do. But before it was decided
that your daughter would be sacrificed,
no sooner had your husband left his home,
than you were fixing your fine locks of hair
seated at your mirror, and any wife
who primps her beauty when her husband's gone,
you can scratch her off the list as worthless.
There's no call for her to show her pretty face
outside the home, unless she's seeking mischief.
Of all the women in Greece, I believe
you were the only one who was happy
whenever Trojan fortunes were successful
and whose eyes would frown when they got worse,
because it was your hope that Agamemnon
would not get back from Troy.But nonetheless,
you could have stayed a truly virtuous woman.
The husband you had was in no way worse
than that Aegisthus, and he'd been chosen
by the Greeks themselves to lead the army.
When your sister Helen did what she did,
you had an opportunity to gain
great glory for yourself, since bad conduct
sets a standard for our noble actions
and makes them something everyone can see.
But if, as you are claiming, our father
killed your daughter, how have you been wronged
by me and by my brother?Why is it,
once you'd killed your husband, you didn't give
our father's home to us, but filled your bed
with someone else's goods and for a price
bought yourself a marriage?And why is it
this husband has not been made an exile
for banishing your son?Why is he not dead
instead of me? The way I'm living now
has killed me twice as often as my sister.
If justice says that murder pays for murder,
your son Orestes and myself must kill you
to avenge our father.If your act was just,
then this one must be, too.Any man
watching out for wealth and noble birth

who gets married to a vicious woman
is a fool.A virtuous, humble marriage
is better for the home than something grand.

CHORUS LEADER
Marrying women is a matter of chance.
Some, I notice, work out well, others badly.

CLYTAEMNESTRA
My child, it was always in your nature
to love your father.That's how thing turn out.
Some are their fathers' children, while others
love their mothers rather than their fathers.
I'll forgive you.I don't get much delight,
my child, from what I've done. But why are you
so filthy, your body dressed in such poor clothes?
You've just been confined and given birth.
Alas, my schemes have made me miserable!
I urged my anger on against my husband
more than I should have.

ELECTRA
Well, it's too late now
to moan about it.There's no remedy.
My father's dead.But why don't you bring back
that exile from this land, your wandering son?

CLYTAEMNESTRA
I'm too afraid.I'm looking after me,
not him.And he's angry, so people say,
about the murder of his father.

ELECTRA
Why let your husband be so cruel to me?

CLYTAEMNESTRA
That's how he is.You've a stubborn nature.

ELECTRA
Because I'm suffering.But I'll stop being angry.

CLYTAEMNESTRA
Then he'll no longer behave harshly to you.

ELECTRA
> He's got ideas of grandeur, living there
> inside my home.

CLYTAEMNESTRA
> You see?Once again
> you're kindling a new quarrel.

ELECTRA
> I'll be silent,
> my fear of him being what it is.

CLYTAEMNESTRA
> Stop this talk.
> Why have you sent for me, my child?

ELECTRA
> You've heard, I think, that I have given birth.
> Please offer up a sacrifice for me—
> I don't know how to do that—on the tenth day,
> as is our custom with an infant child.
> I've had no children before this, and so
> I lack experience.

CLYTAEMNESTRA
> That task belongs
> to the person who delivered the child.

ELECTRA
> I was by myself in labour, so I bore
> the child all on my own.

CLYTAEMNESTRA
> Is this house here
> so remote there are no friendly neighbours?

ELECTRA
> No one wants poor people as their friends.

CLYTAEMNESTRA
> Well, I'll go and make the gods a sacrifice
> for the full term of the child.When I'm done
> carrying out this favour for you, I'll leave,
> off to the field where my husband's offering

sacrifices to the Nymphs.You servants,
take this team away.Put them in the pens.
When you think I've finished sacrificing
to the gods, stand ready.I must satisfy
my husband's wishes, too.

ELECTRA

Enter this poor home.
For my sake take care the soot-stained walls
don't stain your clothes.You'll give the gods
the sacrifice you ought to make.

[Clytaemnestra goes into the house]

And now the basket's ready and the knife is keen,
the one which killed the bull you'll lie beside
when you're struck down.In Hades' home
you'll be wedded to the man you slept with
while you were alive. I'll be offering you
this favour, and you'll be giving me
retribution for my father.

[Electra goes into the house]

CHORUS

Evils are repaid.Winds of fortune
for this house are veering round.
Back then my leader, my very own,
fell murdered in his bath.
Roof and stone walls of the house
resounded, echoing his cries—
"You vicious woman, why kill me
now I've come to my dear land
after ten harvest seasons?"
The flow of justice has reversed itself
and brings to judgment for adultery
the killer of her unhappy husband
when he finally returned back home,
to the towering Cyclopean walls.
With her own hand she murdered him,
the sharpened edge of a keen axe
gripped in her fists.Poor sad husband!
What evils overtook this wretched woman?

She did it like a mountain lion
prowling through a wooded meadow.

CLYTAEMNESTRA *[from inside the house]*
By the gods, children, don't kill your mother.

CHORUS
Do you hear that cry from inside the house?

CLYTAEMNESTRA *[screaming from inside]*
Ah...my god...ah...not me...

CHORUS
I moan, too, as her children beat her down.
The god indeed dispenses justice,
whenever it may come.
You've suffered horribly, sad lady,
but you carried out unholy acts
against your husband.

[Orestes, Pylades, and Electra and Attendants emerge slowly from the house with the bodies of Aegisthus and Clytaemnestra]

CHORUS LEADER
But here they come, moving from the house,
stained with fresh-spilt blood from their own mother,
a trophy, proof of their harsh sacrifice.
There is no house, not now or in the past,
more pitiable than the race of Tantalus.

ORESTES
O Earth and Zeus, who sees all mortal men,
look on these abominable and bloody acts,
these two corpses lying on the ground
struck down by my hand, repayment
for everything I've suffered.

ELECTRA
Too much cause to weep, my brother,
and I have made this happen.
In my wretchedness my fiery rage
burned on against my mother
who gave birth to me, her daughter.

CHORUS
> Alas for fortune, for your fortune,
> a mother who has given birth
> to pain beyond enduring,
> bearing wretched misery and more
> from your own children, and yet it's just—
> you've paid for murdering their father.

ORESTES
> Alas, Phoebus, that justice you sang of
> had an obscure tone, but the pain you caused
> was clear enough—you've given me
> an exile's fate, far from these Greek lands.
> To what other city can I go?
> What host, what man with reverence
> will look at me, who killed my mother?

ELECTRA
> Alas, alas for me!Where do I go?
> To what wedding or what choral dance?
> What husband will take me to a bridal bed?

CHORUS
> Your spirit is shifting back once more
> changing with the breeze.Your thoughts
> are pious now, although profane before.
> You've done dreadful things, my friend,
> to your own reluctant brother.

ORESTES
> Did you see that desperate woman,
> how she threw her robe aside
> and bared her breasts for slaughter?
> Alas for me! The limbs which gave me birth
> collapsing down onto the ground.
> And her hair, I ...

CHORUS
> I understand.
> You had to go through torments,
> hearing your mother's screaming,
> the one who bore you.

ORESTES
>   She stretched her hand toward my chin
>   and cried, "My son, I beg you."
>   She clung onto my cheeks—
>   the sword dropped from my hands.

CHORUS
>   Poor lady! How could you dare
>   to watch your murdered mother
>   breathe her last before your eyes.

ORESTES
>   I threw my cloak over my eyes,
>   then sacrificed her with the sword.
>   I shoved it in my mother's neck.

ELECTRA
>   I was encouraging you—
>   my hand was on the sword, as well.

CHORUS
>   You have inflicted suffering
>   of the most dreadful kind.

ORESTES
>   Take this robe, hide our mother's limbs.
>   Close up her wounds. You gave birth
>   to your own murderers.

ELECTRA *[covering Clytaemnestra's corpse]*
>   There, with this cloak I'm covering up
>   one who was loved and yet not loved.

CHORUS
>   A end of the great troubles for this house.

[Castor and Polydeuces, the Dioscouri, appear above the building on the stage]

CHORUS LEADER
>   But there above the roof beams of the house
>   something's coming. Spirits or gods from heaven?
>   That path does not belong to mortal men.
>   Why are they coming into human view?

DIOSCOURI: *[from the top of the house]*
 Son of Agamemnon, you must listen.
 The twin sons of Zeus are calling you,
 Castor and his brother Polydeuces,
 your mother's brothers. We've just reached Argos,
 after calming down a roaring storm at sea,
 a dreadful threat to ships, after we had seen
 the murder of our sister and your mother.
 She's had justice, but you've not acted justly.
 As for Phoebus, Phoebus, I'll say nothing.
 He is my master. Although he's wise,
 the prophecy he made to you was not.
 You must accept these things and later on
 act on what Fate and Zeus have set for you.
 Give Electra to Pylades as his wife,
 to take back home. And you must leave Argos.
 It's not right for you, who killed your mother,
 to set foot in the city. The Keres,
 those fearful dog-faced goddesses of death,
 will hound you everywhere, a wanderer
 in a mad fit. You must go to Athens
 and embrace Athena's sacred image.
 She'll guard you from their dreadful writhing snakes
 and stop them touching you, by holding out
 her shield with the Gorgon's face above your head.
 And there's the hill of Ares, where the gods
 first sat down to cast their votes on bloodshed,
 when savage Ares slaughtered Halirrothius,
 son of the god who rules the sea, enraged
 at the unholy raping of his daughter.
 That place is where decisions made by vote
 are most secure and sacred to the gods.
 Here you must go on trial for murder.
 The process will result in equal votes
 so you'll be saved from death, for Apollo
 will take responsibility himself.
 His oracle advised your mother's murder.
 This law will be established from then on—
 those accused will always be acquitted
 with equal votes. Struck by the pain of this,
 those fearful goddesses will then sink down

into a chasm right beside the hill,
a reverent and holy shrine for men.
You must settle an Arcadian city
by Alpheus' streams, near the sacred shrine
of Lycaean Apollo, and that city
will get its name from you.I'll tell you more.
As for Aegisthus' corpse, the citizens
in Argos here will place it in a grave.
But in your mother's case, Menelaus,
who's just arrived at Nauplia, so long
after he seized the territory of Troy,
will bury her, with Helen's help.She's come
from Proteus' home, leaving Egypt.
She never went to Troy.It was Zeus' wish
to stir up war and bloodshed among men.
So he sent Helen's image off to Troy.
Since Pylades now has got a virgin wife,
let him go home and leave Achaean land,
with the man they call your brother-in-law
to the land of Phocis.He must give him
a great weight of riches.But as for you,
you must leave along the narrow Isthmus
and go to the blessed hill of Cecrops.36
Once you're completed your appointed fate
for doing the murder, you'll find happiness
and be released from troubles.

CHORUS
> O sons of Zeus, are we permitted
> to come near and speak to you.

DIOSCOURI
> That is allowed—you're not defiled
> by this murder here.

ELECTRA
> And me, sons of Tyndareus,
> may I join in what's said?

DIOSCOURI
> You may.It's to Apollo
> I ascribe this bloody act.

CHORUS
> How is that you two gods,
> brothers of this murdered woman,
> did not keep death's goddesses
> far from her home?

DIOSCOURI
> Destiny and Fate brought what must be—
> and Apollo's unwise utterance.

ELECTRA
> What Apollo and what prophecies
> ordained that I must be
> my mother's murderer?

DIOSCOURI
> You worked together
> and shared a single fate.
> One ancestral curse
> has crushed you both.

ORESTES
> After such a lengthy time
> I've seen you, my sister,
> and immediately must lose
> your love, abandoning you,
> as you abandon me.

DIOSCOURI
> She has a home and husband,
> and will not suffer piteously,
> except she leaves the Argives' city.

ELECTRA
> What else brings one more grief
> than moving out beyond the limits
> of one's native land?

ORESTES
> But I'll go from my father's house,
> then undergo a trial by strangers
> for murdering my mother.

DIOSCOURI

> Be brave. You'll reach
> Athena's sacred city.
> Just keep enduring all.

ELECTRA

> Hold me, my dearest brother,
> your breast against my breast.
> The curses of a slaughtered mother
> divide us from our father's home.

ORESTES

> Throw your arms around me.
> Give me a close embrace.
> Then mourn for me as if I'd died,
> and you were at my burial mound.

DIOSCOURI

> Alas, alas! You've said things
> dreadful even for the gods to hear.
> I and those in heaven have pity
> for mortals who endure so much.

ORESTES

> I'll not see you anymore.

ELECTRA

> I'll not come into your sight.

ORESTES

> These are the final words
> I'll ever say to you.

ELECTRA

> Farewell, my city! A long farewell
> to you my fellow countrywomen!

ORESTES

> Are you going already,
> my most faithful sister?

ELECTRA

> Yes, I'm leaving now
> my soft eyes wet with tears.

ORESTES

Farewell, Pylades.Be happy.
Go and get married to Electra

DIOSCOURI

The marriage will be their concern.
You leave for Athens to escape these hounds,
with their dark skins and hands made up of snakes.
They're on a dreadful hunt to chase you down
and bring you harvests of horrific pain.
We two are off to the Sicilian sea.
We'll hurry there to rescue ships at sea.
As we pass through the flat expanse of air,
we bring no help to those who've been defiled.
We do protect the men who way of their life
reveres what's just and holy, releasing them
from overbearing hardships.Let no one
wish to act unjustly or to get on board
with men who break their oaths.It's as a god
that I address these words to mortal men.

[Castor and Polydeuces disappear. Orestes leaves the stage. Electra and Pylades move off in a different direction. The attendants go with them]

CHORUS

Farewell.Any mortal who can indeed fare well
without being ground down by misfortune,
that man will find his happiness.

[The Chorus carries the bodies back into the house]

—Translated by Ian Johnston

The Apology
Plato
Translated by Benjamin Jowett

Despite what we might think, Plato's The Apology *is not an apology in the way we understand it today. Instead, it comes from the Greek word* apologia, *which refers to a form of rhetoric for the purpose of self-defense in a court of law.*

The Apology *recounts the speech given by Socrates as he is put on trial for his life. The philosopher is accused of corrupting the youth and believing in strange gods, crimes that are punishable by death.*

The real crime of Socrates was that he made certain powerful Athenians look rather foolish. Socrates would often engage in public discourses where he, as well as a combatant, would discuss some essential topic, such as: What is justice? What is piety? What is wisdom?

In the course of these dialogues, Socrates would often entrap his opponents into admitting to contradicting statements or have them sullenly admit defeat altogether. The result of this was that Socrates was regarded as a nuisance, a pest that had embarrassed too many people too many times. This trial would be a means to silence him.

In the course of his speech, Socrates makes several claims that would become central to philosophical thought for centuries to come. Among these are the ideas that "the unexamined life is not worth living" as well as the notion that the only true wisdom is accepting our own ignorance.

"All I know is that I know nothing", is often regarded as a cornerstone of Socratic philosophy.

The verdict is already known by the reader. Socrates will be found guilty and sentenced to die for his crimes. He accepts this outcome willingly. It is possible that he could have requested a lighter sentence, perhaps been exiled from Athens for the rest of his days.

However, to do so would be a tacit admission of guilt, something that the philosopher cannot allow. Socrates believes that it is a far better thing to die whilst in pursuit of wisdom rather than to live ignobly in the shade of ignorance.

SOCRATES' DEFENSE

How you have felt, O men of Athens, at hearing the speeches of my accusers, I cannot tell; but I know that their persuasive words almost made me forget who I was–such was the effect of them; and yet they have hardly spoken a word of truth. But many as their falsehoods were, there was one of them which quite amazed me;–I mean when they told you to be upon your guard, and not to let yourselves be deceived by the force of my eloquence. They ought to have been ashamed of saying this, because they were sure to be detected as soon as I opened my lips and displayed my deficiency; they certainly did appear to be most shameless in saying this, unless by the force of eloquence they mean the force of truth; for then I do indeed admit that I am eloquent. But in how different a way from theirs! Well, as I was saying, they have hardly uttered a word, or not more than a word, of truth; but you shall hear from me the whole truth: not, however, delivered after their manner, in a set oration duly ornamented with words and phrases. No indeed! but I shall use the words and arguments which occur to me at the moment; for I am certain that this is right, and that at my time of life I ought not to be appearing before you, O men of Athens, in the character of a juvenile orator–let no one expect this of me. And I must beg of you to grant me one favor, which is this–If you hear me using the same words in my defence which I have been in the habit of using, and which most of you may have heard in the agora, and at the tables of the money-changers, or anywhere else, I would ask you not to be surprised at this, and not to interrupt me. For I am more than seventy years of age, and this is the first time that I have ever appeared in a court of law, and I am quite a stranger to the ways of the place; and therefore I would have you regard me as if I were really a stranger, whom you would excuse if he spoke in his native tongue, and after the fashion of his country;–that I think is not an unfair request. Never mind the manner, which may or may not be good; but think only of the justice of my cause, and give heed to that: let the judge decide justly and the speaker speak truly.

And first, I have to reply to the older charges and to my first accusers, and then I will go to the later ones. For I have had many accusers, who accused me of old, and their false charges have continued during many years; and I am more afraid of them than of Anytus and his associates, who are dangerous, too, in their own way. But far more dangerous are these, who began when you were children, and took possession of your minds with their falsehoods, telling of one Socrates, a wise man, who speculated about the heaven above, and searched into the earth beneath, and made the worse appear the better cause. These are the accusers whom I dread; for they are the circulators of this rumor, and their hearers are too apt to fancy that speculators of this sort do not believe in the gods. And they are many, and their charges against me are of ancient date, and they made them in days when you were impressible–in childhood, or perhaps in youth–and the cause when heard went by default, for there was none to answer. And, hardest of all, their names I do not know and cannot tell; unless in the chance of a comic poet. But the main body of these slanderers who from envy and malice have wrought upon you– and there are some of them who are convinced themselves, and impart their convictions to others–all these, I say, are most difficult to deal with; for I cannot have them up here, and examine them, and therefore I must simply fight with shadows in my own defence, and examine when there is no one who answers. I will ask you then to assume with me, as I was saying, that my opponents are of two kinds–one recent, the other ancient; and I hope that you will see the propriety of my answering the latter first, for these accusations you heard long before the others, and much oftener.

Well, then, I will make my defence, and I will endeavor in the short time which is allowed to do away with this evil opinion of me which you have held for such a long time; and I hope I may succeed, if this be well for you and me, and that my words may find favor with you. But I know that to accomplish this is not easy–I quite see the nature of the task. Let the event be as God wills: in obedience to the law I make my defence.

I will begin at the beginning, and ask what the accusation is which has given rise to this slander of me, and which has encouraged Meletus to proceed against me. What do the slanderers say? They shall be my prosecutors, and I will sum up their words in an affidavit. "Socrates is an evil-doer, and a curious person, who searches into things under the earth and in heaven, and he makes the worse appear the better cause; and he teaches the aforesaid doctrines to others." That is the nature of the accusation, and that is what you have seen yourselves in the comedy of Aristophanes; who has introduced a man whom he calls Socrates, going about and saying that he can walk in the air, and talking a deal of nonsense concerning matters of which I do not pretend to know either much or little–not that I mean to say anything disparaging of anyone who is a student of natural philosophy. I should be very sorry if Meletus could lay that to my charge. But the simple truth is, O Athenians, that I have nothing to do with these studies. Very many of those here present are witnesses to the truth of this, and to them I appeal. Speak then, you who have heard me, and tell your neighbors whether any of you have ever known me hold forth in few words or in many upon matters of this sort.... You hear their answer. And from what they say of this you will be able to judge of the truth of the rest.

As little foundation is there for the report that I am a teacher, and take money; that is no more true than the other. Although, if a man is able to teach, I honor him for being paid. There is Gorgias of Leontium, and Prodicus of Ceos, and Hippias of Elis, who go the round of the cities, and are able to persuade the young men to leave their own citizens, by whom they might be taught for nothing, and come to them, whom they not only pay, but are thankful if they may be allowed to pay them. There is actually a Parian philosopher residing in Athens, of whom I have heard; and I came to hear of him in this way:–I met a man who has spent a world of money on the Sophists, Callias the son of Hipponicus, and knowing that he had sons, I asked him: "Callias," I said, "if your two sons were foals or calves, there would be no difficulty in finding someone to put over them; we should hire a trainer of horses or a farmer probably who would improve and perfect them in their own proper virtue and excellence; but as they are human beings, whom are you thinking of placing over them? Is there anyone who understands human and political virtue? You must have thought about this as you have sons; is there anyone?" "There is," he said. "Who is he?" said I, "and of what country? and what does he charge?" "Evenus the Parian," he replied; "he is the man, and his charge is five minae." Happy is Evenus, I said to myself, if he really has this wisdom, and teaches at such a modest charge. Had I the same, I should have been very proud and conceited; but the truth is that I have no knowledge of the kind.

I dare say, Athenians, that someone among you will reply, "Why is this, Socrates, and what is the origin of these accusations of you: for there must have been something strange which you have been doing? All this great fame and talk about you would never have arisen if you had been like other men: tell us, then, why this is, as we should be sorry to judge hastily of you." Now I regard this as a fair challenge, and I will endeavor to explain to you the origin of this name of "wise," and of this evil fame. Please to attend then. And although some of you may think I am joking, I declare that I will tell you the entire truth. Men of Athens, this reputation of mine has come of a certain sort of wisdom which I possess. If you ask me what kind of wisdom, I reply, such wisdom as is attainable by man, for to that extent I am inclined to believe that I am wise; whereas the persons of whom I was speaking have a superhuman wisdom, which I may fail to describe, because I have it not myself; and he who says that I have, speaks falsely, and is taking away my character. And here, O men of Athens, I must beg you not to interrupt me, even if I seem to say something extravagant. For the word which I will speak is not mine. I will refer you to a witness who is worthy of credit, and will tell you about my wisdom–whether I have any, and of what sort–and that witness shall be the god of Delphi. You must have known Chaerephon; he was early a friend of mine, and also a friend of yours, for he shared in the exile of the people, and returned with you. Well, Chaerephon, as you know, was very impetuous in all his doings, and he went to Delphi and boldly asked the oracle to tell him whether–as I was saying, I must beg you not to interrupt–he asked the oracle to tell him whether there was anyone wiser than I was, and the Pythian prophetess answered that there was no man wiser. Chaerephon is dead himself, but his brother, who is in court, will confirm the truth of this story.

Why do I mention this? Because I am going to explain to you why I have such an evil name. When I heard the answer, I said to myself, What can the god mean? and what is the interpretation of this riddle? for I know that I have no wisdom, small or great. What can he mean when he says that I am the wisest of men? And yet he is a god and cannot lie; that would be against his nature. After a long consideration, I at last thought of a method of trying the question. I reflected that if I could only find a man wiser than myself, then I might go to the god with a refutation in my hand. I should say to him, "Here is a man who is wiser than I am; but you said that I was the wisest." Accordingly I went to one who had the reputation of wisdom, and observed to him– his name I need not mention; he was a politician whom I selected for examination–and the result was as follows: When I began to talk with him, I could not help thinking that he was not really wise, although he was thought wise by many, and wiser still by himself; and I went and tried to explain to him that he thought himself wise, but was not really wise; and the consequence was that he hated me, and his enmity was shared by several who were present and heard me. So I left him, saying to myself, as I went away: Well, although I do not suppose that either of us knows anything really beautiful and good, I am better off than he is–for he knows nothing, and thinks that he knows. I neither know nor think that I know. In this latter particular, then, I seem to have slightly the advantage of him. Then I went to another, who had still higher philosophical pretensions, and my conclusion was exactly the same. I made another enemy of him, and of many others besides him.

After this I went to one man after another, being not unconscious of the enmity which I provoked, and I lamented and feared this: but necessity was laid upon me–the word of God, I thought, ought to be considered first. And I said to myself, Go I must to all who appear to know, and find out the meaning of the oracle. And I swear to you, Athenians, by the dog I swear!–for I must tell you the truth–the result of my mission was just this: I found that the men most in repute were all but the most foolish; and that some inferior men were really wiser and better. I will tell you the tale of my wanderings and of the "Herculean" labors, as I may call them, which I endured only to find at last the oracle irrefutable. When I left the politicians, I went to the poets; tragic, dithyrambic, and all sorts. And there, I said to myself, you will be detected; now you will find out that you are more ignorant than they are. Accordingly, I took them some of the most elaborate passages in their own writings, and asked what was the meaning of them–thinking that they would teach me something. Will you believe me? I am almost ashamed to speak of this, but still I must say that there is hardly a person present who would not have talked better about their poetry than they did themselves. That showed me in an instant that not by wisdom do poets write poetry, but by a sort of genius and inspiration; they are like diviners or soothsayers who also say many fine things, but do not understand the meaning of them. And the poets appeared to me to be much in the same case; and I further observed that upon the strength of their poetry they believed themselves to be the wisest of men in other things in which they were not wise. So I departed, conceiving myself to be superior to them for the same reason that I was superior to the politicians.

At last I went to the artisans, for I was conscious that I knew nothing at all, as I may say, and I was sure that they knew many fine things; and in this I was not mistaken, for they did know many things of which I was ignorant, and in this they certainly were wiser than I was. But I observed that even the good artisans fell into the same error as the poets; because they were good workmen they thought that they also knew all sorts of high matters, and this defect in them overshadowed their wisdom–therefore I asked myself on behalf of the oracle, whether I would like to be as I was, neither having their knowledge nor their ignorance, or like them in both; and I made answer to myself and the oracle that I was better off as I was.

This investigation has led to my having many enemies of the worst and most dangerous kind, and has given occasion also to many calumnies, and I am called wise, for my hearers always imagine that I myself possess the wisdom which I find wanting in others: but the truth is, O men of Athens, that God only is wise; and in this oracle he means to say that the wisdom of men is little or nothing; he is not speaking of Socrates, he is only using my name as an illustration, as if he said, He, O men, is the wisest, who, like Socrates, knows that his wisdom is in truth worth nothing. And so I go my way, obedient to the god, and make inquisition into the wisdom of anyone, whether citizen or stranger, who appears to be wise; and if he is not wise, then in vindication of the oracle I show him that he is not wise; and this occupation quite absorbs me, and I have no time to give either to any public matter of interest or to any concern of my own, but I am in utter poverty by reason of my devotion to the god.

There is another thing:–young men of the richer classes, who have not much to do, come about me of their own accord; they like to hear the pretenders examined, and they often imitate me, and examine others themselves; there are plenty of persons, as they soon enough discover, who think that they know something, but really know little or nothing: and then those who are examined by them instead of being angry with themselves are angry with me: This confounded Socrates, they say; this villainous misleader of youth!–and then if somebody asks them, Why, what evil does he practise or teach? they do not know, and cannot tell; but in order that they may not appear to be at a loss, they repeat the ready-made charges which are used against all philosophers about teaching things up in the clouds and under the earth, and having no gods, and making the worse appear the better cause; for they do not like to confess that their pretence of knowledge has been detected–which is the truth: and as they are numerous and ambitious and energetic, and are all in battle array and have persuasive tongues, they have filled your ears with their loud and inveterate calumnies. And this is the reason why my three accusers, Meletus and Anytus and Lycon, have set upon me; Meletus, who has a quarrel with me on behalf of the poets; Anytus, on behalf of the craftsmen; Lycon, on behalf of the rhetoricians: and as I said at the beginning, I cannot expect to get rid of this mass of calumny all in a moment. And this, O men of Athens, is the truth and the whole truth; I have concealed nothing, I have dissembled nothing. And yet I know that this plainness of speech makes them hate me, and what is their hatred but a proof that I am speaking the truth?–this is the occasion and reason of their slander of me, as you will find out either in this or in any future inquiry.

I have said enough in my defence against the first class of my accusers; I turn to the second class, who are headed by Meletus, that good and patriotic man, as he calls himself. And now I will try to defend myself against them: these new accusers must also have their affidavit read. What do they say? Something of this sort:–That Socrates is a doer of evil, and corrupter of the youth, and he does not believe in the gods of the state, and has other new divinities of his own. That is the sort of charge; and now let us examine the particular counts. He says that I am a doer of evil, who corrupt the youth; but I say, O men of Athens, that Meletus is a doer of evil, and the evil is that he makes a joke of a serious matter, and is too ready at bringing other men to trial from a pretended zeal and interest about matters in which he really never had the smallest interest. And the truth of this I will endeavor to prove.

Come hither, Meletus, and let me ask a question of you. You think a great deal about the improvement of youth?

Yes, I do.

Tell the judges, then, who is their improver; for you must know, as you have taken the pains to discover their corrupter, and are citing and accusing me before them. Speak, then, and tell the judges who their improver is. Observe, Meletus, that you are silent, and have nothing to say. But is not this rather disgraceful, and a very considerable proof of what I was saying, that you have no interest in the matter? Speak up, friend, and tell us who their improver is.

The laws.

But that, my good sir, is not my meaning. I want to know who the person is, who, in the first place, knows the laws.

The judges, Socrates, who are present in court.

What do you mean to say, Meletus, that they are able to instruct and improve youth?

Certainly they are.

What, all of them, or some only and not others?

All of them.

By the goddess Here, that is good news! There are plenty of improvers, then. And what do you say of the audience,–do they improve them?

Yes, they do.

And the senators?

Yes, the senators improve them.

But perhaps the members of the citizen assembly corrupt them?–or do they too improve them?

They improve them.

Then every Athenian improves and elevates them; all with the exception of myself; and I alone am their corrupter? Is that what you affirm?

That is what I stoutly affirm.

I am very unfortunate if that is true. But suppose I ask you a question: Would you say that this also holds true in the case of horses? Does one man do them harm and all the world good? Is not the exact opposite of this true? One man is able to do them good, or at least not many;–the trainer of horses, that is to say, does them good, and others who have to do with them rather injure them? Is not that true, Meletus, of horses, or any other animals? Yes, certainly. Whether you and Anytus say yes or no, that is no matter. Happy indeed would be the condition of youth if they had one corrupter only, and all the rest of the world were their improvers. And you, Meletus, have sufficiently shown that you never had a thought about the young: your carelessness is seen in your not caring about matters spoken of in this very indictment.

And now, Meletus, I must ask you another question: Which is better, to live among bad citizens, or among good ones? Answer, friend, I say; for that is a question which may be easily answered. Do not the good do their neighbors good, and the bad do them evil?

Certainly.

And is there anyone who would rather be injured than benefited by those who live with him? Answer, my good friend; the law requires you to answer–does anyone like to be injured?

Certainly not.

And when you accuse me of corrupting and deteriorating the youth, do you allege that I corrupt them intentionally or unintentionally?

Intentionally, I say.

But you have just admitted that the good do their neighbors good, and the evil do them evil. Now is that a truth which your superior wisdom has recognized thus early in life, and am I, at my age, in such darkness and ignorance as not to know that if a man with whom I have to live is corrupted by me, I am very likely to be harmed by him, and yet I corrupt him, and intentionally, too;–that is what you are saying, and of that you will never persuade me or any other human being. But either I do not corrupt them, or I corrupt them unintentionally, so that on either view of the case you lie. If my offence is unintentional, the law has no cognizance of unintentional offences: you ought to have taken me privately, and warned and admonished me; for if I had been better advised, I should have left off doing what I only did unintentionally–no doubt I should; whereas you hated to converse with me or teach me, but you indicted me in this court, which is a place not of instruction, but of punishment.

I have shown, Athenians, as I was saying, that Meletus has no care at all, great or small, about the matter. But still I should like to know, Meletus, in what I am affirmed to corrupt the young. I suppose you mean, as I infer from your indictment, that I teach them not to acknowledge the gods which the state acknowledges, but some other new divinities or spiritual agencies in their stead. These are the lessons which corrupt the youth, as you say.

Yes, that I say emphatically.

Then, by the gods, Meletus, of whom we are speaking, tell me and the court, in somewhat plainer terms, what you mean! for I do not as yet understand whether you affirm that I teach others to acknowledge some gods, and therefore do believe in gods and am not an entire atheist–this you do not lay to my charge; but only that they are not the same gods which the city recognizes–the charge is that they are different gods. Or, do you mean to say that I am an atheist simply, and a teacher of atheism?

I mean the latter–that you are a complete atheist.

That is an extraordinary statement, Meletus. Why do you say that? Do you mean that I do not believe in the godhead of the sun or moon, which is the common creed of all men?

I assure you, judges, that he does not believe in them; for he says that the sun is stone, and the moon earth.

Friend Meletus, you think that you are accusing Anaxagoras; and you have but a bad opinion of the judges, if you fancy them ignorant to such a degree as not to know that those doctrines are found in the books of Anaxagoras the Clazomenian, who is full of them. And these are the doctrines which the youth are said to learn of Socrates, when there are not unfrequently exhibitions of them at the theatre (price of admission one drachma at the most); and they might cheaply purchase them, and laugh at Socrates if he pretends to father such eccentricities. And so, Meletus, you really think that I do not believe in any god?

I swear by Zeus that you believe absolutely in none at all.

You are a liar, Meletus, not believed even by yourself. For I cannot help thinking, O men of Athens, that Meletus is reckless and impudent, and that he has written this indictment in a spirit of mere wantonness and youthful bravado. Has he not compounded a riddle, thinking to try me? He said to himself:–I shall see whether this wise Socrates will discover my ingenious contradiction, or whether I shall be able to deceive him and the rest of them. For he certainly does appear to me to contradict himself in the indictment as much as if he said that Socrates is guilty of not believing in the gods, and yet of believing in them–but this surely is a piece of fun.

I should like you, O men of Athens, to join me in examining what I conceive to be his inconsistency; and do you, Meletus, answer. And I must remind you that you are not to interrupt me if I speak in my accustomed manner.

Did ever man, Meletus, believe in the existence of human things, and not of human beings?... I wish, men of Athens, that he would answer, and not be always trying to get up an interruption. Did ever any man believe in horsemanship, and not in horses? or in flute-playing, and not in flute-players? No, my friend; I will answer to you and to the court, as you refuse to answer for yourself. There is no man who ever did. But now please to answer the next question: Can a man believe in spiritual and divine agencies, and not in spirits or demigods?

He cannot.

I am glad that I have extracted that answer, by the assistance of the court; nevertheless you swear in the indictment that I teach and believe in divine or spiritual agencies (new or old, no matter for that); at any rate, I believe in spiritual agencies, as you say and swear in the affidavit; but if I believe in divine beings, I must believe in spirits or demigods;–is not that true? Yes, that is true, for I may assume that your silence gives assent to that. Now what are spirits or demigods? are they not either gods or the sons of gods? Is that true?

Yes, that is true.

But this is just the ingenious riddle of which I was speaking: the demigods or spirits are gods, and you say first that I don't believe in gods, and then again that I do believe in gods; that is, if I believe in demigods. For if the demigods are the illegitimate sons of gods, whether by the Nymphs or by any other mothers, as is thought, that, as all men will allow, necessarily implies the existence of their parents. You might as well affirm the existence of mules, and deny that of horses and asses. Such nonsense, Meletus, could only have been intended by you as a trial of me. You have put this into the indictment because you had nothing real of which to accuse me. But no one who has a particle of understanding will ever be convinced by you that the same man can believe in divine and superhuman things, and yet not believe that there are gods and demigods and heroes.

I have said enough in answer to the charge of Meletus: any elaborate defence is unnecessary; but as I was saying before, I certainly have many enemies, and this is what will be my destruction if I am destroyed; of that I am certain;–not Meletus, nor yet Anytus, but the envy and detraction of the world, which has been the death of many good men, and will probably be the death of many more; there is no danger of my being the last of them.

Someone will say: And are you not ashamed, Socrates, of a course of life which is likely to bring you to an untimely end? To him I may fairly answer: There you are mistaken: a man who is good for anything ought not to calculate the chance of living or dying; he ought only to consider whether in doing anything he is doing right or wrong–acting the part of a good man or of a bad. Whereas, according to your view, the heroes who fell at Troy were not good for much, and the son of Thetis above all, who altogether despised danger in comparison with disgrace; and when his goddess mother said to him, in his eagerness to slay Hector, that if he avenged his companion Patroclus, and slew Hector, he would die himself–"Fate," as she said, "waits upon you next after Hector"; he, hearing this, utterly despised danger and death, and instead of fearing them, feared rather to live in dishonor, and not to avenge his friend. "Let me die next," he replies, "and be avenged of my enemy, rather than abide here by the beaked ships, a scorn and a burden of the earth." Had Achilles any thought of death and danger? For wherever a man's place is, whether the place which he has chosen or that in which he has been placed by a commander, there he ought to remain in the hour of danger; he should not think of death or of anything, but of disgrace. And this, O men of Athens, is a true saying.

Strange, indeed, would be my conduct, O men of Athens, if I who, when I was ordered by the generals whom you chose to command me at Potidaea and Amphipolis and Delium, remained where they placed me, like any other man, facing death; if, I say, now, when, as I conceive and imagine, God orders me to fulfil the philosopher's mission of searching into myself and other men, I were to desert my post through fear of death, or any other fear; that would indeed be strange, and I might justly be arraigned in court for denying the existence of the gods, if I disobeyed the oracle because I was afraid of death: then I should be fancying that I was wise when I was not wise. For this fear of death is indeed the pretence of wisdom, and not real wisdom, being the appearance of knowing the unknown; since no one knows whether death, which they in their fear apprehend to be the greatest evil, may not be the greatest good. Is there not here conceit of knowledge, which is a disgraceful sort of ignorance? And this is the point in which, as I think, I am superior to men in general, and in which I might perhaps fancy myself wiser than other men,–that whereas I know but little of the world below, I do not suppose that I know: but I do know that injustice and disobedience to a better, whether God or man, is evil and dishonorable, and I will never fear or avoid a possible good rather than a certain evil. And therefore if you let me go now, and reject the counsels of Anytus, who said that if I were not put to death I ought not to have been prosecuted, and that if I escape now, your sons will all be utterly ruined by listening to my words–if you say to me, Socrates, this time we will not mind Anytus, and will let you off, but upon one condition, that are to inquire and speculate in this way any more, and that if you are caught doing this again you shall die;–if this was the condition on which you let me go, I should reply: Men of Athens, I honor and love you; but I shall obey God rather than you, and while I have life and strength I shall never cease from the practice and teaching of philosophy, exhorting anyone whom I meet after my manner, and convincing him, saying: O my friend, why do you who are a citizen of the great and mighty and wise city of Athens, care so much about laying up the greatest amount of money and honor and reputation, and so little about wisdom and truth and the greatest improvement of the soul, which you never regard or heed at all? Are you not ashamed of this? And if the person with whom I am arguing says: Yes, but I do care; I do not depart or let him go at once; I interrogate and examine and cross-examine him, and if I think that he has no virtue, but only says that he has, I reproach him with undervaluing the greater, and overvaluing the less. And this I should say to everyone whom I meet, young and old, citizen and alien, but especially to the citizens, inasmuch as they are my brethren. For this is the command of God, as I would have you know; and I believe that to this day no greater good has ever happened in the state than my service to the God. For I do nothing but go about persuading you all, old and young alike, not to take thought for your persons and your properties, but first and chiefly to care about the greatest improvement of the soul. I tell you that virtue is not given by money, but that from virtue come money and every other good of man, public as well as private. This is my teaching, and if this is the doctrine which corrupts the youth, my influence is ruinous indeed. But if anyone says that this is not my teaching, he is speaking an untruth. Wherefore, O men of Athens, I say to you, do as Anytus bids or not as Anytus bids, and either acquit me or not; but whatever you do, know that I shall never alter my ways, not even if I have to die many times.

Men of Athens, do not interrupt, but hear me; there was an agreement between us that you should hear me out. And I think that what I am going to say will do you good: for I have something more to say, at which you may be inclined to cry out; but I beg that you will not do this. I would have you know that, if you kill such a one as I am, you will injure yourselves more than you will injure me. Meletus and Anytus will not injure me: they cannot; for it is not in the nature of things that a bad man should injure a better than himself. I do not deny that he may, perhaps, kill him, or drive him into exile, or deprive him of civil rights; and he may imagine, and others may imagine, that he is doing him a great injury: but in that I do not agree with him; for the evil of doing as Anytus is doing–of unjustly taking away another man's life–is greater far. And now, Athenians, I am not going to argue for my own sake, as you may think, but for yours, that you may not sin against the God, or lightly reject his boon by condemning me. For if you kill me you will not easily find another like me, who, if I may use such a ludicrous figure of speech, am a sort of gadfly, given to the state by the God; and the state is like a great and noble steed who is tardy in his motions owing to his very size, and requires to be stirred into life. I am that gadfly which God has given the state and all day long and in all places am always fastening upon you, arousing and persuading and reproaching you. And as you will not easily find another like me, I would advise you to spare me. I dare say that you may feel irritated at being suddenly awakened when you are caught napping; and you may think that if you were to strike me dead, as Anytus advises, which you easily might, then you would sleep on for the remainder of your lives, unless God in his care of you gives you another gadfly. And that I am given to you by God is proved by this:—that if I had been like other men, I should not have neglected all my own concerns, or patiently seen the neglect of them during all these years, and have been doing yours, coming to you individually, like a father or elder brother, exhorting you to regard virtue; this I say, would not be like human nature. And had I gained anything, or if my exhortations had been paid, there would have been some sense in that: but now, as you will perceive, not even the impudence of my accusers dares to say that I have ever exacted or sought pay of anyone; they have no witness of that. And I have a witness of the truth of what I say; my poverty is a sufficient witness.

Someone may wonder why I go about in private, giving advice and busying myself with the concerns of others, but do not venture to come forward in public and advise the state. I will tell you the reason of this. You have often heard me speak of an oracle or sign which comes to me, and is the divinity which Meletus ridicules in the indictment. This sign I have had ever since I was a child. The sign is a voice which comes to me and always forbids me to do something which I am going to do, but never commands me to do anything, and this is what stands in the way of my being a politician. And rightly, as I think. For I am certain, O men of Athens, that if I had engaged in politics, I should have perished long ago and done no good either to you or to myself. And don't be offended at my telling you the truth: for the truth is that no man who goes to war with you or any other multitude, honestly struggling against the commission of unrighteousness and wrong in the state, will save his life; he who will really fight for the right, if he would live even for a little while, must have a private station and not a public one.

I can give you as proofs of this, not words only, but deeds, which you value more than words. Let me tell you a passage of my own life, which will prove to you that I should never have yielded to injustice from any fear of death, and that if I had not yielded I should have died at once. I will tell you a story–tasteless, perhaps, and commonplace, but nevertheless true. The only office of state which I ever held, O men of Athens, was that of senator; the tribe Antiochis, which is my tribe, had the presidency at the trial of the generals who had not taken up the bodies of the slain after the battle of Arginusae; and you proposed to try them all together, which was illegal, as you all thought afterwards; but at the time I was the only one of the Prytanes who was opposed to the illegality, and I gave my vote against you; and when the orators threatened to impeach and arrest me, and have me taken away, and you called and shouted, I made up my mind that I would run the risk, having law and justice with me, rather than take part in your injustice because I feared imprisonment and death. This happened in the days of the democracy. But when the oligarchy of the Thirty was in power, they sent for me and four others into the rotunda, and bade us bring Leon the Salaminian from Salamis, as they wanted to execute him. This was a specimen of the sort of commands which they were always giving with the view of implicating as many as possible in their crimes; and then I showed, not in words only, but in deed, that, if I may be allowed to use such an expression, I cared not a straw for death, and that my only fear was the fear of doing an unrighteous or unholy thing. For the strong arm of that oppressive power did not frighten me into doing wrong; and when we came out of the rotunda the other four went to Salamis and fetched Leon, but I went quietly home. For which I might have lost my life, had not the power of the Thirty shortly afterwards come to an end. And to this many will witness.

Now do you really imagine that I could have survived all these years, if I had led a public life, supposing that like a good man I had always supported the right and had made justice, as I ought, the first thing? No, indeed, men of Athens, neither I nor any other. But I have been always the same in all my actions, public as well as private, and never have I yielded any base compliance to those who are slanderously termed my disciples or to any other. For the truth is that I have no regular disciples: but if anyone likes to come and hear me while I am pursuing my mission, whether he be young or old, he may freely come. Nor do I converse with those who pay only, and not with those who do not pay; but anyone, whether he be rich or poor, may ask and answer me and listen to my words; and whether he turns out to be a bad man or a good one, that cannot be justly laid to my charge, as I never taught him anything. And if anyone says that he has ever learned or heard anything from me in private which all the world has not heard, I should like you to know that he is speaking an untruth.

But I shall be asked, Why do people delight in continually conversing with you? I have told you already, Athenians, the whole truth about this: they like to hear the cross-examination of the pretenders to wisdom; there is amusement in this. And this is a duty which the God has imposed upon me, as I am assured by oracles, visions, and in every sort of way in which the will of divine power was ever signified to anyone. This is true, O Athenians; or, if not true, would be soon refuted. For if I am really corrupting the youth, and have corrupted some of them already, those of them who have grown up and have become sensible that I gave them bad advice in the days of their youth should come forward as accusers and take their revenge; and if they do not like to come themselves, some of their relatives, fathers, brothers, or other kinsmen, should say what evil their families suffered at my hands. Now is their time. Many of them I see in the court. There is Crito, who is of the same age and of the same deme with myself; and there is Critobulus his son, whom I also see. Then again there is Lysanias of Sphettus, who is the father of Aeschines–he is present; and also there is Antiphon of Cephisus, who is the father of Epignes; and there are the brothers of several who have associated with me. There is Nicostratus the son of Theosdotides, and the brother of Theodotus (now Theodotus himself is dead, and therefore he, at any rate, will not seek to stop him); and there is Paralus the son of Demodocus, who had a brother Theages; and Adeimantus the son of Ariston, whose brother Plato is present; and Aeantodorus, who is the brother of Apollodorus, whom I also see. I might mention a great many others, any of whom Meletus should have produced as witnesses in the course of his speech; and let him still produce them, if he has forgotten–I will make way for him. And let him say, if he has any testimony of the sort which he can produce. Nay, Athenians, the very opposite is the truth. For all these are ready to witness on behalf of the corrupter, of the destroyer of their kindred, as Meletus and Anytus call me; not the corrupted youth only–there might have been a motive for that–but their uncorrupted elder relatives. Why should they too support me with their testimony? Why, indeed, except for the sake of truth and justice, and because they know that I am speaking the truth, and that Meletus is lying.

Well, Athenians, this and the like of this is nearly all the defence which I have to offer. Yet a word more. Perhaps there may be someone who is offended at me, when he calls to mind how he himself, on a similar or even a less serious occasion, had recourse to prayers and supplications with many tears, and how he produced his children in court, which was a moving spectacle, together with a posse of his relations and friends; whereas I, who am probably in danger of my life, will do none of these things. Perhaps this may come into his mind, and he may be set against me, and vote in anger because he is displeased at this. Now if there be such a person among you, which I am far from affirming, I may fairly reply to him: My friend, I am a man, and like other men, a creature of flesh and blood, and not of wood or stone, as Homer says; and I have a family, yes, and sons. O Athenians, three in number, one of whom is growing up, and the two others are still young; and yet I will not bring any of them hither in order to petition you for an acquittal. And why not? Not from any self-will or disregard of you. Whether I am or am not afraid of death is another question, of which I will not now speak. But my reason simply is that I feel such conduct to be discreditable to myself, and you, and the whole state. One who has reached my years, and who has a name for wisdom, whether deserved or not, ought not to debase himself. At any rate, the world has decided that Socrates is in some way superior to other men. And if those among you who are said to be superior in wisdom and courage, and any other virtue, demean themselves in this way, how shameful is their conduct! I have seen men of reputation, when they have been condemned, behaving in the strangest manner: they seemed to fancy that they were going to suffer something dreadful if they died, and that they could be immortal if you only allowed them to live; and I think that they were a dishonor to the state, and that any stranger coming in would say of them that the most eminent men of Athens, to whom the Athenians themselves give honor and command, are no better than women. And I say that these things ought not to be done by those of us who are of reputation; and if they are done, you ought not to permit them; you ought rather to show that you are more inclined to condemn, not the man who is quiet, but the man who gets up a doleful scene, and makes the city ridiculous.

But, setting aside the question of dishonor, there seems to be something wrong in petitioning a judge, and thus procuring an acquittal instead of informing and convincing him. For his duty is, not to make a present of justice, but to give judgment; and he has sworn that he will judge according to the laws, and not according to his own good pleasure; and neither he nor we should get into the habit of perjuring ourselves–there can be no piety in that. Do not then require me to do what I consider dishonorable and impious and wrong, especially now, when I am being tried for impiety on the indictment of Meletus. For if, O men of Athens, by force of persuasion and entreaty, I could overpower your oaths, then I should be teaching you to believe that there are no gods, and convict myself, in my own defence, of not believing in them. But that is not the case; for I do believe that there are gods, and in a far higher sense than that in which any of my accusers believe in them. And to you and to God I commit my cause, to be determined by you as is best for you and me.

The jury finds Socrates guilty.

Socrates' Proposal for his Sentence

There are many reasons why I am not grieved, O men of Athens, at the vote of condemnation. I expected it, and am only surprised that the votes are so nearly equal; for I had thought that the majority against me would have been far larger; but now, had thirty votes gone over to the other side, I should have been acquitted. And I may say that I have escaped Meletus. And I may say more; for without the assistance of Anytus and Lycon, he would not have had a fifth part of the votes, as the law requires, in which case he would have incurred a fine of a thousand drachmae, as is evident.

And so he proposes death as the penalty. And what shall I propose on my part, O men of Athens? Clearly that which is my due. And what is that which I ought to pay or to receive? What shall be done to the man who has never had the wit to be idle during his whole life; but has been careless of what the many care about–wealth, and family interests, and military offices, and speaking in the assembly, and magistracies, and plots, and parties. Reflecting that I was really too honest a man to follow in this way and live, I did not go where I could do no good to you or to myself; but where I could do the greatest good privately to everyone of you, thither I went, and sought to persuade every man among you that he must look to himself, and seek virtue and wisdom before he looks to his private interests, and look to the state before he looks to the interests of the state; and that this should be the order which he observes in all his actions. What shall be done to such a one? Doubtless some good thing, O men of Athens, if he has his reward; and the good should be of a kind suitable to him. What would be a reward suitable to a poor man who

is your benefactor, who desires leisure that he may instruct you? There can be no more fitting reward than maintenance in the Prytaneum, O men of Athens, a reward which he deserves far more than the citizen who has won the prize at Olympia in the horse or chariot race, whether the chariots were drawn by two horses or by many. For I am in want, and he has enough; and he only gives you the appearance of happiness, and I give you the reality. And if I am to estimate the penalty justly, I say that maintenance in the Prytaneum is the just return.

Perhaps you may think that I am braving you in saying this, as in what I said before about the tears and prayers. But that is not the case. I speak rather because I am convinced that I never intentionally wronged anyone, although I cannot convince you of that–for we have had a short conversation only; but if there were a law at Athens, such as there is in other cities, that a capital cause should not be decided in one day, then I believe that I should have convinced you; but now the time is too short. I cannot in a moment refute great slanders; and, as I am convinced that I never wronged another, I will assuredly not wrong myself. I will not say of myself that I deserve any evil, or propose any penalty. Why should I? Because I am afraid of the penalty of death which Meletus proposes? When I do not know whether death is a good or an evil, why should I propose a penalty which would certainly be an evil? Shall I say imprisonment? And why should I live in prison, and be the slave of the magistrates of the year–of the Eleven?

Or shall the penalty be a fine, and imprisonment until the fine is paid? There is the same objection. I should have to lie in prison, for money I have none, and I cannot pay. And if I say exile (and this may possibly be the penalty which you will affix), I must indeed be blinded by the love of life if I were to consider that when you, who are my own citizens, cannot endure my discourses and words, and have found them so grievous and odious that you would fain have done with them, others are likely to endure me. No, indeed, men of Athens, that is not very likely. And what a life should I lead, at my age, wandering from city to city, living in ever-changing exile, and always being driven out! For I am quite sure that into whatever place I go, as here so also there, the young men will come to me; and if I drive them away, their elders will drive me out at their desire: and if I let them come, their fathers and friends will drive me out for their sakes.

Someone will say: Yes, Socrates, but cannot you hold your tongue, and then you may go into a foreign city, and no one will interfere with

you? Now I have great difficulty in making you understand my answer to this. For if I tell you that this would be a disobedience to a divine command, and therefore that I cannot hold my tongue, you will not believe that I am serious; and if I say again that the greatest good of man is daily to converse about virtue, and all that concerning which you hear me examining myself and others, and that the life which is unexamined is not worth living–that you are still less likely to believe. And yet what I say is true, although a thing of which it is hard for me to persuade you. Moreover, I am not accustomed to think that I deserve any punishment. Had I money I might have proposed to give you what I had, and have been none the worse. But you see that I have none, and can only ask you to proportion the fine to my means. However, I think that I could afford a minae, and therefore I propose that penalty; Plato, Crito, Critobulus, and Apollodorus, my friends here, bid me say thirty minae, and they will be the sureties. Well then, say thirty minae, let that be the penalty; for that they will be ample security to you.

The jury condemns Socrates to death.

Socrates Comments on his Sentence

Not much time will be gained, O Athenians, in return for the evil name which you will get from the detractors of the city, who will say that you killed Socrates, a wise man; for they will call me wise even although I am not wise when they want to reproach you. If you had waited a little while, your desire would have been fulfilled in the course of nature. For I am far advanced in years, as you may perceive, and not far from death. I am speaking now only to those of you who have condemned me to death. And I have another thing to say to them: You think that I was convicted through deficiency of words–I mean, that if I had thought fit to leave nothing undone, nothing unsaid, I might have gained an acquittal. Not so; the deficiency which led to my conviction was not of words–certainly not. But I had not the boldness or impudence or inclination to address you as you would have liked me to address you, weeping and wailing and lamenting, and saying and doing many things which you have been accustomed to hear from others, and which, as I say, are unworthy of me. But I thought that I ought not to do anything common or mean in the hour of danger: nor do I now repent of the manner of my defence, and I would rather die having spoken after my manner, than speak in your manner and live.

For neither in war nor yet at law ought any man to use every way of escaping death. For often in battle there is no doubt that if a man will throw away his arms, and fall on his knees before his pursuers, he may escape death; and in other dangers there are other ways of escaping death, if a man is willing to say and do anything. The difficulty, my friends, is not in avoiding death, but in avoiding unrighteousness; for that runs faster than death. I am old and move slowly, and the slower runner has overtaken me, and my accusers are keen and quick, and the faster runner, who is unrighteousness, has overtaken them. And now I depart hence condemned by you to suffer the penalty of death, and they, too, go their ways condemned by the truth to suffer the penalty of villainy and wrong; and I must abide by my award–let them abide by theirs. I suppose that these things may be regarded as fated,–and I think that they are well.

And now, O men who have condemned me, I would fain prophesy to you; for I am about to die, and that is the hour in which men are gifted with prophetic power. And I prophesy to you who are my murderers, that immediately after my death punishment far heavier than you have inflicted on me will surely await you. Me you have killed because you wanted to escape the accuser, and not to give an account of your lives. But that will not be as you suppose: far otherwise. For I say that there will be more accusers of you than there are now; accusers whom hitherto I have restrained: and as they are younger they will be more severe with you, and you will be more offended at them. For if you think that by killing men you can avoid the accuser censuring your lives, you are mistaken; that is not a way of escape which is either possible or honorable; the easiest and noblest way is not to be crushing others, but to be improving yourselves. This is the prophecy which I utter before my departure, to the judges who have condemned me.

Friends, who would have acquitted me, I would like also to talk with you about this thing which has happened, while the magistrates are busy, and before I go to the place at which I must die. Stay then awhile, for we may as well talk with one another while there is time. You are my friends, and I should like to show you the meaning of this event which has happened to me. O my judges–for you I may truly call judges–I should like to tell you of a wonderful circumstance. Hitherto the familiar oracle within me has constantly been in the habit of opposing me even about trifles, if I was going to make a slip or error about anything; and now as you see there has come upon me that which may be thought, and

is generally believed to be, the last and worst evil. But the oracle made no sign of opposition, either as I was leaving my house and going out in the morning, or when I was going up into this court, or while I was speaking, at anything which I was going to say; and yet I have often been stopped in the middle of a speech; but now in nothing I either said or did touching this matter has the oracle opposed me.

What do I take to be the explanation of this? I will tell you. I regard this as a proof that what has happened to me is a good, and that those of us who think that death is an evil are in error. This is a great proof to me of what I am saying, for the customary sign would surely have opposed me had I been going to evil and not to good.

Let us reflect in another way, and we shall see that there is great reason to hope that death is a good, for one of two things:–either death is a state of nothingness and utter unconsciousness, or, as men say, there is a change and migration of the soul from this world to another. Now if you suppose that there is no consciousness, but a sleep like the sleep of him who is undisturbed even by the sight of dreams, death will be an unspeakable gain. For if a person were to select the night in which his sleep was undisturbed even by dreams, and were to compare with this the other days and nights of his life, and then were to tell us how many days and nights he had passed in the course of his life better and more pleasantly than this one, I think that any man, I will not say a private man, but even the great king, will not find many such days or nights, when compared with the others.

Now if death is like this, I say that to die is gain; for eternity is then only a single night. But if death is the journey to another place, and there, as men say, all the dead are, what good, O my friends and judges, can be greater than this? If indeed when the pilgrim arrives in the world below, he is delivered from the professors of justice in this world, and finds the true judges who are said to give judgment there, Minos and Rhadamanthus and Aeacus and Triptolemus, and other sons of God who were righteous in their own life, that pilgrimage will be worth making. What would not a man give if he might converse with Orpheus and Musaeus and Hesiod and Homer? Nay, if this be true, let me die again and again. I, too, shall have a wonderful interest in a place where I can converse with Palamedes, and Ajax the son of Telamon, and other heroes of old, who have suffered death through an unjust judgment; and there will be no small pleasure, as I think, in comparing my own sufferings with theirs. Above all, I shall be able to continue my search

into true and false knowledge; as in this world, so also in that; I shall find out who is wise, and who pretends to be wise, and is not. What would not a man give, O judges, to be able to examine the leader of the great Trojan expedition; or Odysseus or Sisyphus, or numberless others, men and women too! What infinite delight would there be in conversing with them and asking them questions! For in that world they do not put a man to death for this; certainly not. For besides being happier in that world than in this, they will be immortal, if what is said is true.

Wherefore, O judges, be of good cheer about death, and know this of a truth–that no evil can happen to a good man, either in life or after death. He and his are not neglected by the gods; nor has my own approaching end happened by mere chance. But I see clearly that to die and be released was better for me; and therefore the oracle gave no sign. For which reason also, I am not angry with my accusers, or my condemners; they have done me no harm, although neither of them meant to do me any good; and for this I may gently blame them.

Still I have a favor to ask of them. When my sons are grown up, I would ask you, O my friends, to punish them; and I would have you trouble them, as I have troubled you, if they seem to care about riches, or anything, more than about virtue; or if they pretend to be something when they are really nothing,–then reprove them, as I have reproved you, for not caring about that for which they ought to care, and thinking that they are something when they are really nothing. And if you do this, I and my sons will have received justice at your hands.

The hour of departure has arrived, and we go our ways–I to die, and you to live. Which is better God only knows.

THE END

—Translated by Benjamin Jowett

The Battle of Thermopylae
Herodotus
The Histories, Book VII
Translated by G. C. Macaulay

Herodotus, although remembered as "the Father of History", is probably not what we would imagine when we picture a historian. He was not always objective, nor was he picky when it came to selecting which stories made their way into his expansive text, The Histories.

We often find passages from Herodotus that seem, at the very least, implausible. Occasionally, the stories he retells, like a warrior who loses both arms in battle and proceeds to fight with his teeth, seem like pure fiction.

However, Herodotus ought not to be compared to our modern understanding of a "historian", for the simple fact that there was no such thing during his lifetime. Much like other fields of study during the days of classical Greece, historiography was still in its infancy, making Herodotus something of a pioneer.

The man was more of a chronicler. He retold stories that were told to him, no matter how outrageous or unbelievable they might sound.

Still, that is not to say that we ought to abandon The Histories. *It remains one of our best resources for studying the history of the classical Greek civilization.*

Specifically, Herodotus' writings shed light on what has become known as the Greco-Persian wars, a series of engagements between the various city-states of Greece and the massive Persian empire of the fifth century.

Of all of the ancient struggles that raged during this time, there is perhaps none that captures the imagination and inspire awe quite like the battle of Thermopylae.

The allied forces of the Hellenic state, which included King Leonidas and his 300 Spartans, stand fast to defend the pass of Thermopylae in order to prevent King Xerxes of Persia from marching his massive army southward toward the mainland of Greece.

It is a battle with an outcome that is all but assured. While the exact numbers are not known, it is estimated that the Persians outnumbered the allies by at least ten to one.

Still, the Greeks hold fast to their shields and their spears. They are determined to protect their homeland, no matter the cost.

King Xerxes, I say, was encamped within the region of Trachis in the land of the Malians, and the Hellenes within the pass. This place is called by the Hellenes in general Thermopylai, but by the natives of the place and those who dwell in the country round it is called Pylai. Both sides then were encamped hereabout, and the one had command of all that lies beyond Trachis in the direction of the North Wind, and the others of that which tends towards the South Wind and the mid-day on this side of the continent.

These were the Hellenes who awaited the attack of the Persian in this place:—of the Spartans three hundred hoplites; of the men of Tegea and Mantineia a thousand, half from each place, from Orchomenos in Arcadia a hundred and twenty, and from the rest of Arcadia a thousand,—of the Arcadians so many; from Corinth four hundred, from Phlius two hundred, and of the men of Mykene eighty: these were they who came from the Peloponnese; and from the Boeotians seven hundred of the Thespians, and of the Thebans four hundred.

In addition to these the Locrians of Opus had been summoned to come in their full force, and of the Phokians a thousand: for the Hellenes had of themselves sent a summons to them, saying by messengers that they had come as forerunners of the others, that the rest of the allies were to be expected every day, that their sea was safely guarded, being watched by the Athenians and the Eginetans and by those who had been appointed to serve in the fleet, and that they need fear nothing: for he was not a god, they said, who was coming to attack Hellas, but a man; and there was no mortal, nor would be any, with those fortunes evil had not been mingled at his very birth, and the greatest evils for the greatest men; therefore he also who was marching against them, being mortal, would be destined to fail of his expectation. They accordingly, hearing this, came to the assistance of the others at Trachis.

Of these troops, although there were other commanders also according to the State to which each belonged, yet he who was most held in regard and who was leader of the whole army was the Lacedemonian Leonidas son of Anaxandrides, son of Leon, son of Eurycratides, son of Anaxander, son of Eurycrates, son of Polydoros, son of Alcamenes, son

of Teleclos, son of Archelaos, son of Hegesilaos, son of Doryssos, son of Leobotes, son of Echestratos, son of Agis, son of Eurysthenes, son of Aristodemos, son of Aristomachos, son of Cleodaios, son of Hyllos, son of Heracles; who had obtained the kingdom of Sparta contrary to expectation.

For as he had two brothers each older than himself, namely Cleomenes and Dorieos, he had been far removed from the thought of becoming king. Since however Cleomenes had died without male child, and Dorieos was then no longer alive, but he also had brought his life to an end in Sicily, thus the kingdom came to Leonidas, both because was of elder birth than Cleombrotos (for Cleombrotos was the youngest of the sons of Anaxandrides) and also because he had in marriage the daughter of Cleomenes. He then at this time went to Thermopylai, having chosen the three hundred who were appointed by law and men who chanced to have sons; and he took with him besides, before he arrived, those Thebans whom I mentioned when I reckoned them in the number of the troops, of whom the commander was Leontiades the son of Eurymachos: and for this reason Leonidas was anxious to take up these with him of all the Hellenes, namely because accusations had been strongly brought against them that they were taking the side of the Medes; therefore he summoned them to the war, desiring to know whether they would send troops with them or whether they would openly renounce the alliance of the Hellenes; and they sent men, having other thoughts in their mind the while.

These with Leonidas the Spartans had sent out first, in order that seeing them the other allies might join in the campaign, and for fear that they also might take the side of the Medes, if they heard that the Spartans were putting off their action. Afterwards, however, when they had kept the festival, (for the festival of the Carneia stood in their way), they intended then to leave a garrison in Sparta and to come to help in full force with speed: and just so also the rest of the allies had thought of doing themselves; for it chanced that the Olympic festival fell at the same time as these events. Accordingly, since they did not suppose that the fighting in Thermopylai would so soon be decided, they sent only the forerunners of their force.

These, I say, had intended to do thus: and meanwhile the Hellenes at Thermopylai, when the Persian had come near to the pass, were in dread, and deliberated about making retreat from their position. To the rest of the Peloponnesians then it seemed best that they should go to

the Peloponnese and hold the Isthmus in guard; but Leonidas, when the Phokians and Locrians were indignant at this opinion, gave his vote for remaining there, and for sending at the same time messengers to the several States bidding them to come up to help them, since they were but few to repel the army of the Medes.

As they were thus deliberating, Xerxes sent a scout on horseback to see how many they were in number and what they were doing; for he had heard while he was yet in Thessaly that there had been assembled in this place a small force, and that the leaders of it were Lacedemonians together with Leonidas, who was of the race of Heracles. And when the horseman had ridden up towards their camp, he looked upon them and had a view not indeed of the whole of their army, for of those which were posted within the wall, which they had repaired and were keeping a guard, it was not possible to have a view, but he observed those who were outside, whose station was in front of the wall; and it chanced at that time that the Lacedemonians were they who were posted outside. So then he saw some of the men practising athletic exercises and some combing their long hair: and as he looked upon these things he marvelled, and at the same time he observed their number: and when he had observed all exactly, he rode back unmolested, for no one attempted to pursue him and he found himself treated with much indifference. And when he returned he reported to Xerxes all that which he had seen.

Hearing this Xerxes was not able to conjecture the truth about the matter, namely that they were preparing themselves to die and to deal death to the enemy so far as they might; but it seemed to him that they were acting in a manner merely ridiculous; and therefore he sent for Demaratos the son of Ariston, who was in his camp, and when he came, Xerxes asked him of these things severally, desiring to discover what this was which the Lacedemonians were doing: and he said: "Thou didst hear from my mouth at a former time, when we were setting forth to go against Hellas, the things concerning these men; and having heard them thou madest me an object of laughter, because I told thee of these things which I perceived would come to pass; for to me it is the greatest of all ends to speak the truth continually before thee, O king. Hear then now also: these men have come to fight with us for the passage, and this is it that they are preparing to do; for they have a custom which is as follows;—whenever they are about to put their lives in peril, then they attend to the arrangement of their hair. Be assured however, that if thou shalt subdue these and the rest of them which remain behind in Sparta, there is no other race of men which will await thy onset, O king,

or will raise hands against thee: for now thou art about to fight against the noblest kingdom and city of those which are among the Hellenes, and the best men." To Xerxes that which was said seemed to be utterly incredible, and he asked again a second time in what manner being so few they would fight with his host. He said; "O king, deal with me as with a liar, if thou find not that these things come to pass as I say."

Thus saying he did not convince Xerxes, who let four days go by, expecting always that they would take to flight; but on the fifth day, when they did not depart but remained, being obstinate, as he thought, in impudence and folly, he was enraged and sent against them the Medes and the Kissians, charging them to take the men alive and bring them into his presence. Then when the Medes moved forward and attacked the Hellenes, there fell many of them, and others kept coming up continually, and they were not driven back, though suffering great loss: and they made it evident to every man, and to the king himself not least of all, that human beings are many but men are few. This combat went on throughout the day:

And when the Medes were being roughly handled, then these retired from the battle, and the Persians, those namely whom the king called "Immortals," of whom Hydarnes was commander, took their place and came to the attack, supposing that they at least would easily overcome the enemy. When however these also engaged in combat with the Hellenes, they gained no more success than the Median troops but the same as they, seeing that they were fighting in a place with a narrow passage, using shorter spears than the Hellenes, and not being able to take advantage of their superior numbers. The Lacedemonians meanwhile were fighting in a memorable fashion, and besides other things of which they made display, being men perfectly skilled in fighting opposed to men who were unskilled, they would turn their backs to the enemy and make a pretence of taking to flight; and the Barbarians, seeing them thus taking a flight, would follow after them with shouting and clashing of arms: then the Lacedemonians, when they were being caught up, turned and faced the Barbarians; and thus turning round they would slay innumerable multitudes of the Persians; and there fell also at these times a few of the Spartans themselves. So, as the Persians were not able to obtain any success by making trial of the entrance and attacking it by divisions and every way, they retired back.

And during these onsets it is said that the king, looking on, three times leapt up from his seat, struck with fear for his army. Thus they contended

then: and on the following day the Barbarians strove with no better success; for because the men opposed to them were few in number, they engaged in battle with the expectation that they would be found to be disabled and would not be capable any longer of raising their hands against them in fight. The Hellenes however were ordered by companies as well as by nations, and they fought successively each in turn, excepting the Phokians, for these were posted upon the mountain to guard the path. So the Persians, finding nothing different from that which they had seen on the former day, retired back from the fight.

Then when the king was in a strait as to what he should do in the matter before him, Epialtes the son of Eurydemos, a Malian, came to speech with him, supposing that he would win a very great reward from the king; and this man told him of the path which leads over the mountain to Thermopylai, and brought about the destruction of those Hellenes who remained in that place. Afterwards from fear of the Lacedemonians he fled to Thessaly, and when he had fled, a price was proclaimed for his life by the Deputies, when the Amphictyons met for their assembly at Pylai. Then some time afterwards having returned to Antikyra he was slain by Athenades a man of Trachis. Now this Athenades killed Epialtes for another cause, which I shall set forth in the following part of the history, but he was honoured for it none the less by the Lacedemonians.

Thus Epialtes after these events was slain: there is however another tale told, that Onetes the son of Phanagoras, a man of Carystos, and Corydallos of Antikyra were those who showed the Persians the way round the mountain; but this I can by no means accept: for first we must judge by this fact, namely that the Deputies of the Hellenes did not proclaim a price for the lives of Onetes and Corydallos, but for that of Epialtes the Trachinian, having surely obtained the most exact information of the matter; and secondly we know that Epialtes was an exile from his country to avoid this charge. True it is indeed that Onetes might know of this path, even though he were not a Malian, if he had had much intercourse with the country; but Epialtes it was who led them round the mountain by the path, and him therefore I write down as the guilty man.

Xerxes accordingly, being pleased by that which Epialtes engaged to accomplish, at once with great joy proceeded to send Hydarnes and the men of whom Hydarnes was commander; and they set forth from the camp about the time when the lamps are lit. This path of which we speak had been discovered by the Malians who dwell in that land, and

having discovered it they led the Thessalians by it against the Phokians, at the time when the Phokians had fenced the pass with a wall and thus were sheltered from the attacks upon them: so long ago as this had the pass been proved by the Malians to be of no value. And this path lies as follows:—it begins from the river Asopos, which flows through the cleft, and the name of this mountain and of the path is the same, namely Anopaia; and this Anopaia stretches over the ridge of the mountain and ends by the town of Alpenos, which is the first town of the Locrians towards Malis, and by the stone called Black Buttocks and the seats of the Kercopes, where is the very narrowest part.

By this path thus situated the Persians after crossing over the Asopos proceeded all through the night, having on their right hand the mountains of the Oitaians and on the left those of the Trachinians: and when dawn appeared, they had reached the summit of the mountain. In this part of the mountain there were, as I have before shown, a thousand hoplites of the Phokians keeping guard, to protect their own country and to keep the path: for while the pass below was guarded by those whom I have mentioned, the path over the mountain was guarded by the Phokians, who had undertaken the business for Leonidas by their own offer.

While the Persians were ascending they were concealed from these, since all the mountain was covered with oak-trees; and the Phokians became aware of them after they had made the ascent as follows:— the day was calm, and not a little noise was made by the Persians, as was likely when leaves were lying spread upon the ground under their feet; upon which the Phokians started up and began to put on their arms, and by this time the Barbarians were close upon them. These, when they saw men arming themselves, fell into wonder, for they were expecting that no one would appear to oppose them, and instead of that they had met with an armed force. Then Hydarnes, seized with fear lest the Phokians should be Lacedemonians, asked Epialtes of what people the force was; and being accurately informed he set the Persians in order for battle. The Phokians however, when they were hit by the arrows of the enemy, which flew thickly, fled and got away at once to the topmost peak of the mountain, fully assured that it was against them that the enemy had designed to come, and here they were ready to meet death. These, I say, were in this mind; but the Persians meanwhile with Epialtes and Hydarnes made no account of the Phokians, but descended the mountain with all speed.

To the Hellenes who were in Thermopylai first the soothsayer Megistias, after looking into the victims which were sacrificed, declared the death which was to come to them at dawn of day; and afterwards deserters brought the report of the Persians having gone round. These signified it to them while it was yet night, and thirdly came the day-watchers, who had run down from the heights when day was already dawning. Then the Hellenes deliberated, and their opinions were divided; for some urged that they should not desert their post, while others opposed this counsel. After this they departed from their assembly, and some went away and dispersed each to their several cities, while others of them were ready to remain there together with Leonidas.

However it is reported also that Leonidas himself sent them away, having a care that they might not perish, but thinking that it was not seemly for himself and for the Spartans who were present to leave the post to which they had come at first to keep guard there. I am inclined rather to be of this latter opinion, namely that because Leonidas perceived that the allies were out of heart and did not desire to face the danger with him to the end, he ordered them to depart, but held that for himself to go away was not honourable, whereas if he remained, a great fame of him would be left behind, and the prosperity of Sparta would not be blotted out: for an oracle had been given by the Pythian prophetess to the Spartans, when they consulted about this war at the time when it was being first set on foot, to the effect that either Lacedemon must be destroyed by the Barbarians, or their king must lose his life. This reply the prophetess gave them in hexameter verses, and it ran thus:

> *"But as for you, ye men who in wide-spaced Sparta inhabit,*
> *either your glorious city is sacked by the children of Perses, or,*
> *if it be not so, then a king of the stock of Heracleian. Dead shall*
> *be mourned for by all in the boundaries of broad Lacedemon.*
> *Him nor the might of bulls nor the raging lions shall hinder for*
> *he hat might as of Zeus; and I say he shall not be restrained till*
> *one of the other of these he have utterly torn and divided.*

I am of opinion that Leonidas considering these things and desiring to lay up for himself glory above all the other Spartans, dismissed the allies, rather than that those who departed did so in such disorderly fashion, because they were divided in opinion.

Of this the following has been to my mind a proof as convincing as any other, namely that Leonidas is known to have endeavoured to

dismiss the soothsayer also who accompanied this army, Megistias the Acarnanian, who was said to be descended from Melampus, that he might not perish with them after he had declared from the victims that which was about to come to pass for them. He however when he was bidden to go would not himself depart, but sent away his son who was with him in the army, besides whom he had no other child.

The allies then who were dismissed departed and went away, obeying the word of Leonidas, and only the Thespians and the Thebans remained behind with the Lacedemonians. Of these the Thebans stayed against their will and not because they desired it, for Leonidas kept them, counting them as hostages; but the Thespians very willingly, for they said that they would not depart and leave Leonidas and those with him, but they stayed behind and died with them. The commander of these was Demophilos the son of Diadromes.

Xerxes meanwhile, having made libations at sunrise, stayed for some time, until about the hour when the market fills, and then made an advance upon them; for thus it had been enjoined by Epialtes, seeing that the descent of the mountain is shorter and the space to be passed over much less than the going round and the ascent. The Barbarians accordingly with Xerxes were advancing to the attack; and the Hellenes with Leonidas, feeling that they were going forth to death, now advanced out much further than at first into the broader part of the defile; for when the fence of the wall was being guarded,they on the former days fought retiring before the enemy into the narrow part of the pass; but now they engaged with them outside the narrows, and very many of the Barbarians fell: for behind them the leaders of the divisions with scourges in their hands were striking each man, ever urging them on to the front. Many of them then were driven into the sea and perished, and many more still were trodden down while yet alive by one another, and there was no reckoning of the number that perished: for knowing the death which was about to come upon them by reason of those who were going round the mountain, they displayed upon the Barbarians all the strength which they had, to its greatest extent, disregarding danger and acting as if possessed by a spirit of recklessness.

Now by this time the spears of the greater number of them were broken, so it chanced, in this combat, and they were slaying the Persians with their swords; and in this fighting fell Leonidas, having proved himself a very good man, and others also of the Spartans with him, men of note, of whose names I was informed as of men who had proved themselves

worthy, and indeed I was told also the names of all the three hundred. Moreover of the Persians there fell here, besides many others of note, especially two sons of Dareios, Abrocomes and Hyperanthes, born to Dareios of Phratagune the daughter of Artanes: now Artanes was the brother of king Dareios and the son of Hystaspes, the son of Arsames; and he in giving his daughter in marriage to Dareios gave also with her all his substance, because she was his only child.

Two brothers of Xerxes, I say, fell here fighting; and meanwhile over the body of Leonidas there arose a great struggle between the Persians and the Lacedemonians, until the Hellenes by valour dragged this away from the enemy and turned their opponents to flight four times. This conflict continued until those who had gone with Epialtes came up; and when the Hellenes learnt that these had come, from that moment the nature of the combat was changed; for they retired backwards to the narrow part of the way, and having passed by the wall they went and placed themselves upon the hillock, all in a body together except only the Thebans: now this hillock is in the entrance, where now the stone lion is placed for Leonidas. On this spot while defending themselves with daggers, that is those who still had them left, and also with hands and with teeth, they were overwhelmed by the missiles of the Barbarians, some of these having followed directly after them and destroyed the fence of the wall, while others had come round and stood about them on all sides.

Such were the proofs of valour given by the Lacedemonians and Thespians; yet the Spartan Dienekes is said to have proved himself the best man of all, the same who, as they report, uttered this saying before they engaged battle with the Medes:—being informed by one of the men of Trachis that when the Barbarians discharged their arrows they obscured the light of the sun by the multitude of the arrows, so great was the number of their host, he was not dismayed by this, but making small account of the number of the Medes, he said that their guest from Trachis brought them very good news, for if the Medes obscured the light of the sun, the battle against them would be in the shade and not in the sun.

This and other sayings of this kind they report that Dienekes the Lacedemonian left as memorials of himself; and after him the bravest they say of the Lacedemonians were two brothers Alpheos and Maron, sons of Orsiphantos. Of the Thespians the man who gained most honour was named Dithyrambos son of Harmatides.

The men were buried were they fell; and for these, as well as for those who were slain before being sent away by Leonidas, there is an inscription which runs thus:

> *"Here once, facing in fight three hundred myriads of foemen,*
> *thousands four did contend, men of the Peloponnese.*

This is the inscription for the whole body; and for the Spartans separately there is this:

> *"Stranger, report this word, we pray to the Spartans, that lying*
> *here in this spot we remain, faithfully keeping their laws."*

—*Translated by G. C. Macaulay*

The Plague of Athens
Thucydides
The History of the Peloponnesian War, Chapter VII
Translated by Richard Crawley

Thucydides practiced the art of historiography one generation after Herodotus. For this reason, he is sometimes considered a successor to the Father of History. He is also, in some regards, considered something of an improvement.

Unlike Herodotus, Thucydides took care to establish the plausibility of his claims. He reaffirmed his sources and wrote, not as if he were a storyteller, but in the manner that we might expect from a historian.

Consequently, Thucydides is sometimes referred to as "The True Father of History", or as "The Father of Scientific History".

Thucydides, much like Herodotus, sensed the magnitude and importance of the events that were unfolding before him in Greece during the fifth century BC. Only two decades after the end of the Greco-Persian wars, another conflict was brewing within the Hellenic state. Athens and Sparta, classical Greece's two most powerful civilizations, were gearing up for war.

The reasons for the conflict were many. However, Thucydides tells us that it was the sudden growth of the Athenian empire and the fear that it inspired in Sparta that would eventually make war inevitable.

It was then in 431 BC that the Athenian empire and the Peloponnesian League went to war. Spartan armies would regularly invade parts of Attica while the dominant Athenian navy would raid the coasts along the Peloponnese.

However, it was during the second year of the war that a devastating plague would strike the city of Athens. Thucydides describes the effects of the pestilence upon the city. Bodies were left to rot in the streets, corpses were burned by the dozens in the city squares, and rule of law seemed to have no sway over the actions of man.

The plague would mark a point of decline for Athens within the scope of the war. It was a decline that they would never recover from.

Such was the funeral that took place during this winter, with which the first year of the war came to an end. In the first days of summer the Lacedaemonians and their allies, with two-thirds of their forces as before, invaded Attica, under the command of Archidamus, son of Zeuxidamus, King of Lacedaemon, and sat down and laid waste the country. Not many days after their arrival in Attica the plague first began to show itself among the Athenians. It was said that it had broken out in many places previously in the neighbourhood of Lemnos and elsewhere; but a pestilence of such extent and mortality was nowhere remembered. Neither were the physicians at first of any service, ignorant as they were of the proper way to treat it, but they died themselves the most thickly, as they visited the sick most often; nor did any human art succeed any better. Supplications in the temples, divinations, and so forth were found equally futile, till the overwhelming nature of the disaster at last put a stop to them altogether.

It first began, it is said, in the parts of Ethiopia above Egypt, and thence descended into Egypt and Libya and into most of the King's country. Suddenly falling upon Athens, it first attacked the population in Piraeus—which was the occasion of their saying that the Peloponnesians had poisoned the reservoirs, there being as yet no wells there—and afterwards appeared in the upper city, when the deaths became much more frequent. All speculation as to its origin and its causes, if causes can be found adequate to produce so great a disturbance, I leave to other writers, whether lay or professional; for myself, I shall simply set down its nature, and explain the symptoms by which perhaps it may be recognized by the student, if it should ever break out again. This I can the better do, as I had the disease myself, and watched its operation in the case of others.

That year then is admitted to have been otherwise unprecedentedly free from sickness; and such few cases as occurred all determined in this. As a rule, however, there was no ostensible cause; but people in good health were all of a sudden attacked by violent heats in the head, and redness and inflammation in the eyes, the inward parts, such as the throat or tongue, becoming bloody and emitting an unnatural and fetid breath. These symptoms were followed by sneezing and hoarseness, after which the pain soon reached the chest, and produced a hard cough. When it fixed in the stomach, it upset it; and discharges of bile of every kind named by physicians ensued, accompanied by very great distress. In most cases also an ineffectual retching followed, producing violent spasms, which in some cases ceased soon after, in

others much later. Externally the body was not very hot to the touch, nor pale in its appearance, but reddish, livid, and breaking out into small pustules and ulcers. But internally it burned so that the patient could not bear to have on him clothing or linen even of the very lightest description; or indeed to be otherwise than stark naked. What they would have liked best would have been to throw themselves into cold water; as indeed was done by some of the neglected sick, who plunged into the rain-tanks in their agonies of unquenchable thirst; though it made no difference whether they drank little or much. Besides this, the miserable feeling of not being able to rest or sleep never ceased to torment them. The body meanwhile did not waste away so long as the distemper was at its height, but held out to a marvel against its ravages; so that when they succumbed, as in most cases, on the seventh or eighth day to the internal inflammation, they had still some strength in them. But if they passed this stage, and the disease descended further into the bowels, inducing a violent ulceration there accompanied by severe diarrhoea, this brought on a weakness which was generally fatal. For the disorder first settled in the head, ran its course from thence through the whole of the body, and, even where it did not prove mortal, it still left its mark on the extremities; for it settled in the privy parts, the fingers and the toes, and many escaped with the loss of these, some too with that of their eyes. Others again were seized with an entire loss of memory on their first recovery, and did not know either themselves or their friends.

But while the nature of the distemper was such as to baffle all description, and its attacks almost too grievous for human nature to endure, it was still in the following circumstance that its difference from all ordinary disorders was most clearly shown. All the birds and beasts that prey upon human bodies, either abstained from touching them (though there were many lying unburied), or died after tasting them. In proof of this, it was noticed that birds of this kind actually disappeared; they were not about the bodies, or indeed to be seen at all. But of course the effects which I have mentioned could best be studied in a domestic animal like the dog.

Such then, if we pass over the varieties of particular cases which were many and peculiar, were the general features of the distemper. Meanwhile the town enjoyed an immunity from all the ordinary disorders; or if any case occurred, it ended in this. Some died in neglect, others in the midst of every attention. No remedy was found that could be used as a specific; for what did good in one case, did harm in another.

Strong and weak constitutions proved equally incapable of resistance, all alike being swept away, although dieted with the utmost precaution. By far the most terrible feature in the malady was the dejection which ensued when any one felt himself sickening, for the despair into which they instantly fell took away their power of resistance, and left them a much easier prey to the disorder; besides which, there was the awful spectacle of men dying like sheep, through having caught the infection in nursing each other. This caused the greatest mortality. On the one hand, if they were afraid to visit each other, they perished from neglect; indeed many houses were emptied of their inmates for want of a nurse: on the other, if they ventured to do so, death was the consequence. This was especially the case with such as made any pretensions to goodness: honour made them unsparing of themselves in their attendance in their friends' houses, where even the members of the family were at last worn out by the moans of the dying, and succumbed to the force of the disaster. Yet it was with those who had recovered from the disease that the sick and the dying found most compassion. These knew what it was from experience, and had now no fear for themselves; for the same man was never attacked twice—never at least fatally. And such persons not only received the congratulations of others, but themselves also, in the elation of the moment, half entertained the vain hope that they were for the future safe from any disease whatsoever.

An aggravation of the existing calamity was the influx from the country into the city, and this was especially felt by the new arrivals. As there were no houses to receive them, they had to be lodged at the hot season of the year in stifling cabins, where the mortality raged without restraint. The bodies of dying men lay one upon another, and half-dead creatures reeled about the streets and gathered round all the fountains in their longing for water. The sacred places also in which they had quartered themselves were full of corpses of persons that had died there, just as they were; for as the disaster passed all bounds, men, not knowing what was to become of them, became utterly careless of everything, whether sacred or profane. All the burial rites before in use were entirely upset, and they buried the bodies as best they could. Many from want of the proper appliances, through so many of their friends having died already, had recourse to the most shameless sepultures: sometimes getting the start of those who had raised a pile, they threw their own dead body upon the stranger's pyre and ignited it; sometimes they tossed the corpse which they were carrying on the top of another that was burning, and so went off.

Nor was this the only form of lawless extravagance which owed its origin to the plague. Men now coolly ventured on what they had formerly done in a corner, and not just as they pleased, seeing the rapid transitions produced by persons in prosperity suddenly dying and those who before had nothing succeeding to their property. So they resolved to spend quickly and enjoy themselves, regarding their lives and riches as alike things of a day. Perseverance in what men called honour was popular with none, it was so uncertain whether they would be spared to attain the object; but it was settled that present enjoyment, and all that contributed to it, was both honourable and useful. Fear of gods or law of man there was none to restrain them. As for the first, they judged it to be just the same whether they worshipped them or not, as they saw all alike perishing; and for the last, no one expected to live to be brought to trial for his offences, but each felt that a far severer sentence had been already passed upon them all and hung ever over their heads, and before this fell it was only reasonable to enjoy life a little.

Such was the nature of the calamity, and heavily did it weigh on the Athenians; death raging within the city and devastation without. Among other things which they remembered in their distress was, very naturally, the following verse which the old men said had long ago been uttered:

A Dorian war shall come and with it death.

So a dispute arose as to whether dearth and not death had not been the word in the verse; but at the present juncture, it was of course decided in favour of the latter; for the people made their recollection fit in with their sufferings. I fancy, however, that if another Dorian war should ever afterwards come upon us, and a dearth should happen to accompany it, the verse will probably be read accordingly. The oracle also which had been given to the Lacedaemonians was now remembered by those who knew of it. When the god was asked whether they should go to war, he answered that if they put their might into it, victory would be theirs, and that he would himself be with them. With this oracle events were supposed to tally. For the plague broke out as soon as the Peloponnesians invaded Attica, and never entering Peloponnese (not at least to an extent worth noticing), committed its worst ravages at Athens, and next to Athens, at the most populous of the other towns. Such was the history of the plague.

—Translated by Richard Crawley

On Happiness
Aristotle
The Nicomachean Ethics, Book X
Translated by W.D. Ross

A student of Plato, Aristotle is often considered to be the greatest philosopher that ever lived. This is partly due to the fact that there was almost no field of philosophical study that he did not either revolutionize, build upon, or invent; mathematics being the glaring exception.

Aristotle wrote on everything from the movement of the cosmos to the structure of the soul. He concisely defined systematic logic, is credited with establishing the study of zoology, and even examined the function and structure of tragedy.

His work was so expansive and so prolific that it wasn't until the Italian Renaissance, some 1700 years later, that commentators were finally able to raise any meaningful criticisms to his works.

It was in the field of Ethics, however, that Aristotle's contribution is most apparent. The Nicomachean Ethics, *which was dedicated to his son, Nicomachus, is often considered to be his crowning achievement. It is within these pages that Aristotle, perhaps for the first time in recorded history, attempts to give us an answer to that confounding question, "what is the meaning of life?"*

Chapter 4: On Pleasure

(Pleasure is an activity, not a process)

What pleasure is, or what kind of thing it is, will become plainer if we take up the question again from the beginning.

Seeing seems to be at any moment complete, for it does not lack anything which coming into being later will complete its form; and pleasure also seems to be of this nature. For it is a whole, and at no time can one find a pleasure whose form will be completed if the pleasure lasts longer. For this reason, too, it is not a movement.

For every movement[1] (e.g. that of building) takes time and is for the sake of an end, and is complete when it has made what it aims at. It is complete, therefore, only in the whole time or at that final moment. In their parts and during the time they occupy, all movements are incomplete, and are different in kind from the whole movement and from each other. For the fitting together of the stones is different from the fluting of the column, and these are both different from the making of the temple; and the making of the temple is complete (for it lacks nothing with a view to the end proposed), but the making of the base or of the triglyph is incomplete; for each is the making of only a part.

They differ in kind, then, and it is not possible to find at any and every time a movement complete in form, but if at all, only in the whole time. So, too, in the case of walking and all other movements. For if locomotion is a movement from to there, it, too, has differences in kind-flying, walking, leaping, and so on. And not only so, but in walking itself there are such differences; for the whence and whither are not the same in the whole racecourse and in a part of it, nor in one part and in another, nor is it the same thing to traverse this line and that; for one traverses not only a line but one which is in a place, and this one is in a different place from that.

We have discussed movement with precision in another work, but it seems that it is not complete at any and every time, but that the many movements are incomplete and different in kind, since the whence and whither give them their form. But of pleasure the form is complete at any and every time. Plainly, then, pleasure and movement must be different from each other, and pleasure must be one of the things that are whole and complete.

This would seem to be the case, too, from the fact that it is not possible to move otherwise than in time, but it is possible to be pleased; for that which takes place in a moment is a whole[2].

---

[1]   ...**for every movement:** "Movement" may also refer to "process". The building of a temple may take time to acquire all the things that make it a complete temple. It is therefore a process. Pleasure is not a process because it does not take time or a procedure to be realized and complete.

[2]   ...**is a whole:** there is no coming into being of pleasure. Coming into being requires that parts come into being one after the other. Pleasure is complete all at once and as a whole.

From these considerations it is clear, too, that these thinkers are not right in saying there is a movement or a coming into being of pleasure. For these cannot be ascribed to all things, but only to those that are divisible and not wholes; there is no coming into being of seeing nor of a point nor of a unit, nor is any of these a movement or coming into being; therefore there is no movement or coming into being of pleasure either; for it is a whole.

(Pleasure Completes and Activity)

Since every sense is active in relation to its object, and a sense which is in good condition acts perfectly in relation to the most beautiful of its objects (for perfect activity seems to be ideally of this nature; whether we say that it is active, or the organ in which it resides, may be assumed to be immaterial), it follows that in the case of each sense the best activity is that of the best-conditioned organ in relation to the finest of its objects. And this activity will be the most complete and pleasant.

For, while there is pleasure in respect of any sense, and in respect of thought and contemplation no less, the most complete is pleasantest, and that of a well-conditioned organ in relation to the worthiest of its objects is the most complete; and the pleasure completes the activity.[3]

But the pleasure does not complete it in the same way as the combination of object and sense, both good, just as health and the doctor are not in the same way the cause of a man's being healthy.[4] (That pleasure is produced in respect to each sense is plain; for we speak of sights and sounds as pleasant. It is also plain that it arises most of all when both the sense is at its best and it is active in reference to an object which corresponds; when both object and perceiver are of the best there will always be pleasure, since the requisite agent and patient are both present.)

Pleasure completes the activity not as the corresponding permanent state does, by its immanence, but as an end which supervenes as the

---

[3]   **...completes the activity:** There is pleasure in perception. Viewing beautiful objects is pleasurable to us. The pleasure of perception is most perfect when the organs of perception (eye, ear, etc...) are in good working condition and the object of our perception is beautiful or in good condition.

[4]   **...being healthy:** The doctor is the efficient cause (a cause of change apart from the thing being changed) while health is the formal cause (cause of change that is by virtue of the thing being changed, i.e., it's shape or arrangement) of being healthy.

bloom of youth does on those in the flower of their age. So long, then, as both the intelligible or sensible object and the discriminating or contemplative faculty are as they should be, the pleasure will be involved in the activity; for when both the passive and the active factor are unchanged and are related to each other in the same way, the same result naturally follows.[5]

How, then, is it that no one is continuously pleased? Is it that we grow weary? Certainly all human beings are incapable of continuous activity. Therefore pleasure also is not continuous; for it accompanies activity. Some things delight us when they are new, but later do so less, for the same reason; for at first the mind is in a state of stimulation and intensely active about them, as people are with respect to their vision when they look hard at a thing, but afterwards our activity is not of this kind, but has grown relaxed; for which reason the pleasure also is dulled.

One might think that all men desire pleasure because they all aim at life; life is an activity, and each man is active about those things and with those faculties that he loves most; e.g. the musician is active with his hearing in reference to tunes, the student with his mind in reference to theoretical questions, and so on in each case; now pleasure completes the activities, and therefore life, which they desire. It is with good reason, then, that they aim at pleasure too, since for every one it completes life, which is desirable. But whether we choose life for the sake of pleasure or pleasure for the sake of life is a question we may dismiss for the present. For they seem to be bound up together and not to admit of separation, since without activity pleasure does not arise, and every activity is completed by the attendant pleasure.[6]

Chapter 5: Different Types of Pleasure

(Pleasures Differ)

For this reason pleasures seem, too, to differ in kind. For things different in kind are, we think, completed by different things (we see this to be

---

[5]   **...naturally follows:** Perceiving is good as an end in itself, so is contemplation. Pleasure is an added end, a good in itself that naturally completes an activity.

[6]   **...attendant pleasure:** Pleasure completes activities. Life is an activity and therefore is completed with pleasure. Humans aim at pleasure because it is the natural end to the activity of life. It is unclear, however, if we aim at pleasure for the sake of life or life for the sake of pleasure.

true both of natural objects and of things produced by art, e.g. animals, trees, a painting, a sculpture, a house, an implement); and, similarly, we think that activities differing in kind are completed by things differing in kind. Now the activities of thought differ from those of the senses, and both differ among themselves, in kind; so, therefore, do the pleasures that complete them.

This may be seen, too, from the fact that each of the pleasures is bound up with the activity it completes. For an activity is intensified by its proper pleasure, since each class of things is better judged of and brought to precision by those who engage in the activity with pleasure; e.g. it is those who enjoy geometrical thinking that become geometers and grasp the various propositions better, and, similarly, those who are fond of music or of building, and so on, make progress in their proper function by enjoying it; so the pleasures intensify the activities, and what intensifies a thing is proper to it, but things different in kind have properties different in kind.[7]

This will be even more apparent from the fact that activities are hindered by pleasures arising from other sources. For people who are fond of playing the flute are incapable of attending to arguments if they overhear some one playing the flute, since they enjoy flute-playing more than the activity in hand; so the pleasure connected with fluteplaying destroys the activity concerned with argument. This happens, similarly, in all other cases, when one is active about two things at once; the more pleasant activity drives out the other, and if it is much more pleasant does so all the more, so that one even ceases from the other. This is why when we enjoy anything very much we do not throw ourselves into anything else, and do one thing only when we are not much pleased by another; e.g. in the theatre the people who eat sweets do so most when the actors are poor. Now since activities are made precise and more enduring and better by their proper pleasure, and injured by alien pleasures, evidently the two kinds of pleasure are far apart. For alien pleasures do pretty much what proper pains do, since activities are destroyed by their proper pains; e.g. if a man finds writing or doing sums unpleasant and painful, he does not write, or does not do sums, because the activity is painful. So an activity suffers contrary effects from its proper pleasures and pains, i.e. from those that supervene on it in virtue of its own nature.

---

[7]   **...different in kind**: Since activities are different (e.g. though vs perception) the pleasures that accompany these activities will be different. We must identify the appropriate pleasure that compliments each activity.

And alien pleasures have been stated to do much the same as pain; they destroy the activity, only not to the same degree.

(Which Pleasures are Good?)

Now since activities differ in respect of goodness and badness, and some are worthy to be chosen, others to be avoided, and others neutral, so, too, are the pleasures; for to each activity there is a proper pleasure. The pleasure proper to a worthy activity is good and that proper to an unworthy activity bad; just as the appetites for noble objects are laudable, those for base objects culpable. But the pleasures involved in activities are more proper to them than the desires; for the latter are separated both in time and in nature, while the former are close to the activities, and so hard to distinguish from them that it admits of dispute whether the activity is not the same as the pleasure. (Still, pleasure does not seem to be thought or perception-that would be strange; but because they are not found apart they appear to some people the same.) As activities are different, then, so are the corresponding pleasures. Now sight is superior to touch in purity, and hearing and smell to taste; the pleasures, therefore, are similarly superior, and those of thought superior to these, and within each of the two kinds some are superior to others.

Each animal is thought to have a proper pleasure, as it has a proper function; viz. that which corresponds to its activity. If we survey them species by species, too, this will be evident; horse, dog, and man have different pleasures, as Heraclitus says 'asses would prefer sweepings to gold'; for food is pleasanter than gold to asses.

So the pleasures of creatures different in kind differ in kind, and it is plausible to suppose that those of a single species do not differ. But they vary to no small extent, in the case of men at least; the same things delight some people and pain others, and are painful and odious to some, and pleasant to and liked by others. This happens, too, in the case of sweet things; the same things do not seem sweet to a man in a fever and a healthy man-nor hot to a weak man and one in good condition. The same happens in other cases. But in all such matters that which appears to the good man is thought to be really so.

If this is correct, as it seems to be, and virtue and the good man as such are the measure of each thing, those also will be pleasures which appear so to him, and those things pleasant which he enjoys. If the things he finds tiresome seem pleasant to some one, that is nothing surprising; for men

may be ruined and spoilt in many ways; but the things are not pleasant, but only pleasant to these people and to people in this condition.[8]

Those which are admittedly disgraceful plainly should not be said to be pleasures, except to a perverted taste; but of those that are thought to be good what kind of pleasure or what pleasure should be said to be that proper to man? Is it not plain from the corresponding activities? The pleasures follow these. Whether, then, the perfect and supremely happy man has one or more activities, the pleasures that perfect these will be said in the strict sense to be pleasures proper to man, and the rest will be so in a secondary and fractional way, as are the activities.[9]

Chapter 6: Happiness and Intellectual Activities

(Happiness and Virtuous Action)

Now that we have spoken of the virtues, the forms of friendship, and the varieties of pleasure, what remains is to discuss in outline the nature of happiness, since this is what we state the end of human nature to be.

Our discussion will be the more concise if we first sum up what we have said already. We said, then, that happiness it is not a state; for if it were it might belong to some one who was asleep throughout his life, living the life of a plant, or, again, to some one who was suffering the greatest misfortunes. If these implications are unacceptable, and we must rather class happiness as an activity, as we have said before, and if some activities are necessary, and desirable for the sake of something else, while others are so in themselves, evidently happiness must be placed among those desirable in themselves, not among those desirable for the sake of something else; for happiness does not lack anything, but is self-sufficient. Now those activities are desirable in themselves from which nothing is sought beyond the activity. And of this nature virtuous actions are thought to be; for to do noble and good deeds is a thing desirable for its own sake.

---

8   **...in this condition**: Aristotle aims at finding which pleasures are "good". The "good person", insofar as he is good, will be a benchmark of sorts. Since this person is excellent, that which he finds pleasurable, will really *be* pleasurable. Vicious people will mistake vice for pleasure. This is to be expected since they are in a depraved state and cannot perceive true pleasure.

9   **...are the activities**: Aristotle ends this chapter by asking what type of pleasure is most appropriate for people. Certainly there will be one pleasure that is supremely best for us.

Pleasant amusements also are thought to be of this nature; we choose them not for the sake of other things; for we are injured rather than benefited by them, since we are led to neglect our bodies and our property. But most of the people who are deemed happy take refuge in such pastimes, which is the reason why those who are ready-witted at them are highly esteemed at the courts of tyrants; they make themselves pleasant companions in the tyrants' favourite pursuits, and that is the sort of man they want. Now these things are thought to be of the nature of happiness because people in despotic positions spend their leisure in them, but perhaps such people prove nothing; for virtue and reason, from which good activities flow, do not depend on despotic position; nor, if these people, who have never tasted pure and generous pleasure, take refuge in the bodily pleasures, should these for that reason be thought more desirable; for boys, too, think the things that are valued among themselves are the best. It is to be expected, then, that, as different things seem valuable to boys and to men, so they should to bad men and to good.[10]

Now, as we have often maintained, those things are both valuable and pleasant which are such to the good man; and to each man the activity in accordance with his own disposition is most desirable, and, therefore, to the good man that which is in accordance with virtue.

Happiness, therefore, does not lie in amusement; it would, indeed, be strange if the end were amusement, and one were to take trouble and suffer hardship all one's life in order to amuse oneself. For, in a word, everything that we choose we choose for the sake of something else-except happiness, which is an end. Now to exert oneself and work for the sake of amusement seems silly and utterly childish. But to amuse oneself in order that one may exert oneself, as Anacharsis puts it, seems right; for amusement is a sort of relaxation, and we need relaxation because we cannot work continuously. Relaxation, then, is not an end; for it is taken for the sake of activity.

The happy life is thought to be virtuous; now a virtuous life requires exertion, and does not consist in amusement. And we say that serious

---

10   ...and to good: Aristotle claims that bodily amusement is not the same as true pleasure. Amusement may seem desirable in itself, but amusement does not flow from virtue or knowledge, which is the source of all truly good things. Just as the pleasures differ from men and boys, so to pleasures differ from good people and bad people.

things are better than laughable things and those connected with amusement, and that the activity of the better of any two things-whether it be two elements of our being or two men-is the more serious; but the activity of the better is ipso facto superior and more of the nature of happiness. And any chance person-even a slave-can enjoy the bodily pleasures no less than the best man; but no one assigns to a slave a share in happiness-unless he assigns to him also a share in human life. For happiness does not lie in such occupations, but, as we have said before, in virtuous activities.

Chapter 7: Theoretical Study and Happiness

If happiness is activity in accordance with virtue, it is reasonable that it should be in accordance with the highest virtue; and this will be that of the best thing in us.

Whether it be reason or something else that is this element which is thought to be our natural ruler and guide and to take thought of things noble and divine, whether it be itself also divine or only the most divine element in us, the activity of this in accordance with its proper virtue will be perfect happiness. That this activity is contemplative we have already said.[11]

Now this would seem to be in agreement both with what we said before and with the truth. For, firstly, this activity is the best (since not only is reason the best thing in us, but the objects of reason are the best of knowable objects); and secondly, it is the most continuous, since we can contemplate truth more continuously than we can do anything. And we think happiness has pleasure mingled with it, but the activity of philosophic wisdom is admittedly the pleasantest of virtuous activities; at all events the pursuit of it is thought to offer pleasures marvellous for their purity and their enduringness, and it is to be expected that those who know will pass their time more pleasantly than those who inquire. And the self-sufficiency that is spoken of must belong most to the contemplative activity.

For while a philosopher, as well as a just man or one possessing any other virtue, needs the necessaries of life, when they are sufficiently

---

[11]   **...already said:** Aristotle makes the claim that true happiness is an active expression of that which is most appropriate for us given our status as rational creatures. The activity of study is our most appropriate pleasure and therefore our means to a truly happy life.

equipped with things of that sort the just man needs people towards whom and with whom he shall act justly, and the temperate man, the brave man, and each of the others is in the same case, but the philosopher, even when by himself, can contemplate truth, and the better the wiser he is; he can perhaps do so better if he has fellow-workers, but still he is the most self-sufficient. And this activity alone would seem to be loved for its own sake; for nothing arises from it apart from the contemplating, while from practical activities we gain more or less apart from the action.[12]

And happiness is thought to depend on leisure; for we are busy that we may have leisure, and make war that we may live in peace. Now the activity of the practical virtues is exhibited in political or military affairs, but the actions concerned with these seem to be unleisurely. Warlike actions are completely so (for no one chooses to be at war, or provokes war, for the sake of being at war; any one would seem absolutely murderous if he were to make enemies of his friends in order to bring about battle and slaughter); but the action of the statesman is also unleisurely, and-apart from the political action itself-aims at despotic power and honours, or at all events happiness, for him and his fellow citizens-a happiness different from political action, and evidently sought as being different. So if among virtuous actions political and military actions are distinguished by nobility and greatness, and these are unleisurely and aim at an end and are not desirable for their own sake, but the activity of reason, which is contemplative, seems both to be superior in serious worth and to aim at no end beyond itself, and to have its pleasure proper to itself (and this augments the activity), and the self-sufficiency, leisureliness, unweariedness (so far as this is possible for man), and all the other attributes ascribed to the supremely happy man are evidently those connected with this activity, it follows that this will be the complete happiness of man, if it be allowed a complete term of life (for none of the attributes of happiness is incomplete).

But such a life would be too high for man; for it is not in so far as he is man that he will live so, but in so far as something divine is present in him; and by so much as this is superior to our composite nature is its

---

[12] **...from the action**: The virtue of wisdom is not only the most pleasant, but it is the most self-sufficient. For while the charitable man must have others to receive his charity, and the just man must have others to receive his just acts, the wise man needs nothing other than himself and his human desire for contemplation.

activity superior to that which is the exercise of the other kind of virtue. If reason is divine, then, in comparison with man, the life according to it is divine in comparison with human life. But we must not follow those who advise us, being men, to think of human things, and, being mortal, of mortal things, but must, so far as we can, make ourselves immortal, and strain every nerve to live in accordance with the best thing in us; for even if it be small in bulk, much more does it in power and worth surpass everything.

This would seem, too, to be each man himself, since it is the authoritative and better part of him. It would be strange, then, if he were to choose not the life of his self but that of something else. And what we said before' will apply now; that which is proper to each thing is by nature best and most pleasant for each thing; for man, therefore, the life according to reason is best and pleasantest, since reason more than anything else is man. This life therefore is also the happiest.

—Translated by W.D. Ross